SOLDIERS AND SHERPAS

'Brummie' Stokes follows in the great tradition of English adventurers, men who have braved the elements to snatch triumph from the jaws of almost inevitable disaster. Now, for the first time, he tells the full and frank story of an extraordinary life, ranging from poverty-stricken childhood through military campaigns all over the globe to the ultimate challenge – the assault on Everest.

Stokes enlisted in the Green Jackets at the age of seventeen and subsequently realised his dream of joining the SAS, and was decorated several times for bravery. Mountaineering is his real passion, however and together with fellow SAS climber Bronco Lane, he has climbed many of the world's most demanding peaks, including the mountaineer's greatest prize – Everest.

Defying death, frostbite and many other hazards, Brummie made several expeditions to Everest and the high Himalayas. In this dramatic, funny, intensely moving book, he talks us through the various stages of preparation for a big climb, revealing the psychological and physical stress it entails, and relives the dangers and the thrills of conquering a summit.

D1343281

About the author

John Henry 'Brummie' Stokes is one the the world's most daring and determined mountaineers. Born in 1945 in the mining village of Hamstead near Birmingham, he lived in a colliery-owned terrace house with his sister and three brothers. He joined the Green Jackets in 1963, and in 1966 the SAS. In 1976 he reached the summit of Everest via the South Col route with fellow SAS climber Bronco Lane. He made his first attempt on Everest's Northeast Ridge in 1986 with Mo Anthoine and Joe Brown.

In 1988 he returned to Everest with a team made up of many of the old hands from the previous trip. Although Brummie Stokes himself had to be evacuated through illness, his team cracked the last great challenge of Mount Everest's Northeast Ridge.

Brummie Stokes lives in Hereford with his wife and two sons.

Soldiers and Sherpas

A Taste for Adventure

Brummie Stokes

Foreword by Colonel David Stirling

CORONET BOOKS
Hodder and Stoughton

Dedicated to Lynn,
Sam and Ben,
and to my long-term
friend Bronco Lane

Copyright © 1988 by Brummie Stokes

First published in Great Britain in 1988
by Michael Joseph Ltd.

Coronet edition 1990

British Library C.I.P.
Stokes, Brummie 1945-
 Soldiers and Sherpas : a taste for
adventure. 1. Asia Everest. North-east
face. Mountaineering expeditions.
Biographies
I. Title
915.49'6

ISBN 0 340 51117 6

Printed and bound in Great Britain
for Hodder and Stoughton
paperbacks, a division of Hodder and
Stoughton Ltd., Mill Road,
Dunton Green, Sevenoaks, Kent
TN13 2YA (Editorial Office:
47 Bedford Square, London
WC1B 3DP) by Cox & Wyman Ltd.,
Reading.

Contents

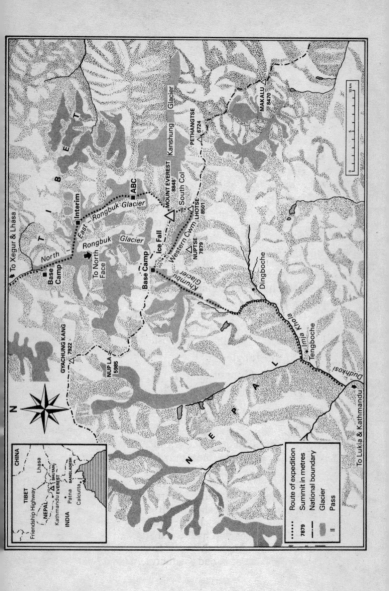

Foreword

Contemplating even for a moment the implications of failure in any bold endeavour spurs the will to succeed. There must, however, be limitations to that spur to avoid failure if you are leading an expedition. Responsibility for those accepting your leadership requires the exercise of sound judgement. To induce high morale so as to keep your team at its highest capability, there must be confidence in that judgement. It is true that not all you believe in succeeds, but nothing at all is achieved if you do not start out with faith.

When I first met Brummie Stokes, what most struck me was his positive attitude. Brummie is a fighter; single-minded and resilient he keeps battling on whatever the obstacles in his way. And, as this book tells, life has cast some formidable barriers across Brummie's path. One thing that shines out very clearly from his narrative is that whatever the misfortune, whatever the pain or hardship to be endured, there are certain values that, for him, are fixed and can never be compromised: loyalty to your companions, straight dealing and personal integrity.

In his youth, Brummie sometimes won the day on what he calls 'sheer aggression', but there were other days, plenty of them, when his natural pugnaciousness only added detours to his route. His long struggle to get into the SAS Regiment is a case in point when, having finally made it through the selection course, he suffered the ignominy of being 'Returned to Unit' for picking an argument with a sergeant who he felt had treated him unfairly. Over the years Brummie has learned to harness his fighting spirit into a force for action and it has served him well as a soldier and a mountaineer. It took him to the top of Everest in 1976 and saw him through an epic descent in bad weather, appalling frostbite injury

I

and the long road to recovery; it still drives him to return to the mountain in the hope of scaling its last and hardest unclimbed ridge.

Since climbing Everest, Brummie has already been back to the mountain only to be caught on one occasion in a devastating avalanche that broke his neck and killed a friend. Many people cannot conceive why he should want to go again. For Brummie it is unfinished business; the Northeast Ridge must be climbed, not so much to prove that he can still do it, even without toes – though that does come into it – but more as a tribute to lost companions. Such determination I can understand and applaud.

His fascination with Everest, that too I can understand. When I was young and Everest was still unclimbed, I dreamed of being the first to reach its lonely summit; I even formulated a five-year plan that was to enable me to do so. I trained in the Swiss Alps and the Rocky Mountains but after two years my plans were interrupted by the outbreak of war. By the time the war was ended, my life had taken a different turn and Everest could no longer be part of it, but I am proud now to be Patron of Brummie Stokes' Northeast Ridge Expedition. If only vicariously I can at least identify with his struggle. I wish him and his team well. He deserves reward for his courage and his persistence and, above all, for his moral guts.

David Stirling
Founder of the SAS
London, May 1988

Preface

T HE ALERT reader may notice one or two gaps in the narrative of this story, but will appreciate that much of the work undertaken by the SAS is of a sensitive nature. Many a good tale has had to be left out for reasons of security and some names omitted or changed so as not to identify soldiers still serving with the Regiment. Places, dates, times may on occasions have been merged with one another, but in the main, events are related in the order of their happening. This is my story, seen through my eyes. I have few notes at the time and kept diaries only of some of my climbing expeditions; memory is notoriously selective and time dims and rounds off much of the detail. Others, who shared these adventures with me, may perhaps have seen things differently.

My education was patchy and most of what I have learned I picked up after I left school; my style and vocabulary consequently are not that of a Will Shakespeare. It's tough, but it can't be helped. I was an adventurer and soldier first, not a book-writer, though I have enjoyed this journey back to my roots and trust others will find something to interest them, too. But the book would probably never have been finished without the assistance of Audrey Salkeld, who has spent hours typing and editing my manuscript and advising me generally.

I am indebted to everyone who appears in these pages. Each in his or her own way has contributed towards my growing up, and towards the shaping of my character. My love and thanks go to my parents, to my brothers and sister and other close family and friends for the support and encouragement they have given me over the years, but most especially to my wife Lynn and my boys Sam and Ben, who have had to endure so many weeks of waiting and worrying on my behalf, but who have never urged me to abandon my taste for adventure.

I would like to thank the following friends and fellow climbers for providing photographs where needed: J. Bond, Meryon Bridges, Joe Brown, Bronco Lane, Eddie Lillicoe, Paul Nunn, J. Peacock, A. Scott and V. Timu.

Expeditions rely heavily upon their sponsors, and I take this opportunity to place on record my gratitude to all those who have helped me and my teams get to faraway places, particularly George Williams of Anglian Window Centres, and to my patrons, The Lord Hunt of Llanfair Waterdine, the Hon. Angus Ogilvie and the Rt. Hon. Lord Jellicoe. I have a special thank you for Colonel David Stirling, the founder of the SAS, who has stood firmly by my side during the 'rough bits'.

Though it is the good times one mostly remembers, I can never forget those lost friends, fellows-in-adventure, who did not come back. Andy, Tony, Steve, Benny, Ollie, Terry, David, Pasang, Jerry and Richard will always hold a special place in my memory and regard.

BRUMMIE STOKES
Hereford
April, 1988

Introduction

HEARD Merv scream a warning, but it came too late. A chunk of ice whistled through the tent in front of my face and the whole world went crazy.

The tent, with me inside, was picked up and thrown down the mountainside by what I took at the time to be a big wind. I felt myself being lifted from the ground and rolled around inside the small blue capsule as it was flung down the hill, my kit tossing and tangling around me as we went. I was screaming with panic, convinced I was going to die without seeing anyone ever again. My mind was racing: I had to do something.

Bouncing off the snow, I felt my shoulder jar as it hit something. I then noticed that a small hole had been made by the ice when it flew through the tent earlier. Pushing my hand into this hole, I ripped a large tear down the side of the bubble I was in, deflated it quickly and was half outside as tons of snow began piling in on top of me. I blacked out.

When I came to I was swimming for the surface through the suffocating snow. I fought my way clear, knelt up and opened my eyes. What I saw horrified and scared me. Snow and ice blocks were piled up everywhere, bodies lay crumpled and half-buried in the snow, and there were such strong winds blowing, it was almost impossible to scramble to my feet. A loud rumbling noise echoed in my ears and the high-pitched whine of wind as it tore savagely at my clothing. I stood up, but was immediately bowled over again.

'Oh, no!' I thought. 'It's starting again!' Any minute now I expected to be blown away once more, and cried out in anguish, 'God! No! No! Please don't make it now! Please, please don't make it now!'

I was shouting at the wind to stop, like a crazy man. I couldn't understand what was going on, what had happened. Later I learned that Merv, who had screamed the warning, had been standing outside his tent and had seen a 400-foot frontage of serac high on the mountain start to tumble towards us. The crash that followed after it had toppled in freefall a thousand feet shook the whole amphitheatre and triggered off avalanches of powdered snow from both Mount Everest and Changtse. The whole lot poured on to us, completely devastating our camp and sweeping it almost half a mile down the hill.

Still numb with fear and shock, I looked up the hill to where Merv was waving and yelled over the wind, 'I'm all right!' But he continued to wave, obviously trying to tell me something. I made out the words: 'Help me! Help me! Bring an axe!'

Dazed, I looked round at the tatters of my tent: no axe, no anything. It had all gone, all been buried.

Early Days

WE LIVED in Hamstead when I was young, just outside Birmingham. It was a mining village, but my dad did not work down the pit. He had seen what a lifetime underground had done for his own father, who was worn out and crippled before he was fifty, and decided it was not for him. Instead, when he returned home after the war, he settled into a series of factory jobs. The work was hard, even so, and the hours long. He would come home exhausted at the end of his shift, his clothes spattered with little blobs of metal from the furnaces. But tired as he was, my father could always somehow pull out enough energy to play football in the street with his kids. He was proud of his family and enjoyed it when we did things together.

'The village', as it was called, was a very close-knit community, for even though we were surrounded by city, Hamstead was almost cut off from the rest of the world and went along at its own pace. It can only be approached by coming downhill from any direction and is very reminiscent of one of the old Welsh mining valleys. The area it covered was perhaps no more than a square mile, within which everyone knew everyone else and all their business intimately. The whole community revolved around the pit, no one talked of much else. It had its own community centre and miners' club owned by the colliery. Life was conducted to the shrill sound of the pithead hooter and the 'knocker-uppers', men whose job it was to wake up the shift workers in the early hours of the morning by banging on doors and upstairs windows with long poles. Generations of villagers had worked in the mines and most people knew very little of life outside their own little part of the world. We were almost a nation apart, despised by the majority of people who lived outside the village, who looked down on us as a dirty, scruffy lot – which in comparison to some of them, I suppose we were. But their main grouse went back to the time of the two world wars when, being miners, the male population of our village was in the main exempt from conscription. Of necessity, such insularity made us fiercely proud, and we would be prepared at the drop of a hat to fight to defend our honour or that of fellow 'Hamsteadonians'.

Number 111 Back Row, where we lived, was the end-house of a colliery-owned terrace, two up, two down. There were seven of us, but pushed as we were for space, no one was allowed into the 'best room' except on special occasions. The toilet and the 'bake house', where my mum did all the washing, were across the yard. Baths were taken in a tin tub in front of the fire, and as all the water had first to be laboriously heated in a coal-fired boiler out the back, there was only ever enough to fill the bath once. It wasn't much fun if you came last in line of such a large family. The only 'fixture' in the kitchen was the blacklead grate, used for heating and cooking. Blacking the grate was a monumental and messy task. We kids were all expected to give a hand, though we did our best to disappear whenever the time came round.

My mother came from Merthyr Tydfil. I don't ever remember her enjoying really good health and she always suffered badly with her nerves. It meant that often when I should have been at school, I was at home instead, looking after her and the house, and preparing meals for my younger brothers and sister, and for my father when he came in from work.

Money was always scarce, but mother lived firmly by the belief that 'If the Lord don't send, he will give'. With her Welsh valley background she set great store by God and we were made to go to Sunday School every week. I would get myself ready, then help prepare my younger brothers and sister and take them across the field to the church hall – which doubled as a scout hut, youth club and anything else that was required of it – but once I had deposited them there, I would be away out the back, making my way to the canal to be with my friends. We would spend the time smoking stolen cigarettes or swimming in the rat- and dead-cat-infested water, before it was time for me to go back and collect the kids.

My father was from Birmingham. He was always a very fair-minded man, though he would never hesitate to do battle with

8

anyone out to make trouble – particularly if one of us kids were threatened. It was an unwise neighbour who came round to complain about our behaviour. Our dad would be out there like a shot, swinging the punches. He'd always been something of a street fighter; to him that was the natural way of resolving arguments. And he was a big man, too, with hands like shovels. It was no joke getting into a fight with him.

There was one time, when we were quite small, word got to him that my grandfather had been attacked at work and kicked to the ground. It wasn't long before my dad caught up with the chap who had done it. We were out walking along the canal when my father spotted the bully a few hundred yards away. Telling us to stay out of sight, he took off like a greyhound and brought the man down before he knew what had hit him.

'The Cut', as the canal was called, was a retreat for all the sons of the village. In the early days it was used for the transportation of coal by barge. These barges would pick up their loads from the basin, a large area of dock-like bays close to the pit stockyards, where the coal would be poured down chutes into the barges anchored below. Sometimes the mine workers would put so much coal on to the vessels that it would spill over the side and into the water as the horsedrawn boat was pulled along the canal. This was done deliberately so that we kids could dive into the murky depths and retrieve the precious anthracite, bag it up and sell it off later to assist with the weekly wage.

There were many days when I would take my old 'Trambo', a boxcar on four old pram wheels, up to the 'Marlhole' on my way to school to pick a bag of coal, hide it and collect it at lunch time. The 'Marlhole' was an area of land owned by the colliery which was used as a dumping ground for all the waste and slag that came out of the pit. This was transported for over a mile via an overhead cableway of tubs, each containing half a ton of rubble and bits of waste coal that the sorters had missed (or shut a blind eye to). The tub would hit a trigger device hanging from the cable and deposit its contents in a steadily growing heap on the ground.

As soon as the dust settled, there would be a mad scramble as miners' wives and kids began fighting for the pieces of black rock before the next tub arrived thirty seconds later. This was called 'scratting'. We would stuff the booty into our little collecting sacks, and all around the heap of rubble there would be prams, old pushchairs, bikes and 'trambos' loaded up with half-filled sacks of coal, jealously guarded as often as not by grimy little youngsters of five and six who played quite unconcerned among the slagheaps. All this activity was watched by Mr Dukes, the caterpillar driver and watchman, whose job it was, when the pile got too large, to bulldoze the waste into a huge hole some 150 feet below in readiness for use in the kilns or to be made up into bricks in the brickyard.

Old 'Dukesey' would have to chase us off every now and then, especially if there was an overseer about. But we were like a flock of carrion crows after a rotting carcase: chased off by a predator one minute, we would come skulking back for more as soon as his back was turned.

In the late evening after the watchman had gone home and the tubs were no longer bringing up slag was the time for distractions and dares. A cleaning period of about an hour was required at the pithead to service the tubs and this was all we needed to enable us to climb to the top of the 'tower'. This tower, which housed the giant wheel that carried the heavy-duty cable, on to which the tubs were fixed, stood just over 200 feet high.

One dare was to climb up the inspection ladders and touch the wheel as it rotated above you. Another was to climb to the top of the slagheap and grab hold of a tub as it passed by. The object then was to lodge yourself on top of the, by now, upside-down tub and hang on for dear life as you were carried on an ever-rising traverse, up to and around the tower and wheel, before returning to the slag heap and dropping to the ground. The trick was not so much in doing it, but in getting away with it without being spotted by someone who would tell your parents.

The most impressive dare of all, however, was not one of the Marlpit ones: what drew the most admiration was to climb to the top of the chimney stack in the grounds of the brickyard. This could only be done at night or on a Sunday when no one was around. It entailed first getting into the yard, avoiding the guard dogs and patrol man, and then ascending the stack by the steeplejack's ladder and lightning conductor, which were anchored to its side. We had been told that there was a gold coin cemented into the top of the chimney, but this was either taken by the builder or was just a story, for we saw no sign of it at all.

Much kudos could be gained by completing these dares, and despite the many accidents, most boys tried, because the worst thing in the world was to be considered unmanly or a coward.

Unwanted and broken bricks would be dumped by the ton to the side of the yard. This created an ideal adventure playground for kids, where we would build gang huts out of the red and blue waste bits of brick. These could be camouflaged by piling hundreds of other bricks on top, leaving just a small entrance hole known only to gang members. The whereabouts of these sanctuaries were always kept a closely-guarded secret, even to the extent of 'bombing them in' and relocating if a member defected to a rival gang.

We were five kids at home, four boys and a girl. I was the eldest, born in 1945, and for some reason or other could never seem to keep out of trouble. By the time I was a teenager, I was hanging around with a pretty tough bunch and really going off the rails. There was one time when a couple of mates and I stole a car and went for a joyride. We had set fire to a haystack already that day and the next thing we did was crash the car. In the evening a policeman called round at the house, wanting to speak to me.

'What do you want him for?' my father asked.

The policeman related our trail of havoc.

'Will you wait a minute?' My father showed him into the kitchen and called up the stairs to me.

'What's all this about stealing cars?' he demanded.

I thought I could bluff it out. 'Not me, dad,' I replied. 'No way.'

The words seemed to hang in the air; I couldn't believe my dad did not detect their falseness right away, but he didn't question it. As far as he was concerned, my word was good enough, and with that, he asked the policeman to leave.

Next night, however, the man was back. This time he had positive proof; one of the other lads had fingered me. There was no way out. I confessed, and was taken down to the police station to be charged. Later my father was allowed to bring me home. His face was white as we walked back to the house and he did not say a word. I was scared stiff.

Once inside, he gave me a good walloping.

'Do you know what that was for?' he demanded afterwards.

'B-because I stole the car and that,' I muttered.

'No!' He was shouting now. 'Not just for that! Yes, because you stole the car, and yes, because you got caught doing it, but most of all, for telling me lies. I trusted you, and you let me down!

'I can tell you this, son,' he continued, 'I'll never trust you again. Go on, get upstairs to bed.'

I disappeared quickly, relieved that I wasn't going to get beaten any more. But it hurt far more that I had disappointed my father. I cried bitterly before I finally fell asleep.

Next morning my father took me aside and apologised for hitting me. He said he was sorry he had lost his temper, and promised we would work it out together. Weeks later, good as his word, he spoke up for me in the juvenile court. I was put on probation for one year.

Not long after, when I was fourteen, I was running my own gang and had worked out a plan to rob the local supermarket. When I look back at it now, it was quite an elaborate plan with all the ingredients of a military raid.

Using a ladder to reach a rear window, smeared with grease to stop it falling out as I smashed it, we would be in and out in ten minutes, taking just cigarettes and money. That way no one would suspect that kids had done it. We even had a look-out in the main road.

Once we had got the stuff out we were to make our way separately to the gang den up in the brickworks. We would leave everything untouched for two months until things had calmed down, and then divide it up. We rehearsed the whole thing. Everything seemed fine.

All went according to plan until I smashed the window and slipped inside. Instead of just two of us going in and passing stuff to the others, everyone started to pile through the window and ransack the place. My plan was breaking up. Giggling hysterically, people started to pull down cakes, sweets, pop, cigarettes, cash, anything they could lay their hands on. It was all going crazy.

'Come on, get out! That's enough!' I said after ten minutes.

I could feel my heart thumping with excitement and fear. With cigarettes stuffed up my jumper and carrying a supermarket bag full of goodies, I was left alone to dispose of the ladder.

'Bloody fools! Bloody fools!' I kept repeating. 'They spoiled it. Why didn't they stick to the plan?'

Sure enough, the next morning on the bus going to school, everyone had cigarettes. People who had never had two ha'pennies to rub together were suddenly barons, handing out sweets and smokes to all and sundry. In the school grounds at break, groups could be seen all over, selling off fags cheaply.

The policeman was soon back knocking at our front door. It was the moment I had been dreading but knew with increasing certainty that it had to come. My mother was in tears and my father was raging. There was no good-hiding this time.

All he said was, 'That's it! I've finished with you!' and left for his night shift.

Locking myself in the bedroom, I felt terrible. I was sure he meant it. I'd really gone too far this time and sacrificed any respect he held for me. Only then did I realise just how important my father's support and respect was. It was all I wanted – and I had thrown it away! I was no good to anyone and would be better off dead. On my way upstairs I had grabbed a jar of my mother's sleeping tablets from the kitchen. I had had enough; I would finish it for once and for all.

All my life till then I had felt in some way special, convinced I was going to be someone one day. Now I could see it was not true: I was bad, bad all through. Once again I had let everyone down. I swallowed the whole jar of pills, and lay down on the bed waiting to die. Before long the room was spinning. The light was so bright and I felt sick, sicker than I ever thought possible.

I must have blacked out, for the next thing I remember was having fingers forced down my throat. And I was being made to drink really strong, black coffee. I was vomiting everywhere. My dad, who had been summoned from work, was slapping my face.

'How many did you take? How many did you take?' he asked. He was cradling me in his arms and forcing me to be sick.

'I'm sorry dad. I'm so sorry!' I cried.

I saw he was crying, too, and his big face wore a strained look. I loved him so much, and I had failed him.

The sound of an ambulance wailed into the night as it rushed me off to hospital and the stomach pump.

The next day I lay deep in the bed, too ashamed to answer the man in the next bed when he enquired kindly what I was in for. I would not speak to anyone. I felt so wretched and hated everything about myself. How was I ever going to face people again?

Later that day, my mother arrived with my father, who again hugged me in his big arms and said. 'You don't ever need to do that, John. We thought we had lost you. Don't ever do that again.'

We both cried, and that night I grew even closer to my dad. He persuaded me there was always some way of putting difficulties behind you and trying to make a go of things. I still felt very ashamed, though, and do even to this day. Not only that, I have never been able to stomach strong coffee since!

Climbing for dares on the chimney stacks and the wheeltower of the 'Marlhole' had given me a taste for scrambling. The excitement I get from confronting danger, a blend of fright and exhilaration, and the need I constantly have to urge myself on to see how far I can go – these, when I look back, must have all originated during those early years in Hamstead. There were no mountains, as such, anywhere near the village, but I took to wandering along the towpaths of the old canal where it was always very quiet. I found that I really enjoyed being on my own; I would stroll along taking in the wonder of it all, listening to birds and watching the swans gliding on the scummy waters. I would walk for miles, often finishing up somewhere near Dudley where the canal cut its way beneath a large hill, on which Dudley castle stood.

I had long ago sought out odd bits of rocky outcrop and old quarries in the vicinity, where I could scramble about undisturbed and pretend that I was Sir Edmund Hillary or Sherpa Tenzing scaling the highest mountain in the world. The very name of Everest filled me with a longing to see it; I both envied and hero-worshipped the two men who had been the first to climb it.

I was eight years old, the year of the Coronation of the Queen, when the news of the conquest of Everest was announced. Taking part in the celebrations many of the youngsters in the village had been dressed up as climbers and driven on floats through the streets. I looked very smart in the scarlet uniform of a soldier with a guardsman's hat made of cardboard, but I can remember taking a rope from one of the boys dressed as climbers and draping it proudly across my shoulders, just as Sherpa Tenzing might have done. Holding up a small Union Jack as I stood on the back of the float pretending that I was on the roof of the world, was, had I but known it, a prophetic moment, encapsulating everything that later was to become important in my life – soldiering, climbing, Sherpas – and Mount Everest.

The small outcrops on which I was teaching myself to climb were not very high, fifty or sixty feet at most, but I was ever conscious of the fact that if I did fall, it could be enough to kill me. Not having anyone else to climb with, I never gave a moment's thought to the extra dangers involved in climbing alone. The gear I wore was the same as I wore every day, with the exception of an old pair of cricket boots that my mother had bought for me in a jumble sale. I had no time for cricket, but I removed the studs and found that the stiff leather adhered well to the crumbling rock of the crags. Rope was something that I had no need of on my own, nor knew how to use. For the time being, I was content to scramble about on this easy stuff, and when I could not get out there (it was a five-mile walk along the towpath), I would scale the sides of the High Bridges, which spanned the canal close to our house, where the canal went through a steep-sided gorge covered with trees. Towers of imported stone, cut into large blocks, supported the bridges, and lying-back against the side of the gorge at an angle of sixty degrees, they were crying out to be climbed. The difficulty was negligible, but they provided exposure, rising as they did to 150 feet above the towpath. One of the most exciting climbs on the bridges was a straightforward traverse on metal struts underneath the road that this structure supported. Vehicles could be heard thundering inches above your head and the view below was breathtaking as horse-drawn barges and the people out walking the towpath appeared so tiny.

Always having to wash my clothes, dirty and oily from scrambling over the rocks and bridges, my mother would scold me for being 'climbing mad'. She would invariably relate to me the story of how, when I was three, I had climbed out of a bedroom window in my aunt's house and got myself stuck on top of a porchway for more than an hour before I was found and rescued, quite unperturbed by the incident.

My first venture into the bigger hills came when I was invited to join the Sunday School on its 'chara' trips to North Wales. This gave me my chance to climb to the summit of Snowdon, and a taste for adventure. I followed the line of the railway track to the top of the mountain in the company of hordes of other tourists, but in my mind, they were not there. And this was not Snowdon. To me, in my private world, I was alone with Hillary and it was Everest we were tackling for the first time.

Time spent in Wales gave me an opportunity to see how real climbers did it and I watched in amazement as human flies clung effortlessly to rocky buttresses and faces along the Llanberis Pass. Persuading one of these 'professionals' to 'give me a go', I tied on a rope for the first time and half-climbed, half-crawled up the rock face after him, trembling with the strain. It was marvellous! It had frightened me, but at the same time it had elated me. It had made me feel many things, but most of all it had given me pleasure. I was hooked.

By now I was working so I could afford to pay my own train fares out of Birmingham and get off into the hills at every opportunity. I never shared what I was doing with my parents for fear that they might try to stop me, even though it had been my father who had pointed out most of the bridges and crags to me during our many adventure walks at weekends. I was not to know then that it would be these walks and trips to the outlying areas of Birmingham, where it was less built up, that would lead eventually to my unquenchable thirst for open and high places.

The Green Jackets

CAN still vividly remember the thrill as the train pulled out of Snow Hill Station on that spring day in 1963. Now I was seventeen and a half and off to be a solider.

I had always wanted to join the Army, but to my surprise, my father said, 'No'. He urged me to try as many jobs as I could, then if I still wanted to be a soldier, I could go off when I reached the age of seventeen and a half. For two years I worked in factories, offices, the pit, at panel-beating, in bowling alleys. Whenever I moved into something I liked, dad urged me on.

He was very astute, my old man. He gave me a good grounding. By the time I went into the military, I had seen many different ways of life and taken a look at a lot of occupations. I may have mastered none of them, but I have never regretted the insight they gave me.

Three weeks earlier, I had walked into an army recruiting office and informed the hefty sergeant on duty there that I wanted to sign up for the SAS.

'Not as easy as that, mate,' he'd said, and with a hint of relish had gone on to explain how it was not The Regiment's policy to mess around training yobos off the streets. Let some other branch of the army do that; the SAS could always skim off the cream later.

That was a bit of a blow. I have never liked hanging around. I like to get stuck in right away once I've made up my mind. But, if that was the system, I was prepared to go along with it.

'How long does this training take?' I asked him.

'Three years.'

Three whole years? But that was forever! Sensing my dismay, the sergeant moved in for the hard sell. The Green Jackets, he recommended, were the next best thing. No coincidence, of course, that the Green Jackets happened also to be his own regiment, and he went on to enthuse about the honour that went with wearing its black belt and infantry green beret.

I signed.

Now, here I was, a raw recruit with the 3rd Battalion The Royal Green Jackets Rifle Brigade, on a train bound for Winchester to start my training. Several other lads had joined on the way, so that by the time we pulled into the little station, there was quite a group of us. We scrambled out on to the platform and stood around hesitantly, wondering what to do next. A uniformed soldier soon arrived to round us up.

'Hey! John Lennon!'

I looked round.

'Yes, you! Come here!'

John-bloody-Lennon! Who did he think he was? I didn't even like the Beatles. Maybe, like most lads of my age, my hair was combed forward and I was wearing tight blue jeans, a jacket without a collar and winkle-picker shoes, but they were all I had to my name – apart, that is, from a small plastic Masons carrier bag which contained some socks, my washing kit and a brand new razor Mum and Dad had bought me as a going-away present.

'Yeah, mate, what's up?'

'What's your name then, son? Stokes, eh? Well then, Stokes, see this on my arm?' He pointed to the black and green tape slanting two ways on his bicep. 'That's called a stripe, and that makes me a Lance Corporal, see. Something you will never be if you call me your mate again. I ain't your mate now; I never will be your mate. Understand? It's Corporal to you. Right! Get over there by the truck with the rest of these soldier boys.'

I mentally marked him down as a power-crazed idiot, someone I only thought to find in comic strips. Any more like him, I thought, and I wasn't too sure I was going to like it in the army. Just in time I remembered the last thing my old man said when I left: 'Look, listen, learn – and keep yer mouth shut, son. At least till you see the way the land lies.' It was probably sound advice, and I resisted the urge to take a swing at this big-mouth, but I wasn't going to forgive him for having a go at me so soon.

The next three months were spent picking up the basics: weapon training, boxing, marching about and being shouted at, getting into better condition than I had ever been in before and making new friends. We were out of doors most days, in the country, chasing about woods and doing things with guns, maps and compasses. It was good to be away from the city. I did not miss Birmingham – not the pit, the dirt, nor the rut I was in. The only thing that I was not happy about was having to say, 'Yes, Corporal. No, Corporal,' when I really meant the opposite. Still, no harm in stringing them along, just so long as I remained my own man – and became the best at everything I did.

The competition was keen. Evil Pete, our squad corporal and instructor, had everyone striving towards the ultimate goal, to become the best recruit of the intake, and it did not take long for my professional pride to take over. My kit became the tidiest, my boots the shiniest and my creases the sharpest. I was taking great pleasure in being first in everything. Then, with only a week to go before we passed out of our training phase and moved on to join the Regular Battalions, tragedy struck. I fractured my leg racing to finish first over the obstacle course.

'Oh, no,' I thought, 'I'll be back-squadded and have to wait for the next intake before I can complete the last week's training.'

Fortunately, this was not the case. Evil Pete proved to be not as black as we painted him. I learned later he had himself attempted an SAS selection course, which may be what made him sympathetic to my endeavours. He had seen enough, he said, to convince him and the School Commander that I would not require any further training before joining the Battalion. Even with my leg in plaster I had done enough to earn the honour of being Best Recruit.

My first posting was to the Mediterranean island of Cyprus. Sun, sea, sand and mountains – it sounded idyllic. The only trouble was that I had chosen to join up during a small war between the Greeks and the Turks. I soon learned that the reality of limited wars was different from the movies, and not that exciting. Most of the time was spent sitting in small sandbagged observation posts on the top of buildings, reporting once an hour by radio to an operations room you never saw. Only occasionally, did we come close to any real action.

Moving in convoy along the road from Dekhelia to Nicosia one morning, our vehicles were stopped at a roadblock manned by a small band of armed Greek Freedom Fighters. Our directive was to sit between the Greek and Turkish factions on what became known as the 'Green Line' to prevent them from ripping each other's throats out. In this instance, the roadblock formed a barrier between us and our position on 'the line'. Our command-ing officer strolled over to the obstacle and demanded it be pulled down so that we could proceed on our way. The Greeks refused, whereupon our CO then produced his pistol and called up one of our Wombat Anti-Tank weapons. This was duly deployed and aimed at the pile of vehicles blocking our way. He then asked again that the barricade be removed. This time, on being told 'no', the Wombat was ordered to be loaded and made ready for firing. The Greek guard was told he had until the count of ten to open up the barrier or it would be blasted apart.

Five minutes later, we were on our way.

I was impressed. 'So that's the way it's done, eh? These officers really knew their stuff.' But I qualified this, later, to only some of them.

Sitting in my little sandbagged rooftop perch at two o'clock one morning, the static on the radio was interrupted by the excited voice of one of the regiment's younger lieutenants.

'Quick, quick, get me the CO!'

My ears pricked up. This must be something big. I looked round the area, checking for signs of mass activity. The night was silent and the sky crystal clear, every planet plain to see. Slightly disappointed that we were not under attack, I listened in to the rest of the conversation. What on earth could warrant getting the big man up at this hour in the morning?

'The North Star has moved,' the lieutenant went on. 'When I went to sleep at eleven o'clock, it was off to my left, and now it is across on my right.'

I could not believe my ears: was it some sort of joke? Here was a man who had attended an expensive school, university, Sandhurst and then officer training school, but where had he *been* all that time to remain so completely unaware of the phenomenon of the earth's rotation?

'See me in the morning,' was all the CO said, his voice quietly dangerous.

The lieutenant was supposed to be my *leader*. I thought, I would not follow this man to the toilet, let alone to war; and it was then I realised I should never take for granted everything that one of these plum-in-the-mouth 'doughballs' told me.

Every now and then, we would have to do a guard on one of the various ammunition dumps on the island to ensure that they were not broken into. Guard duties as a rule are quite boring, so to alleviate them we used to have to try and amuse ourselves in a variety of ways.

The section corporal in charge of us was a chap we nicknamed 'Toe' Bristow, who was not a bad lad, but had a tendency to be dictatorial. His great joy was fire drill. He would call us out at any time of the day or night to go through the ritual. It necessitated everyone in the compound, whether in bed at the time or not, to run out of the guardroom in whatever they were wearing and take up positions on the fire engine. Everyone had his own special place to go to. The Toe took great delight in lodging himself head and shoulders through the ladder section which overhung the back of the engine, from where he would direct operations.

We would drive at great speeds around the compound, cornering as though we were taking part in a Grand Prix – all this, so that our corporal, hanging on the back, could feel the exhilaration of charging around on his very own fire engine.

I must admit that this was quite fun when it first began, but it began to pall after we'd had no sleep for days on end because we were constantly called out to play on this stupid green fire machine. After long discussions, a plan was hatched.

The very next time we were called out was around midnight. It was a warm, clear night. Out we tumbled to take up our positions on the vehicle and, as usual, the Toe adopted his prominent position through the ladder rungs at the back.

'Drive out to the back gate,' he ordered the driver.

Bells ringing and lights flashing, we set off at a great rate. The back gate was nearly a mile away – this could not be better! Hanging on to the side of the vehicle opposite Charlie, I grinned at him as I released the extending-ladder retaining pin. As we gathered speed, so the ladder started to slip back, taking poor old Toe with it. Losing his footing, he very quickly found himself suspended in mid-air, screaming, 'Stop! Stop!'

Staring directly in front, laughing and pretending not to hear him, we noticed that the second section of ladder had started to slip out as well. Sneaking a quick look back, I could see that our gallant fire chief was hanging on for dear life, with his feet just coming into contact with the ground every now and then. With the momentum of the ladder swaying up and down, he was having to bound along the road for a few paces and would then take off into the air, all the time shouting for us to stop the vehicle.

Of course, pretending not to *know* what was happening, there was nothing we could do! Just as we approached the first bend, laughing hysterically at each other, Charlie asked, 'Shall I?' and released the clip that retained the ladder's sideways movement. As we rounded the next left-hand bend, so too did the ladder, only a little faster. The corporal was really raging as he loped on to the dirt on the side of the road. Everyone on the wagon was by now openly screeching with laughter at the sight of this poor man with his head and shoulders stuck through a ladder which was by now trailing some forty feet behind us, and bounding to the left and right as we tore around bend after bend.

When we at last came to a standstill, people fell about on the ground, weak from laughing so much.

'Right, you bastards, you will pay for this!' said our budding fireman, as he extricated himself from the end of the ladder which had come to rest in a pile of dust off to the right of us.

'If we get twenty-eight days for this, it will have been worth it,' I said to Charlie.

Fire drill was never the same again after that, nor as frequent.

Not long after our return to the United Kingdom, we were sent on a tour of duty to Hong Kong, from where we would go on to Singapore, Malaya and finally, undertake a six-month operational stint in Borneo on Active Service duties against communist terrorists in that country's protracted conflict with Indonesia.

Hong Kong! As nineteen-year-olds we could hardly wait. Oh, oh, the bright lights, wine, women in Chinese split-up-the-side-to-the-armpit dresses, and song! We would show them. Just let us loose on this town!

Landing at Hong Kong's Kai Tak Airport, we could see skyscrapers, shops and bars everywhere. We were bundled through customs and on to three-ton wagons, then driven in convoy *past* all the bright lights, through a long tunnel and out into the countryside.

'Hey, what's going on here? I thought we were posted to Hong Kong,' I demanded of one of the sergeants who had come to pick us up.

'Fan Ling, son, Fan Ling is where you're going.' He added, 'You'll love it.'

With a broad smile, he turned to look out the back at the miles and miles of paddy and semi-cultivated fields we were passing on our journey westwards, towards the border with China.

Even with the draught blowing through the open front of the canopy, it was hot and sticky inside the lorry, and since we had landed there had been an ever-present smell I could not fathom out, nauseating and redolent of rotting flesh.

'I shan't be sorry to get through this lot,' someone muttered out of the darkness of the wagon.

By now, we were all feeling queasy and we were relieved when the vehicle started to pull in through a barbed-wire gate, drove on to a concrete hard-standing, and stopped.

'Welcome to Fan Ling,' said the sergeant as he let down the tailboard. 'Get your kit off and fall in in three ranks over here. Come on, now, jump about a bit! Don't want to be here all night messing about, do we?'

We were marched to our various platoon rooms in old wooden buildings that looked as though they had not been used for years. Twenty beds were set out ready with blankets and sheets, and there was a great rush to grab a bed and get sorted out.

'What's this thing here?' I asked. It looked like a giant butterfly net.

One of the old sweats who had served in the tropics before put me wise. 'It's your mosquite net, young 'un,' he said, 'and you'll be needing it here tonight, I think.' With that he kicked the side of the dusty old building, disturbing a swarm of minute transparent insects, which were soon whining about our ears.

Fan Ling is in the New Territories and our time there was spent acclimatising, training, and doing duty on the border observation posts, checking for illegal immigrants and keeping an eye on Chinese Army activity on the other side. It was during this period that I started to box again. Cyprus had given me the opportunity to establish myself on the Regimental Team. I had no real skill, but used to win most of my fights by sheer aggression. Being a member of the team brought certain privileges. You did not have to do guard duties as most of the day was spent in the gym and – better still – you got to go down into the city every now and then when there was an inter-battalion tournament.

I didn't make many close friends during those years. I had always been a bit of a loner, and the folk I struck up with were all much the same – self-contained, self-reliant, and anti-officer. We were always bucking the system and getting into trouble, and it usually ended up with short forays to the guardhouse. Many were the times that two or three of us would take off in a Chinese bus to

Hong Kong Island and throw ourselves into a drinking spree that ended in the arms of some bar floozie, to whom we would swear undying love and devotion. We would pawn a watch or some other item to pay her, and when the money ran out, wander around till we were picked up by the Military Police. Like packs of hounds, the MPs constantly roamed the streets looking for such prey. After a good kicking by this gang of heroes-who-never-went-to-war, we would be deposited back at the Regimental Guardroom in Fan Ling. It was as good a place as any to dry out and get fit again.

Four months in Hong Kong passed very quickly, the only real action taking place when we were called out to help keep order during riots in the Kowloon-side backstreets. I found it very unsettling at that age, standing in ranks of three with inadequate anti-riot equipment while hordes of Chinese advanced upon us, armed with bamboo spears and molotov cocktails. I had no idea then why the Chinese were rioting, nor why they should want us to leave Hong Kong, but it did give me a taste of what it felt like to have adrenalin pumping excitement around my body.

Then it was on to Singapore, the Lion City, where we went through Changi and Nee Soon, names that we had all heard about during our short service lives. Changi was the infamous prison where, in the last war, most of the British troops were held after Singapore fell to the Japanese. A feeling of depression lingers over it still. Nee Soon was the site of another camp, one which featured in the book and film *The Virgin Soldiers*. That story did not seem very far removed from our own experiences, but after a fairly short time there, we were moved by vehicle across the causeway to Johore Baru in Malaya to start a period of intense jungle training in preparation for our duties in Borneo.

Billeted in open-ended tin huts, we spent three weeks being taught how to live, move, eat and fight in the jungle. This was a doddle since most of the training was done in the open sunshine out on a massive football field.

I was getting impatient. 'When are we going to stop messing about and get down to some real soldiering and patrolling in the trees?' I wanted to know.

The answer came a few days later when we were told to pack up and get ready for 'jungle-familiarisation patrols'. We were going to be away for a week under the supervision of our sergeant-major, Bill Bagley, a Brummie who had served with the SAS and who wore parachute wings on his chest to denote that he had made operational parachute descents somewhere in the world. I was never able to find out where, since as a lance corporal, I was not allowed to talk socially with people of his rank.

We were dropped off along an old logging track and the first thing I noticed as the noise of the engines died down were the many varied sounds around us. Birds, crickets, running water, wind through the trees – there were hundreds of different noises. I was going to like this place. The jungle seemed so very vast yet peaceful, too.

'Come on then, off yer bums! Pick up yer kit and follow me.'

In single file, we walked along a smaller track for about five minutes, before coming to a small camp made out of trees and branches. Putting my kit down on the first shelter I came to, I was surprised to be attacked by the sergeant-major.

'You can bugger off from there, sunshine,' he roared. 'That's mine.'

It would appear that all the ready-built shelters were for the officers. We had to construct our own. Thirty inexperienced men were set loose on the jungle with their *parangs* to hack out the necessary materials. It was a recipe for disaster. Sweating from the effort, the starch began to run out of our jungle uniforms, raising an ugly itching rash wherever it trickled. Some fool decided to play at Tarzan and, swinging on a length of vine, managed to dislodge a branch which fell on to one of the other lads, breaking his arm. It also brought down a tree snake, which we immediately encircled and began beating with sticks. The snake struck out and bit two people before it was killed.

We had been in the jungle for only an hour, and already three people had to be sent back to hospital. Before we finished that night, two more had to leave after slicing themselves with their *parangs*.

As it began to grow dark, the whine of the mosquitoes became more insistent, and it was difficult to hear much over the sound of people swatting away at the blood-hungry little monsters.

'For Chrissake, put on your insect repellent,' shouted the sergeant-major. 'It sounds like a Bavarian thigh-slapping contest around here.' Certainly, any enemy could have taken us by surprise; we would never had heard him approach.

Once it became really dark, everything on the ground took on a green, fluorescent glow, and I could see torches moving everywhere, tiny green ones.

'Can you see those lights out there, Charlie? I asked the man next to me.

With a chuckle he replied, 'They're fireflies, mate, not lights.'

And that was when the sky opened up, releasing torrents of monsoon rain.

'OK, into your shelters,' yelled the sergeant-major, already, I suspected, safely within the sanctuary of his own. Later, lying in my half-completed hideaway, trying to adjust the waterproof roof to keep out some of the rain at least, I could not resist a snigger over the comic aspect of it all. We were a right bunch of novices, I thought, like boy scouts out on their first camping trip. I was soon soaked through and did not sleep a wink all night, but I had learned a lot. I took to the jungle quite naturally, recognising that you can't fight it. You have to bend and live in harmony with it.

To the Land of
the Headhunters

THREE WEEKS of continuous jungle work qualified us as fit for active service duty in Borneo. We had been taught how the infantry lives, moves and fights in a jungle environment, had learned how to build helicopter landing sites, how to abseil into the jungle, and how to get an injured man winched out, should the need ever arise. There were a thousand and one small 'tricks of the trade' for making life in the trees more comfortable, that I had picked up from looking and listening to the older and more experienced members of the company. At the end of the day, though, the message was always the same: the jungle is neutral. If you don't try to fight it, it can be a pleasant place, but equally, if you don't learn to live side by side with it, then it can be most unpleasant and will eventually wear you down. I couldn't see that being a problem for me, as I quite enjoyed it. The closeness of nature, seeing birds, plants and animal life at such close quarters was, for me, an adventure. The fact that I would be studying this fascinating environment in an area where a limited war was taking place only added to the excitement. I could not wait to get to grips with the Wild Men of Borneo.

After a week's preparation and packing, the Regiment boarded a flat-bottomed tug called HMS *Aubery*, bound for Kuching, Borneo's main town. The boat had at one time been a minesweeper and had been retired to the South China Sea because it was of no further use anywhere else in the world. It was a rusting old bucket that, in the words of one of the crew 'should have been in the scrapyard years ago. It's got so many holes in it, it's like sailing in a colander.'

'Cheers, mate,' I thought, 'that's all I need, done my confidence the world of good, that has!' Not being a very good sailor, I spent the majority of the trip hanging over the side, feeding the fishes. I wasn't alone. It would appear that I had enlisted with a regiment of landlubbers.

For two days we bumped, crashed and swayed our way across the South China Sea, our faces turning ever greener, until at last, mercifully, we docked in the smelly fishing port of Kuching. We had arrived on the war front. I did hope that I wouldn't be needed for any immediate battles, as the way I felt I would not have been much good to anyone.

I need not have worried on that count. As I was to learn during our briefing sessions over the next couple of days, the only fighting that was taking place was miles away to the north, way up on the border with Indonesia. Communist terrorists (CT) were apparently infiltrating across the border, setting up training camps, and intimidating the local villagers into becoming communist. If they objected, a headman (*Pengulu*) would be taken out and shot and replaced with someone more sympathetic to the communist cause. It would be our job to stop this happening by setting up company positions along the border, liaising closely with the *Pengulus* and setting up ambushes at all the likely crossing points. The 'confrontation', as this was called, had been going on for quite some time before we arrived and we were to take over a base that had already been set up by the Parachute Regiment at a place called Gunong Gajah (Elephant Hill). The only way into this location was by helicopter and it would take several hours' flying to get there.

On the morning of the third day, we loaded all our kit and equipment into the twin-engined Belvedere helicopter, a monster sausage of a machine with a set of rotor blades at each end. After a long flight, we descended like locusts swarming over a vegetable patch on a bare hillock hacked out of the jungle. Throughout the journey I had sat quietly by the window watching the vast expanse of rainforest below me, my eyes following the lines of the muddy rivers as they wound their way towards the sea. Dotted here and there along the banks of these rivers were tiny villages, or, as my limited Malay had now taught me, *kampongs*. My eyes strained at groups of people in the water fishing or washing. Having heard all the stories of Wild Men, I was expecting to see tattooed head-hunters and was not at all sure what my reaction would be when eventually the time came to meet one face to face.

As we were coming into land I noticed that there was a small *kampong* not too far from the foot of our hillock and that a long high ridge of jungle-covered mountain ran in almost straight line a couple of miles to the north. This I guessed must be the border ridge.

We had arrived at what was to become our home for the next six months. Men of the Parachute Regiment, whom we had come to relieve, clambered aboard in our place, and before long the noise of the helicopters had droned away in the distance, allowing the natural sounds of the jungle to take over.

We were shown to our new quarters.

'Bit grim here, innit?' commented someone as I descended into an underground bunker which acted as both sentry post and sleeping quarters.

'This one'll do for us,' I said to Charlie, Vic and Mac, as I placed my kit on one of the four bamboo-built bunk beds inside the gloomy interior. It smelled of damp and earth and was lit by the light of a single, flickering candle in a makeshift candle-holder, fashioned from an old beer can by one of the previous tenants. The other three scrambled in after me and claimed their spots.

'Hope we don't have to spend too much time cooped up in this prison,' remarked Vic, a scouse who had been a friend since our training days in Winchester.

It did not take us long to familiarise ourselves with the new surroundings. The little hill we were on was only a couple of hundred feet above the river and the *kampong*, and had two points of entry and exit: one that went down to the water, and another at the other end of camp that led towards the border. The camp was some 300 yards across, surrounded by barbed wire with a four-foot-deep trench inside. The four-man sentry posts stood at intervals of thirty feet around the perimeter. Beyond the barbed wire, firmly implanted in the earth and pointing outwards menacingly, were row upon row of *pangees*, thousands of razor-sharp, bamboo spears about eighteen inches long, that would cut into the shins of any enemy attempting a frontal attack on our base. One of the Parachute Regiment lads had informed us that at a place called Plan an Mapu, the next position along the border, just such an attack had been made only a week earlier by a band of about thirty CT. It had lasted for about three hours and been unsuccessful because the enemy was unable to breach the barbed wire and *pangee* pits. Over the next few days our defences were reinforced by mines and trip flares to give us advanced warning of any impending attack.

After settling in and familiarising ourselves with the immediate area, I took over the job of Lead Scout. This was a professional honour in that it meant I must have proved to the hierarchy that I had the necessary skills and natural ability to lead the rest of the company, or platoon, through the jungle and avoid walking into enemy ambushes. Either that, or I was the only one daft enough to put myself up front to be the first to come into contact with the enemy. Personally, it suited me to have this measure of command over the situation and not to have to rely on the judgement of anyone else if it came to life-or-death decisions. I felt pretty confident of my own abilities to detect any enemy presence, but not so happy to rely on others. Being up front was more exciting, too. It meant that if we moved slowly and quietly enough, I could creep up on and get a good look at some of the wildlife in the woods before it was disturbed by our presence.

One day when I was leading the platoon up to the border ridge on patrol, I heard the excited chatter of a troop of monkeys coming my way and the sound of a hornbill screaming its warning as it flew out of harm's way above my head. Prickling with excitement, I dropped to the ground, released the safety catch from my rifle and pointed it up the track. Charlie, my back-up man, quietly moved up beside me, copying my movements. I sensed, rather than knew, that things were not quite right. I gave the thumbs-down sign to indicate that there were enemy in front of us and waited with bated breath and heart pumping for them to appear in my sights. The monkeys disappeared over the side of the ridge between us and whatever they were running from. Casting a quick glance at Charlie who had also taken aim, I caught sight of a brownish uniformed soldier cautiously making his way along the track, and lined up my foresight to his middle.

Just as I was about to squeeze the trigger, I was startled by the voice of the troop officer storming his way along the line of men who were by now all taking up firing positions behind me.

'What's going on here?' he boomed, coming to an abrupt halt as I fired at the fleeing figure of the CT in front of me. Both Charlie and I rushed forward to try and get off another couple of shots, but we were too late. The enemy had gone. Bringing forward our Iban tracker, a small, sinewy, raw-boned man with tattoos on his neck and face indicating that he originated from the ferocious headhunter tribe, we learned that there had been about six in the enemy party, and judging by the blood on the ground, we had managed to put a hole in one of them.

I had been blooded. This was the first time I had taken part in any real action in which I was allowed to shoot back. I felt elated, but at the same time I was disappointed with the officer, who, by his untimely action, had ruined what otherwise have been a 'good contact'. It was the same officer who had spotted the North Star moving in Cyprus, so I should not have been surprised by this turn of events.

After working with our Iban trackers and visiting various *kampongs*, the myth of cannibalistic Wild Men of Borneo had long since been diluted in my mind. True, I had seen skulls hanging from poles in the longhouse where we squatted to smoke and take tea with the *Pengulu* on our visits, but I had been assured that although headhunting used to be common practice, it was not something that happened these days. All the same, I was never really convinced after spotting one skull that did not look all that old, and which had gold teeth glinting in the sunlight. What I was sure of, though, was that our own trackers were a great bunch of characters and that by watching them closely in the jungle, I would be able to learn an awful lot. To the untrained eye, the jungle is a leafy mess of intertwining vines and trees, but to the Iban it is an orchard. I learned to spot fruit hanging twenty to thirty feet away from me, but perhaps the most important lesson was to understand that I had to look *through* the jungle and not at it.

There are not many things living in the jungle that cannot be eaten, and this was demonstrated to me one night by our Iban when we were sleeping out on the border ridge. Wrapped in my poncho I had fallen asleep on the ground, only to be woken by a warm heavy object on my leg. Nudging Charlie, I told him to stop messing about.

I moved my leg gently and the heavy, warm thing took up a new position higher up my body. I switched on my torch and let out a scream as the beam of light fell upon the brown coiled form of a snake. Kicking out with my feet, I leapt out of the poncho and scampered along the track, closely followed by several of the others who had been woken by my cry and also seen the creature. Laughing like a demon, the Iban killed the snake with his sharp *parang* and after skinning it and cutting it up, cooked and ate it. I declined his kind offer to try it, and had problems sleeping for the rest of the night. He later informed me that snakes hunt at night, but that sometimes they will move in close to humans or animals, just to snuggle up to their body warmth. The thing he had just killed and eaten was not of the poisonous variety, so I had no need to feel concerned, he assured me.

In the jungle for four months, working out of firm bases, I was really becoming attuned to the environment, learning fast from the Ibans. The body has five natural senses: sight, smell, sound, touch and taste, with which to detect an enemy or find its way through the jungle, but I learned that it is possible to develop a sixth sense, which only comes in moments of danger – and only when you are in perfect harmony with your surroundings. At least, that's what I put the outcome of this next incident down to.

Patrolling one of the ridges along the border, checking for signs of enemy activity, I came across one of our old helicopter pads and making the recognised signal, sank to one knee to listen for sounds that would indicate the presence of anyone other than ourselves in the locality. It was all quiet. Straining my eyes, I peered through the jungle, scanning the area across and around the helipad. All was still. After five minutes looking and listening to only the natural sounds of the jungle, I started to move forward. A large log barred the way on to the open area of the landing pad. My back-up had moved into a position from where he could give me covering fire should the need arise, and the rest of the platoon were ready to react, stretched out along the track behind us.

With my rifle held in my right hand, pointing across the pad, I cocked my left leg over the fallen tree, preparing to step across when, for no explicable reason, I froze. I could not for the life of me put my foot down on the other side. The hairs on the back of my neck were all on end and tingling. I just felt that things were not right. Something inside me was repeating, 'Don't put your foot down! Don't put your foot down! Look down! Look down!'

Leaning forward over the trunk, at exactly the point where my next step would have been, I saw the shape of a green plastic box, the size of a cigar tin. Recent rains had washed away the soil that had been burying it and it was now exposed to my view. Letting out a long, low sigh, I drew back my leg, recognising the object for an anti-personnel mine, capable of blowing my foot clean off. They were not designed to kill, only maim. Retracing my steps exactly, I made my way back to the rest of the platoon and reported my find. Later, leaning against a tree as the mine-detector squad cleared the pad, I reflected on how lucky I had been, and how I owed it all to my new-found sixth sense.

That day we found mines scattered about the area of the helipad.

These helipads were also used by the SAS whenever they did their 'cross-border operations'. Our job would then be to secure the pad to make sure it was clear of enemy and mines so that their four-man teams could land and infiltrate across the border ridge into Indonesia on information-gathering patrols. It was during one such operation, while we were holding a helipad for the SAS, that I decided I was ready to join them. My three years in the Green Jackets was almost up and the recruiting sergeant had said that after three years I could apply for selection. When the helicopter had deposited its four men and they were dragging their Bergen rucksacks off to one side of the pad, I strode over to make enquiries about how to join. I also asked about the job they were now embarking on and was given a very sharp answer to the effect that it was none of my business. My business or not, I knew that I was good enough and, come what may, would soon be joining them. As they moved off along the track, so I followed on behind. After a short while the rear man spotted me and waited till I caught up.

'What's you game then, pal?' he demanded.

Telling him that I had come to join their cross-border op, I was told in no uncertain terms that I was not, and that I should get myself back to my own lot before they missed me. I suppose I never really expected them to take me along, but I was still disappointed that my long shot had failed and slunk dejectedly back to where I had left the others. But when I reached the spot, they had gone.

I was now alone in the jungle for the first time in my life: it was an eerie feeling. I knew that all I had to do was follow the tracks left by the platoon and that they were headed for our firm base, anyway. Nevertheless, the vastness of the forest hit me for the first time, as I sat, quietly rooted to the spot, off to one side of the helipad, listening to the sounds of people moving through the trees towards me.

'You fool!' I thought. 'What have you done? Left yourself out on a limb, cut off from the rest of the platoon, and now the enemy are creeping up on you along the track!'

My mind focused on the words that had just run through my

mind: 'people moving through the trees'. But how could they? People don't move through trees; only animals do that. This realisation hit me just as a troop of orang-utans came swinging through the branches. Big, gingery things, they were heading straight for me.

'Oh, no! After all this I am going to be eaten by a bunch of monkeys!' I muttered to myself. Of course, I need not have worried as orang-utans are vegetarians, if I'd only stopped to think. However, crouched in my hiding place, ready to shoot if they approached too close, their dietary habits were the last thing on my mind. Dropping surprisingly lightly to the ridge floor, the biggest one led the way and started to poke around the freshly dug earth where all the empty tins and food packets from the platoon's lunch break were buried. Rooting out the garbage from the fresh soil, they licked and sucked at the remnants for a while, before moving off along the ridge and climbing again into the trees above me, swinging from branch to branch and uttering peculiar hooting sounds. Their noise gradually faded as I emerged from my hidey-hole. I felt privileged to have witnessed the spectacle, yet very alone and rather vulnerable here by myself.

By the time I rejoined the platoon a few hours later, I had seen more wildlife than I had seen in the months of patrolling around in large, noisy groups. Charlie had covered for me and I had not been missed, but I was glad to be back in the fold. The day after, I went in to see the Company Clerk to request that he send off my SAS selection application form. My mind kept wandering back to the four-man patrol that even now must be moving deeper into enemy-held territory, and I wondered how long it would be before I, too, could be one of them.

The information gathered by these SAS patrols was sometimes acted upon by regiments like ours. Such was the case with an operation that went slightly wrong. The SAS had been across the border and located an Indonesian base with about twenty soldiers in it just 2,000 yards over the border. We were asked if we would go across and 'take it out'. Cross-border operations were very sensitive politically, and I do not know if this one had the sanction of the powers-that-be or was the idea of our Company Commander. But whatever the politics, we were anxious to do it and plans were made accordingly.

The company, armed to the teeth, crossed the border without any problems and moved down to surround the camp. All night we lay in ambush, just watching, and at first light, when the soldiers inside started to move, the order was given for action. The smell of smoke and the rapid cracking of bullets as they sped towards their targets were everywhere. It was all over in a very short while and an order to withdraw towards the border was given just as mortar bombs started to land around us. Hot splinters of shrapnel began flying about, striking the trees and giving the effect of an air burst. We split into smaller groups and each platoon commander led his own patrol on different tracks towards the ridge and safety. The mortars continued to rain down as they searched the jungle in square firing patterns, hoping to catch our fleeing troops. Up until then, we had only taken minor casualties, but some of the mortars began finding their mark and a couple of men were hit, though thankfully none of them fatally.

Leading one of the other platoons along a well-worn track, one of the regiment's best footballers, a well-liked young man called Ronnie, stepped on a mine and had his foot blown off. The next few hours turned frantic as everyone fought to get him attended to and carried to a winch spot from where a helicopter could fly him out to the hospital in Kuching.

When everyone was back in the firm base, our thoughts were not that the mission had been successful. This paled into insignificance against thoughts of poor old Ron, who lived for his football and would never be able to play again.

Just before the end of our tour in Borneo, wading up a small river, I felt really sick and weak and collasped in a heap. My companions helped me back to the base, and I was looked at by the medic, but he was unable to diagnose the problem. They helicoptered me back to Kuching to see a 'real' doctor in the hospital. By now I was drifting in and out of delirium and ranting on about snakes, ambushes and head hunters.

The doctor, after making some tests, reported that I was suffering from *Leptospirosis* and exhaustion. I had refused to take any rest and recuperation breaks during my time in the jungle and had run my body right down, leaving my resistance too low to combat the effects of the *Leptospirosis*. This, I learned, was contracted from rat's urine, which had entered the bloodstream via the numerous tiny leech bites on my legs. I had probably picked it up in the river we were patrolling on the day that I collapsed. I had been in the jungle for five and a half months and found it very difficult to adjust to the clean surroundings of the hospital I was now recovering in. After a week I was allowed out and moved into a small hotel in Kuching that had been taken over by the military for soldiers' rest and recuperation leave.

For a while, I was like an animal in an environment it did not understand. I was frightened of traffic and found it hard to cross roads for fear of being knocked over. I found myself longing for the peace and quiet of the jungle again. Life there was much slower and easier to cope with.

For the first time in a while I got to have a drink, and this resulted in my meeting some members of the SAS in the Market Square one night after curfew. They were living in the Palm Grove Hotel, one of the nicer hotels, and would mount their operations direct by helicopter to the jungle helipads from there. This, it seemed to me, was a very sensible way to run a war and I explained to them my desire to join the SAS. Insisting that I was one of them, they waved off the Military Policeman who had arrived to arrest any soldiers still on the streets after curfew. The SAS at that time were the only ones exempt from the rules of the curfew and at about three o'clock the next morning they dropped me off, drunk as a skunk, at the door to my hotel.

Revitalised but hungover, I tried next day to chase up the answer to my application to attend the SAS selection courses and was told I would have to wait until we arrived back in the UK, as all the documentation had been packed ready for the move in two weeks' time. I had waited this long I supposed another couple of weeks would not make that much difference. I needed the rest anyway. I had enjoyed my time in the jungle but I had to admit I was a little tired.

Who Dares Wins

D URING ALL those early years in the army, my desire to get into the SAS had never wavered. My first application to attend a selection course for the Regiment went in towards the end of my third year in the army. I heard nothing. After a while I applied again, then again, and again. When I had submitted five applications and still not received any reply, I began to get very suspicious and spoke to the Chief Clerk, who was a friend of mine.

'You won't hear nothing neither, mate,' he told me. 'All your forms go straight in the bin. They don't want you to leave.'

I could not for the life of me think why not. I caused them more trouble than most – when we were in barracks, anyway. I must admit things were different when we were on active service. I was quite useful then, but even so, I would have thought that the back of me was what the hierarchy would have preferred.

Angry that I was being held back, I would sit in the NAAFI every night, brooding into my beer and trying the hatch up ways to short-circuit the system. All the same, I reckoned I had better keep up pressure along the legitimate channels as well, and applied once more for a transfer. When, two days later, the Chief Clerk reported that this request, too, had joined the others in the wastepaper basket, I could contain myself no longer.

Storming past the desk of the Regimental Sergeant-Major, I burst into the CO's office and, waving the paperwork under his nose, demanded to know what he was playing at. It was a court martial offence even to come into this sanctum without an appointment, and already the RSM outside was roaring for the duty officers to come and arrest me. I was obviously going to have to say what I'd come to say quickly, but that was no problem: years of frustration were doing the talking for me. He had not only behaved dishonorably, I told the CO, he was guilty of breaking military rules. My words rained upon him, and to his credit he did not add to the pandemonium. In fact, though the significance of it did not strike me at the time, he looked, if anything, bemused by my outburst. He heard me through, and when I had calmed down, told me he would be prepared to overlook the incident if I showed him I could keep out of trouble. In return for evidence of good conduct, he promised to forward my forms to Hereford, the headquarters of the SAS.

This was 1966 and we were stationed in Belfast. It was before the troubles there flared up again seriously, and life was fairly normal apart from disruption in the docks because of a threatened shipping strike. Two days before our tour of duty was to end, I spoke again to my friend, the Chief Clerk.

'Look, Brum,' he said, 'I'm sorry, mate, but I hadn't the heart to tell you before. Your latest application ended up in the shredder even before it got to the CO's office.'

So that was it! I should have known. That bastard Sergeant-Major had it in for me; he must have been the one behind all the blocked applications right from the beginning. No wonder, the CO had seemed baffled.

'Well, OK,' I thought, 'we shall see who has the last laugh!'

The next night I went down to the docks and made arrangements to get a passage on an old cargo barge that was leaving for Scotland in the morning, the same day that the battalion was to sail to England by ferry. These would be the last vessels to leave before the strikes. My plan was simple: I would disappear in Ireland, but while the police were looking for me there, I'd be safely across the water and stating my case to the SAS in Hereford!

When the battalion was all aboard the ferry, waving goodbye to the lines of girlfriends along the quay, I stood quietly by the gangplank, biding my time. The ferry hooter sounded just as the plank was being hauled aboard. Off I went, as if from starting blocks.

'*Stokes! Get back here!*'

The Sergeant-Major's voice floated to me over the cheers of the assembled battalion and the band struck up the Regimental March.

What a way to go! The adrenalin was thudding round my body as I panted and pushed through the ranks of giggling girls, racing to make good my escape. By now I was being pursued by both military and civilian police.

Rounding a corner not far from where my barge was moored, I came face to face with two members of the Royal Ulster Constabulary. One of them had a pistol pointed directly at my middle.

'I'm no hero,' I declared lamely, and gave myself up.

'Well, that's a fine start to your SAS career,' I told myself as I was led away in handcuffs to be handed over to the Military Police. At least my ignominy had not been witnessed by the rest of the lads; the ferry had long since departed. As far as they were concerned, I had got clean away and made a monkey out of the officers. But locked up in a cell that night, I was informed by the corporal who was in charge of our regimental rear party, that he and two others would shortly be escorting me back to Felixstowe to face charges of desertion.

We flew into Heathrow a few days later, where we were met by two Military Policemen and accompanied to Waterloo. They took their leave once they had settled us aboard the train, no doubt thinking that I was sufficiently outnumbered. I'm only a small bloke, after all, and safely handcuffed, how could I possibly pose a threat with three people to guard me?

There was over half an hour to go before the train left and I persuaded the corporal that I needed to visit the toilet. Of course, it is a well-known fact that you must not use the loo when the train is standing in a station. So, with two of the men to escort me, we went back down the platform and descended into the Gents.

'Come on then,' I said, 'take them off,' indicating the cuffs.

After a short protest, they were removed. I went into the toilet and locked the door. Immediately I got down on my belly and began crawling under the side panels. To my dismay I came to a barrier of feet with trousers around the ankles, and I was still not far enough away from where the two guards were faithfully standing outside the, by now, empty *khazi*.

'Oh, well,' I thought, 'in for a penny, in for a pound.'

Under I went. The bloke gave the game away, letting out a startled shriek as I scurried between his legs. I opened the door and made for the stairs. Racing up, three at a time, I crossed the station and dived into the Underground, where I jumped the queue and rushed past the ticked inspector with a 'Can't stop, mate, emergency!' I was on a train before anyone could catch me.

I did not dare go home for fear that was the first place the police would look for me. Instead, I made my way to the house of a girlfriend in Hamstead. All I had was the uniform that I stood up in. She lent me some money and a few of her brother's old clothes. From there, I hitched to Hereford and made my way to 'Bradbury Lines', the headquarters of the Special Air Service Regiment.

Back in my Green Jackets' uniform, now all pressed up, I stood outside the door looking as 'smart as a carrot', but with butterflies going crazy inside my stomach. At long last, I was about to enter what had become for me, hallowed portals. This was where the élite of the world's military forces came from, the true professionals. Would I be able to measure up?

'What are you looking for, Boyo?' said a small soldier with an unmistakable Welsh accent. He was wearing olive green trousers, putties, a heavy-duty pullover with blue belt, and the coveted beige beret and winged dagger badge of the SAS soldier. He wore no rank as he stood outside the Guardroom.

'I've come to do Selection,' I said, trying to make the words sound as normal as possible.

'Oh, oo 'ave, 'ave oo?' And he directed me to the Training Wing.

This was a complex of wooden buildings around which I noticed a few headstones with cryptic inscriptions:

Here lies the body of Sam Smith, died when his throat was cut after falling asleep on guard duty;

R.I.P. Dan Davies. (You would still be here, if your rifle had been clear!)

Just then I heard a loud bang. Around a corner I could see a plume of smoke slowly rising and a crowd of soldiers excitedly examining a stretch of old railway line they had just blown up.

'You've arrived, old son,' I told myself, and was surprised to hear, as if in echo to my thoughts, a voice saying, 'John, what on earth are you doing here?'

It was 'Brummie' Hassal, another lad from Hamstead, whom I had not seen since he had gone off to join the Paras some years before. I explained everything to him and asked what was going on. Demolition training, he said, and took me off to see the man in charge of Selection.

'What do yo' want?' asked this huge six-footer with a broad and gravelly Birmingham accent. I told him.

'Wait here. I'll go and have a word with The Boss.'

I had never heard a commanding officer addressed in that manner before. I was later to learn that it was a name only given to the few officers who earned the respect of their men.

Raised voices could be heard from the inner room. Things did not bode too well for me, I thought. I stood up as the large man came back to his desk. He motioned me to sit down and reached across for the phone.

'What's the name of your Barracks?' he asked.

Once he got through, he demanded to speak to the adjutant. Young Stokes had just turned up on the doorstep of the SAS to do Selection, he told him. All I could hear coming down the phone was a high-pitched scream, 'Throw him in jail, throw him in jail!'

'Now yo' just calm down a bit, sir,' he said, holding the instrument away from his ear and winking at me as yet another tirade came cascading through the wires.

'We are going to keep him here and let him have a go,' he said. 'If he passes, we will deal with it; if he fails, yo' can have him back and lock him up forever as far as we're concerned.' With that, he put down the phone.

'When did yo' last eat?' he asked. It was hard to remember. A long time ago, anyway.

'Right then, young 'un. Get yerself fed. Yo' start next Monday. Till they yo' are on leave.' He added, 'Are you fit?'

'Could be fitter,' I replied.

'Up to yo',' he murmured, 'up to yo'.'

The regimental motto of the SAS is 'Who dares, wins.' I had done both and, as the sergeant had said, it was now up to me. I liked the way things got done around here. This was my kind of army.

It was now mid-June and 135 soldiers from all units of the British Army stood in an excited huddle outside the Training Wing. There were all ranks from Private to Major under a large sign that had been pasted on the wall. 'Selection,' it said.

Out of the building walked the big Brummie sergeant I had met on my first day. 'All right yo' lot,' he addressed the mixed assembly, 'get in three lines over here.'

The order came with no screaming and shouting and stamping

of feet, as it would have done in my old regiment. It was all very matter-of-fact. The officers formed a line of their own off to one side.

'Something different about yo' lot, is there?' the sergeant asked them. 'Got something we oughtn't to catch? Come on now, sirs, join in with the rest. We're all one happy band here.'

By the look of one or two of them, they were anything but happy at the prospect of having to stand next to ordinary enlisted men. But my rebellious anti-system steak was loving every minute of it.

'Because there are so many of yo', we are not goin' to issue yo' with kit just yet, until we have had a look at yo'. Mau-Mau here is going to take you all for a little trot first.' He indicated the little Welsh soldier I had seen outside the Guard Room on that first day.

'There won't be as many of yo' by this afternoon. Anytime yo' want to leave, just say the word and come and collect your ticket for the *Golden Express* back to yo'r own unit. Don' worry about it.' He continued, as much to himself as us, as he nodded to Mau-Mau and disappeared back inside the building, 'We've sin um cum and we've sin um goo!'

'OK, face that way and let's go, boyos!'

The stocky little Welshman, with the weatherbeaten face of a man from the hills, directed us on to the parade ground. Unlike other squares I had 'bashed' on, this one was being used as a car-park and helicopter landing site. Not much drill done around here, I was glad to note. As we jogged around the outside edge of the square, I could not help remarking the prominent tower with four clock faces on it. About the tenth time around the quarter-mile circuit, Mau-Mau told us that all the names on the brass plate underneath the clock were those of SAS soldiers killed in action in different small wars around the world – all those, in fact, he said, who had 'failed to beat the clock'.

By this time about twenty people had already packed it in. I could not believe it. Two and a half miles and it had creased people. Admittedly, it did not make life any easier wearing gas masks you could hardly breath in, but even so . . . A voice in my head said, 'Never mind them, son, just you make sure you're still here at the end.' I was determined I would be.

An hour and a half later, we were still running around. The pace was not so fast and Mau-Mau had long since positioned himself in the centre where he could keep an eye on everyone. We were constantly encouraged to give in.

'Pack in whenever you like, boyos,' Mau-Mau would chant. 'Death is nature's way of saying you have failed selection.'

When we eventually did stop to shower off and have lunch, our numbers had dwindled to ninety-three.

During the next three weeks, we were put through an intense physical programme in the countryside around Hereford, designed to test our stamina, endurance, patience, sense of humour, team spirit, resourcefulness and a whole host of other things I never even knew that I had. The whole purpose was to find the point where you say 'Enough!' And then you were given the ticket for the *Golden Express*.

A typical regimen would be one when, after a full day's running from point A to point B, over the hills with a forty-five-pound Bergen rucksack on your back, and getting into bed by one o'clock in the early hours, you would be called out at five on to the wagons and driven to Pen-y-Fan, the highest hill in the Brecon Beacons. There, at intervals along the road, you would be dropped off, on your own, with your sack, and told to navigate yourself to the high point where you would be given instructions. When you got there, Mau-Mau, or one of the other instructors, would appear out of the early morning mist and tell you that you had fifteen minutes to get back down to a rendezvous point on the road in order to meet up with the vehicle to transport you back to Hereford. Just as you were within fifty yards of the vehicle, sweating and panting and looking forward to a rest, it would take off and stop half a mile further on. Eventually, when you did catch up with it, Mau-Mau would again appear, and you were left wondering how he managed to get there before you. He really was a mountain goat.

Instead of heading for home, you would then be told to take a five-gallon jerrycan of water to someone who would be waiting back at the top of the hill.

'Be a bit fly here,' I thought. 'Get out of sight, empty the water, and fill up at a waterpoint nearer the top.'

They had obviously seen through that one a long time ago. As I slowly started to pour out the liquid, I could see it was dyed red.

'No easy way out, is there?' a voice said from behind a rock. They were everywhere! 'You can always pack it in.' As he came out of his hiding place, I saw it was the RSM.

'Never happen, sir,' I vowed, as I scrambled to get the top back on the jerrycan and my arse up the hill.

The course culminated in a forced march over the Beacons,

moving from checkpoint to checkpoint over a distance of fifty-five miles. The problem was that all these points were either at the top of a hill, or right at the bottom. Then came the crippler: it had to be done in under eighteen hours, or you failed!

Three months later, after continuation training and combat survival, fifteen of us stood in front of the CO's desk to receive our SAS berets. We were all desperately tired, but proud to a man.

'Don't think that this is the finish,' said The Boss, 'because it isn't. You are always learning new things and training in the Regiment. And remember, the only discipline here is self-discipline. We will back you all the way if you are right, but bring the name of the Regiment into disrepute and you will be on the *Golden Express* so fast your feet won't touch the ground.'

With that, he threw us each a beige beret and said, 'Welcome to the SAS!'

I wished he had not said that bit about the *Golden Express*.

Because I was not yet parachute-trained, the first thing for me was to do a course at Abingdon No. 1 Parachute Training School. The course was run by instructors from the RAF, but all administration was carried out by a sergeant from the Parachute Regiment. He was to be my downfall.

Standing on parade one morning, ready to march to the training hangers and be handed over to the RAF (who were really good fun), the sergeant took it into his head to have a go at me and called me a liar. The reaction he got was not the one he expected. (You are not supposed to challenge senior ranks out for a punch-up). The outcome was that once more I ended up in the 'Pokey'.

Visited by the Parachute Regiment's RSM, who ran the school, I learned that our Sergeant Ripcord (as I shall call him) had once failed to pass SAS Selection and since then held a grudge against everyone who had. This did not help me very much, though. I was banished from the SAS and RTU'd (Returned to Unit) for twelve months.

'Oh, no!' I railed against bitter fate. 'I don't think I can face it. Back into the ordinary army again!'

Six months later, on leave in the UK, I was back at SAS Headquarters, begging forgiveness. I was in luck.

'OK. So long as you have learned your lesson,' said the CO. 'But just to make sure you're still fit, you can re-do the first three weeks of Selection!'

When I next came to do my parachuting course, there were no hitches. Sergeant Ripcord had moved on.

Some people describe parachuting as fun. I never actually got around to calling it that – a challenge, yes; hard, no; fun? No way! The build-up to the first jump is strenuous but exciting. The RAF instructors, I found, did their best to ease you through it.

'Knowledge dispels fear,' our group's instructor would say. 'Think of the parachute as just another means of transport, a vehicle to get you from point A to point B.'

'OK,' I thought, 'that makes sense, I can buy that.' But what did not add up was why I should be driving this vehicle out of a fast-moving aircraft (Point A) and rocketing to earth (Point B) in the first place. It was surely safer to land with the plane?

During the first couple of days we were taught by Kirk-baby, our instructor, how a canopy develops as it opens. We had it drummed into us how we must land: 'Feet and knees together, chin in, elbows in, knees bent! And keep looking at the ground!' The words imprinted themselves on the brain, as did those others with more sinister ring, 'Stand in the door. Red on. Green on. *Go!*' (this last syllable screamed in your ear). It did not take long to 'condition' us; soon that little word '*Go!*' would be all it required to make us (otherwise, apparently sane men) step out into thin air.

The next stage in the training cycle, however, was 'the fan', a wire cable strapped on to your body by means of a harness, and attached at the other end to a windmill-like contraption. This was designed to slow down your rate of descent when you jumped from a lofty platform. The harness is attached only after you have climbed the long forty- or fifty-foot ladder up to the little stage. The instructor gives you a cursory check-over, and then comes the order, 'Stand in the door!' You find yourself launching into the air at the word '*Go!*'

Landing on the matting and executing a near-perfect roll, you walk away feeling quite pleased with yourself and happy that this parachuting lark is after all quite a doddle!

Some days later still, all that changes. You assemble in the hanger to draw a parachute for your very first drop. What a horrible word 'drop' is! It's not once uttered by any of the ashen-faced recruits, I can vouch for that, and the usual round of wisecracks about falling off logs or being scraped off tramac like lumps of strawberry jam are conspicuous by their absence today.

Never was so much time taken over checking any piece of equipment. Every stitch of the parachute is inspected by its wearer and then a friend is invited to take a look as well.

'Just to make sure. Not that I'm concerned, you understand.'

Reassured that your chute is not going to fall apart on you, the group – or 'stick', as it is known – shuffles off in the direction of the Balloon. This huge air-filled monster is tethered by a wire hawser to a winch, so that it cannot fly off out of control; a metal 'cage' is suspended by cords underneath it.

Kirk-baby shepherded six of us into it, jollying us along, and sorted us into the order in which we were to be 'dispatched'. (There's another word I never did like – has an uncomfortable air of finality about it.) I found myself in the 'Number Two' position. 'Oh well,' I thought, 'at least I get to see someone else go first.'

'Up eight hundred. Six men jumping,' shouted Kirk.

The winch started to wind out, the cage of the tethered Balloon tilted forward and the butterflies worked overtime in my stomach. I felt very, very nervous, but excited too. We swayed slightly as the open-sided cage parted company with the ground and creaked and groaned its way slowly upwards. I looked around – to appear nonchalant – and saw the horizon widen. Casting a glance down, I could see the cable had small marker flags on it every hundred feet or so, and was surprised by the angle at which it ran away from us, until my brain engaged and I realised that even the slight breeze we had that day would be enough to carry us downwind.

We came to an abrupt halt and swayed as the winch stopped paying out. It suddenly became very quiet. The reality of the situation hit me hard. 'They really do mean it,' I panicked. 'The training is over. This one's for real!'

'Tell off for equipment check,' screamed Kirk, shattering the silence. The only other noise was a steady whine as the wind brushed past the cage. We each made a last check of our own gear and then that of the man behind.

'Number One – OK!'

'Number Two – OK!'

Right round the cage to 'Number Six – OK!' the voices sounded strained.

'Number One – step forward,' ordered Kirk (who was leaning casually against the single bar in the doorway that separated us from the sky). The first man stepped forward hesitantly. I felt for him, knew just how his inside was knotted up as he edged towards the door. Kirk hooked his parachute strop to the wire anchor point at the top of the cage.

'I don't want to go first!' Number One started to back off from the door.

'Oh, no!' I thought. I was in a bad enough state as it was, I could do without this. It was doing my confidence no good at all. Kirk, who was obviously a very experienced instructor and no doubt had had to handle situations like this many times in the past, proceeded very gently to persuade Number One to move forward again, but he was not going to wear it.

Knowing that he would have to defuse this fast-escalating situation quickly, Kirk simply said, 'There is absolutely nothing to be apprehensive about. This is what all your training has been for – and to prove it, young Stokes here is going to demonstrate to all of us how it's done. Aren't ya, Stokes?'

I nearly buckled at the knees and could feel the blood draining from my face, but I moved into position in front of the cage as he hooked me up and stood the first man to one side. After checking me over and making some sort of signal to the people on the ground, Kirk-baby then opened the bar that acted as a safety barrier.

'Stand in the door!' he screamed.

I took up the position with the toe of my left boot on the lip of the doorway, my eyes fixed upwards towards the tail of the barrage balloon, heart pounding fast.

'Red on! Green on! *Go!*'

I launched my body as far from the cage as I could. Immediately I started to plummet downwards. Heart in my mouth, stomach churning, every muscle tensed. I was ready for the inevitable drop into the ground. Eyes tightly squeezed shut, face screwed up. I was surprised to hear a sound escape from somewhere deep inside me, 'Urghhhhhh!'

I gasped as I felt a jolt and my torso was arrested by the parachute deploying. Relief flooded through me. 'It works! It actually works!' I was talking to myself as I floated gently towards the earth, grinning broadly.

'Check your canopy!' A thin voice said from somewhere below. The RAF captain on the landing zone was urging me to go through my drill. Training took over and I made the check. Everything in order. I started to relax a little.

'Pull down on your back lift-webs,' he said. 'You are drifting forwards.' The horizon started to disappear quickly as the ground loomed closer. My brain was telling me what to do (I was talking to myself again). 'Feet and knees together . . . head in . . . chin in . . . elbows in . . . knees bent . . . look at the ground!'

The grass rushed to meet me and I collapsed in a heap on the welcome earth. As I sat up and looked around, my parachute billowed about me. I had done it! I had done it! By now, my grin stretched from one ear to the other: I was a parachutist! It was easy . . .

'Are you going to sit there all day with that silly expression on your face?' the captain shouted through his megaphone. Come on, finish the drill. Get yourself out of the harness. Pick up your chute and watch for the next person landing!'

I could see someone else floating gently down, and another exiting from the balloon with his chute already opening.

'Drive yourself off from the cage next time, Stokes,' said the captain. 'You looked like porridge dribbling over the side!' He added, 'Enjoy it?' The fixed smile on my face must have given him his answer.

During the next two weeks, we made a further seven descents, mostly from C-130 aircraft, which were slightly easier, because of the constant noise and the fact that after leaving the door, instead of dropping, you were carried away by the slipstream. The last two were at night with equipment. The course completed, we were then presented with our wings.

Hotfooting it back to Hereford, these Parachute Regiment wings were proudly exchanged for SAS ones. I now considered myself a fully fledged SAS soldier. It had taken a long time, and I'd had to work very hard for it, but it was all worth it. Calling in at the Adjutant's Office, I was told I had been posted to 'A' Squadron. I was walking on air.

The Troop

'**A**' SQUADRON OFFICE was housed on the opposite side of camp from the Training Wing, at one end of a wooden 'spider'. (The whole camp was of the wooden hutted variety.) Even as I stepped in through the door, I fancied I could sense the special character of the place. The CO's office was to the left of a small corridor, and sharing a room at the end of the passageway were the Sergeant-Major and the Clerk. To the right was a door marked 'Interest Room'. Always inquisitive, I could not resist having a quick peep inside and pushed the door open with the toe of my boot. Photos were pinned to the walls of members of the Squadron in live action around the world, and of men free-falling, diving, crossing sand dunes in vehicles, climbing mountains. There were bits of old weapons, swords, and bayonets pinned all over the walls and rafters, as well as buffalo horns, a skull, snake skins and all manner of other curiosities. I decided I had better not let myself get caught snooping around, and went to knock on the door of the office. Strange that I was now part of all this but still felt out of place.

The Sergeant-Major looked up as I entered the room and introduced myself.

'Ah, Stokes,' he said, shaking my hand. 'What's your first name – Brummie, isn't it?' His manner caught me off guard, it was all so civilised. Where I had just come from, it took men of his rank all their time to look at you, let alone welcome you by your first name. I knew I was going to like it here.

'Now I know you had a little bit of trouble before you came to us,' the Sergeant-Major said, referring to my RTU. 'We shall put all that behind us and forget about it. But if you try anything on here, you will be on yer bike right sharpish, son. OK?' Then with a smile, he added, 'By the way, my name's Lawrence.' Turning to push his head through a small sliding hatch in the wall, I heard him say, 'All right to bring the new bloke in now, sir?'

He motioned me to go inside. I marched through the door and stood rigidly to attention in front of a well-built, ruddy-faced man with a bristling moustache. This was Major Henry, the command-ing officer.

'No need for that,' he said irritably, waving his hand for me to stand at ease. 'Welcome to the Squadron.'

He proceeded to give me a complete rundown on what the squadron was all about. If I had been a visiting General, I don't think I could have asked for more. When he finally came to a halt, he asked me which troop I wanted to go into.

I was dumbstruck. The last thing I had expected was to have a choice. 'Mountain troop,' I said without hesitation.

The Squadron Sergeant-Major (SSM) told me to wait in the Interest Room so that the Clerk could take all my details – next of kin, blood group and all that – then he would get someone to come over and show me where the troop lines were.

Half an hour later, a thin-faced lad about the same age as myself appeared through the door and introduced himself. 'Bronco Lane,' he said, reaching out to shake my hand. He was a little taller than me, with blue eyes and a weather-beaten face. 'Where's your kit?'

He led me across to 'A' Squadron Lines and on the way told me that he had been on the previous selection. They had been told all about me by two of the blokes on my first selection course: Scouse O'Neal and Ricky Gayle were also now in the Mountain Troop (I Troop) and had regaled everyone with the story of my quick departure back to unit after the fiasco with the Parachute Ser-geant. 'Hope you made a good job of it,' Bronco smiled.

We had reached the entrance of the barrack room, which was to become my home base for the next seven years.

'Welcome to One Troop *Basha*,' said Bronco, as he pushed open the door.

Inside was a long wooden-floored room with a set of fire doors at the far end; lockers and beds lining each side wall were afforded a measure of privacy by partitions of old curtain and parachute fabric. The sound of Irish folk music blasted out from inside one of these makeshift cubicles.

'Turn it down a bit, Scouse,' yelled Bronco, 'There's a mate of yours here.' A round laughing face appeared from behind the curtain, followed by the short stocky figure of Scouse O'Neil.

During the next six months I learned how the Regiment operated, both in peacetime and in war. We had very little time to ourselves. Each day brought fitness training, exercises, courses. I fast learned that it was going to take three years before I was qualified enough to be considered fully operational. But by then I should be an all-rounder with something to put back into the Regiment; I would have taken courses in medicine, signals, demolition and learned a language. This training would be interspersed by trips abroad for extra experience and involvement in 'limited wars'. I was quite excited at the prospect. It did not take long before I moulded into the troop and gained the confidence of the 'old sweats'. During this time, too, I struck up a firm friendship with Bronco.

His background was not that dissimilar to my own. Our thoughts on the main issues of life were very much in accord, and we soon found our love for the hills and open countryside was identical. He had higher academic qualifications than me and a natural bent towards books that I did not share, at that time at least. Both of us were single lads, with no plans for early marriage, and when others of the troop disappeared home in the evenings or at weekends to see wives and girlfriends, Bronco and I would be off to nearby Symonds Yat to go climbing, or wandering around in the hills. Neither of us had much experience of climbing in those days, but as time went by we taught ourselves most of what we needed to know.

Symonds Yat stands on the banks of the River Wye; it is a picturesque spot, tucked away in trees. There were no guidebooks to the cliffs when we started, so we just began putting up routes all over the place, ripping ivy from some of the less-obvious faces. Sometimes we would spend weeks forcing a new route up a crag.

Money was scarce as we were only earning fifteen pounds a week, which in 1967 was well below the national average. Most of our pay went down at the local pub, so there wasn't a lot left for purchasing climbing gear. Out of necessity, we took to making a lot of our own kit from old parachute harnesses and nuts and bolts from the vehicle workshops.

Competition on the crags grew as other members of the Squadron's Mountain Troop joined us and we all tried to put up harder and harder routes. This inevitably led to wider friendships being forged and to our venturing further afield. We would make frequent climbing trips to North Wales, where we would head for Llanberis at the foot of Snowdon to cut our teeth on such routes as Sabre Cut and Shadow Wall. One of the Tigers of the Regiment's climbing fraternity was Paddy Freaney, who impressed us all by shinning up Cemetery Gates and later the same year, making an ascent of the Old Man of Hoy in the Orkneys in order to establish a signals base during a TA Exercise. His exploits spurred us on considerably and brought home to me that anything was possible. It was all within my grasp: all I had to do was go out and get it.

But before I could go and do anything, there were one or two basics to get under my belt. I still did not hold a driving licence, so while we were up in North Wales one weekend, I asked Bronco to teach me. It was during one of the subsequent training sessions that I had an insight into his sense of humour. Driving from Llanberis towards Bangor one evening after we had finished climbing for the day, I pulled the Landrover into a lay-by and told Bronco that I was just popping outside to take a leak. There was nowhere else to go, so I started to relieve myself against the back wheel of the truck, out of sight of the passing traffic. Half-way through, I was shocked to hear the vehicle start up and slowly drive off, leaving me exposing myself to the rush-hour traffic. I could hear Bronco cackling like a maniac as he steered out into the road. 'I'll get you for this!' I thought.

The lessons continued for the next two weeks, after which I passed my test and took Bronco for a pint in a nearby pub to celebrate. While he was finishing his beer I sneaked out and started up the vehicle. He came rushing out, but as he approached, I drove away slowly, waving and shouting out of the window. 'That's the one I owe you! See you back at the ranch, pal.' His face was a picture; his words, choice.

Returning to Hereford, I found that I had been allocated space on a Signals Course. My days were now filled with hours of classroom work, learning aerial theory, morse code, and how to fix defective radios in remote locations using razor blades and odd bits of wire. Although it was always interesting to be learning something new, I found it a real drag to be indoors all the time. To make ends meet, most of the blokes did part-time work in the evenings – some in the bakery, some as bouncers in pubs, and some, like me, loading, packing or catching poultry at the chicken factory. The money was not that good, but by doing four night shifts a week, we could almost double our military wages. It meant, though, that we would only be getting two or three hours' sleep a night and we had a tendency to nod off during the day's instruction. This was not too bad on a Signals Course, but resulted in some untimely bangs on the demolition cadres.

One member of the troop who was doing a medical course in the daytime, also used to slaughter chickens at night. By the end of his second week he was absolutely on his last legs, but on getting paid for the fortnight on the Saturday morning, decided to have a few pints with the rest of us down at the local before catching up on his sleep. Wearily we all crawled into bed later that afternoon, numbed by drink and exhaustion. Soon there was nothing to hear but snores. But it was not long before I was aroused from the deepest of slumbers by the sound of bells ringing and men laughing and shouting. As my eyes opened, I saw our chicken-slaughterer dancing about the room, trying to beat out a pair of flaming trousers. He was stamping up and down on them in a frantic attempt to put out the fire, but instead of helping him, all the other chaps were propped up on their elbows, laughing hysterically. It was a well known fact that after a few drinks, this character would regularly stumble into the *Basha*, hang his clothes on the floor next to the bed and crawl in, mumbling to himself as he lit a cigarette. This occasion had been no different, except that he had dropped the lighted end onto his trousers as he fell asleep. His two week's wages went up in smoke with the breeks, and there was no way he was going to see the funny side of that. 'Never mind, mate,' a voice came from the far end of the room. 'Look on the bright side. That's probably saved you half a dozen big hangovers.'

The days seemed to fly by during those early years. There were never enough hours in a day to complete all the things that we wanted to do, and everything amused us, even down to Scouse's old van that was always stranding us high and dry somewhere. It ran, when it did run, on army petrol that had somehow found its way into the tank, and its tax disc was a Guinness label. The whole Regiment was full of colourful personalties, individualistic misfits, each with his own idea of how to make life tolerable. Take Mel Parr from 'B' Squadron.

One Sunday morning as we were crossing the Old Bridge that connected the Funny Farm (as the barracks was known) with the city centre, we were surprised to see Mel in the River Wye, doing battle with a huge tree that was floating gently downstream. 'Come on in and give me a hand,' he shouted. 'We need this.' Such was the trust we all had in each other that without demur, we all waded in. The mighty oak was anchored to the underside of the bridge until later in the day when we had enlisted the aid of a three-ton truck, complete with winch, with which to haul it ashore.

Finally someone put the question that had been puzzling all of us. 'What are we going to do with it, Mel?'

'It's a table,' he said.

And sure enough, within twenty-four hours, it had been down to the saw mills and cut into three planks with the rough edges and bark left in place on their sides. These, over the next month, were planed and sanded down, and fixed on to trestle legs to form a thirty-foot-long table. A drying room in 'B' Squadron Lines was denuded of all its hot pipes, cleaned out and painted to receive this magnificent piece of woodwork. It soon dominated the centre of the room where it was joined by rough-hewn benches along each side of its length. By now the plan that had been hatched by Mel was made known to all. The drying room, which was little used, was to be converted into a private drinking hall. And the SAS Other Ranks Club was born.

Ideas poured in from all quarters on a theme for the club, but Mel had already settled this in his mind and was not about to be swayed. He was obsessed with the history of Welsh bowman and invading hoards; his desire was to recreate a warriors' hall. Everyone became caught up on the project and soon shields, swords, helmets and skins started to appear on the walls as people donated treasured trophies from around the world. One morning as I stumbled bleary-eyed to the wash-house, I caught the pungent smell of butchered flesh and nearly shed my towel in astonishment when I discovered a freshly skinned and gutted ram hanging inside the shower cubicle, the remains of its belly slopping out on to the floor. It was not a pretty sight to encounter first thing in the morning and I hastily fled to the next cubicle, only to be greeted by a similar apparition.

'What do you think of this lot, then, Brum?' asked Taff, who had just returned from a shooting trip to North Wales. 'The skins can be hung on the walls of the club, the horns can be used to drink from, and we can barbecue the meat on Opening Day.' He grinned.

'Great,' I replied, not bothering to ask him how he had come across these little finds.

First named the Viking Drinking Hall it soon became more commonly known as Valhalla and was a very popular and unique meeting place after normal drinking hours, not only for the Regiment, but for half the citizens of Hereford as well. Something the Regiment set great store by was winning over the hearts and minds of the locals; we did a pretty good job of that. Friendships burgeoned with farmers, publicans and the local police. The bond which the Regiment struck up with the people of Hereford was one of which we were quite proud. We were often called out during flood alerts to rescue livestock and ferry them to higher ground. It was considered privileged extra training to assist the police in crowd control at the local football ground on a Saturday afternoon, where many a visiting hooligan found himself leaving the game unexpectedly early.

Girlfriends came and went in my life; I wanted nothing more than casual relationships at that time. I had been in love with a girl back home in Birmingham, but had mismanaged the whole affair and she had walked out on me. Now I felt slightly uncomfortable and insecure whenever friendships got beyond the being-good-mates or having-a-good-time stage. This was the Sixties, the hippy era of making love, not war; and I found myself in the confusing position of trying to be on both sides of the fence at once – a short-haired, hippy soldier.

There was a teacher training college nearby, which needless to say drew us like a magnet. One morning I was trying to leave the room of a girlfriend without being spotted, when I bumped into one of our Fijians attempting the same manoeuvre. Before we could make good our escape, however, the college head entered the building with a group of new student teachers. We quickly made for the safety of a large assembly room and hid behind the stage curtains. The girls were ushered into the room and the head took up a position on the stage to deliver her speech of welcome. And a very eloquent five minutes it was, too, during which both of us were surprised to learn why it was that our local pub was discovered and frequented by her new students so soon after their arrival in Hereford.

'One word of warning, girls' the old dear said, 'you may not be aware of it, but Hereford is the headquarters of the Special Air Service Regiment. They live in a camp on the opposite side of the river; Bradbury Lines, it's called but it's known to everyone around here as the Funny Farm. I am afraid to say these are depraved young men, quite sex-mad and will take advantage of you, if you are not careful. They frequent a public house in the city centre, known as The Grapes, which I'm sure you will understand is out of bounds to you – for your own good.'

The giggling of the girls was almost drowned out by our own laughter as we appeared from behind the curtain at the back of the headmistress, waved to the assembly, and made away through the side door. We both knew that the first place those girls would head for after classes would be the watering hole of the SAS. It was most welcome advertising and I often wondered if the good lady ever realised that she was indirectly responsible for so many 'chance meetings' between her 'gels' and the lads of the 'Funny Farm'.

It was during this early stage of my SAS career that I learned there were three different types of people in the service: the 'Trogs' who were the 'other ranks' and the backbone of the troop, and among whom a close bond of comradeship existed; then there were the Officers, or 'Ruperts' as we called them. These came in two different varieties – the good ones we all looked up to and referred to as 'Boss' as a mark of our respect, and the 'Doughballs' (or 'Clowns', or just plain 'Sirs'), who may have passed the same selection course as the rest of us, but sadly lacked that little extra something that makes a true SAS soldier, the ability to fit in and work in close harmony with a small group for long periods under adverse conditions.

The first Troop Officer that I had was, I'm afraid, of the doughball variety. Bronco informed me mysteriously that I need not worry about this, because he would not be staying long. Such was the power of decision in the day-to-day running of the Troop by the Troop Sergeant in those days, that it was not long before Bronco's prophecy came true and we saw the back of our Rupert. I learned quickly that the power and stability of the SAS rested mainly on the shoulders of its senior ranks. My own sights were set on becoming a sergeant-major one day.

Probably the most likeable Rupert was our Squadron Commander, Major Henry, a big jovial man, whose thoughts on doughballs matched our own. The squadron he commanded, in common with the others in the Regiment, was made up of five troops: Mountain, Freefall, Landrover, Boat and an attached Signals Troop. 'Our Henry', as he was affectionately known, was not personally very keen on parachuting, swimming or driving and would invariably end up with the Mountain Troop during our training trips abroad. These trips would provide excellent climbing opportunities, and hours of laughter when he was along, most of it – though we think he never realised it – at his expense. If he did, he was far too gracious to mention it.

One winter we were told we should take advantage of the snow conditions in Scotland and spend two weeks around Aviemore, learning to ski. This we thought a great idea and could not wait to get going. Things began to lose their appeal, however, when the Troop Rupert suddenly hatched a hare-brained plan to combine the trip with a little driver training. Instead of travelling north on the train, we would drive up in 'Pink Panthers'. These are the SAS's open-topped, stripped-down Landrovers, festooned with gun mountings and specially adapted for desert work; and as the name might suggest, they are pink in colour. Apart from the fact that driving around in such outlandish vehicles would make us look like a load of big time show-offs, having recently arrived back in the UK from three months in the deserts of Sharjah, we would most likely freeze to death before we got past Carlisle. Adamant that we do it his way, the young Captain outlined his plan to Major Henry, who, without making him change it, let it be known that he thought it was a silly idea. His only proviso was that no uniforms or SAS insignia were to be worn.

This suited the Trogs down to the ground as we found that wearing SAS gear invariably acted as an invitation to some yob or other to pick a fight. It was the dream of every young tough, it seemed, to make a name for himself by defeating a member of the SAS Regiment. It put us in an impossible situation, for it was strict SAS policy that anyone caught fighting with civilians was automatically RTU'd. If an incident did flare up, we had either to deal with it quickly and quietly, or else walk away from it, and that was very difficult. Better to travel inconspicuously and avoid the problem; who wanted to go skiing in uniform, anyway?

Arriving in the village of Grantown-on-Spey, we found that we were to be accommodated at the local TA Drill Hall, and that instruction in the art of how to ski would be provided for us by our very own corporal, Geordie Shipfields. Geordie, who we later learned was not the best skier in the world, was not pleased to have been given the job either, but took it very seriously. Once we had settled ourselves into what was to be our home for the next two weeks, the programme started.

We had been provided with skis, poles and boots from the Army Adventure Training Stores and having kitted ourselves up, we presented ourselves outside in the snow. Some of us had skied before and wanted to go off on our own, but that did not fit in with Geordie's plan at all. He had been told to give us all instruction and that was precisely what he intended to do.

In his Newcastle accent, he told us, 'Yaw've got ta knoo the exercises ta mak yer bo-ans soopple. Ef yaw doan' get soopple, yaw'll brak yer bo-ans.' Geordie gave us a demonstration on how to board the ski tow which was to take us up the nursery slopes. When at last he had us all safely deposited at the top of the hill; the tow-bar operator sighed with relief; it had taken half an hour to get us there. We kept falling off and knocking over whole rows of experienced skiers in the process, and though we all thought this was desperately funny, the other people, strangely, did not see it in the same light.

Eventually, when we were all standing in a ragged line on the top of the slope, Geordie urged us to 'Remember what I toald ya. Now do the same as me and yaw'll be alreet.'

He pointed his skis downhill and started to descend. Within seconds, we could see that our man was no Franz Klammer; with his skis about two feet apart, knees locked together and bottom sticking out as though he were about to sit down, he sped downwards, gathering momentum. It was then we noticed the smart-looking ski instructor half-way down the hill, with his equally well-dressed and equipped class lined up and watching the whole proceedings intently. His expression of superior amusement gave way to one of horror as Geordie shouted a warning, 'Get oot the way, man, I kanney stop!' The class panicked and toppled over like ninepins as Geordie zoomed towards them. He managed to steer a course between the instructor and his pupils but it was the last act over which he had any direct influence. After that he was totally out of control, unable to turn left or right. Like something out a cartoon strip, he left the piste completely, flew over an embankment, executed a beautiful somersault and crashed into a snowdrift – breaking his leg. Remembering to keep our own 'bo-ans soople', we carted him off to the nearest hospital.

Two years went by, interspersed with trips to various countries and participation in small 'brush fire' wars throughout the world, the majority of which never came to the attention of the British press 'for political reasons', a fact of which we were very aware, and accounts for the unexplained gaps in this narrative. I have always firmly believed that our national secrets should remain secret. There is a song that I used to hum to myself as I trudged over the hillsides and it seems to sum it all up for me: 'For what's done is done, and what's won is won, and what's lost is lost and gone forever.' In the main, these, words, I think, echoed the thoughts of the rest of the members of the Troop as well.

One of the climbing trips that took place in those early years and which I still look back on now with affection was an ambitious attempt to scale our first Alpine peak. At the time we had no Troop Officer, which meant we had practically a free hand when it came to planning the expedition, submitting to our Squadron Commander a proposal to climb Mont Blanc and the Matterhorn in the Summer of 1968. He was absolutely delighted at the prospect and decided to join us. With 'Our Henry' along, we knew we were in for a bit of fun.

None of us had done any serious Alpine routes at that time, except for the Troop Corporal, Alex, who had been on a German mountain training exercise. On the strength of this, he was given the job of guide to the rest of us. Scraping together enough gear was an effort as the mountain store in Hereford held next to nothing at that time. We borrowed a large tent from another unit and commandeered ice-axes and crampons from the Adventure Training Pool. Weighed down with everything we needed for four weeks, we set off from Hereford.

There were ten of us in the party, all dressed up in jeans and the new trekking boots we had just bought at a discount from Nobby Clark. Nobby, who had once served with the Regiment, now ran the Joe Brown climbing shop in North Wales, so we were always OK there for a spot of shop-soiled gear. In London, we lugged our rucksacks, tents and a huge tinker's basket of food and cooking pots across town, to connect with the Dover boat train. Our problems started when we tried to negotiate the Paris Metro in the middle of the rush hour. French business men shrank into corners of the train, trying to avoid impalement on the spikes of our ice-axes. 'Our Henry', insisting he could speak the 'Frog-lingo', undertook to get us off at the right station, assuring us that all we needed to do was to follow him. As we pulled into station after station, nine pairs of eyes could be seen straining in the direction of our illustrious leader. At the Gare de Lyon, the doors opened with a hiss, but Henry made no move. This couldn't be it, then. Just as they were slamming shut, however, Henry suddenly changed his mind and jumped out. It was too late for us, we were stranded on the train as it began to pull away once more. 'Get out at the next stop,' shouted Dick, one of our number who we found really could speak French. 'That was the wrong one anyway.'

Sure enough, ten minutes later, along came Henry. 'Just testin',' he said with a sheepish grin.

Tired and hungry, we arrived at the little station in Chamonix. It was already dark as we unloaded our kit from the guard's van and wandered off up the road, looking for our campsite. It was in the woods, not too far from the railway track, and we spent the next hour in pitch darkness fighting to erect the tent we had borrowed. It was a huge bell tent that could have accommodated twenty or thirty boy scouts. At least it was blue, so we stood a chance of being mistaken for inexperienced tourists rather than impoverished soldiers who couldn't afford anything better. Eventually, the thing stood upright with our sleeping bags rolled out on karrimats inside it. We had settled in. Just time to stroll down into town for a much-needed beer before turning in.

I stopped and looked up at the black shapes in the sky thousands of feet above our heads. 'Clouds look a bit black,' I thought to myself, but then, as my eyes became accustomed to the light, I realised that they were not clouds at all, but the mountains towering black and forbidding on either side of the valley. I found it hard to believe that they could be so high. The sheer enormity of the Mont Blanc massif hit me like a slap in the face as I tried in vain to take it all in. I had flown over this range on my way to far-flung outposts, but seeing it from the air was no preparation for standing now at its foot. Overawed, I made my way quietly into town behind the others, who I could tell were equally impressed.

Inevitably we found our way to the Bar National, which we were soon to learn was the most popular haunt of visiting climbers. The wine and beer were cheap and you could gather news here of local weather conditions and who was doing what. After a few beers and a plate of French Fries, we staggered back to the campsite and a good night's sleep.

The next week was spent exploring the glaciers and learning how to cope with crampons and ice-axes. We encountered crevasses and taught ourselves how to extricate ourselves if we should ever have the misfortune to fall into one. We were all familiar with abseiling and jumaring, so most of it was simply a question of putting what we knew into practice. The setting was magnificent. I had never seen anything like this in my whole life: some of the glaciers were miles across, great rivers of crushed ice tumbling down the mountainside; peaks rose steeply into the air, sharply silhouetted against a pale blue sky. We quickly learned how to spot the tell-tale signs of a snow-covered crevasse, how to cross a *Bergschrund*, and that it was no good putting on a heavy Bergen rucksack and trying to race up these slopes, as we might back home. We learned that at altitude everything has to be done at a steady, plodding pace, so that energy can be conserved, and so that we do not run out of breath.

By listening to other climbers in the Bar Nat. at night, and reading up reports of climbs in the area, it soon became apparent that we would need to start a climb early in the morning while it was still dark, in order to be back down in the valley by midday when the weather tended to turn a bit nasty. We practised this theory out on a couple of smaller peaks in the valley over the next few days. It was hard to get used to moving up snowfields and snow gullies and finding the most direct and easy routes up the mountain, rather than climbing on the inviting-looking, but harder rock routes. Climbing in the Alps, we learned, was all about getting to the top and not putting up new rock routes. We could easily see why this was, standing on the summits of some of these peaks early in the morning, just as the sun started to nose its way over the horizon. For the first time I was experiencing the thrill of being out on a limb in a vast expanse of mountains. Above the billowing cloud, the miracle of a new day would unfold before my wondering eyes as the sky passed through a million shades of grey, blue and yellow before the vermilion rays of the sun reached out into all corners of the heaven and the welcome warmth began to seep into my body. My love of sunrises and sunsets dates from that time; these special times when the world is still, are when it seems to me possible to get closest to nature and the meaning of life.

I had enjoyed climbing for a long time. But now I fell in love with the mountains. I became hooked on 'big hills'. It did not matter that hundreds of people may have stood on this very spot before me. For me, the moment was mine alone.

Several days later we made our attempt on Mont Blanc. Not being able to afford the cost of the *téléférique*, we plodded steadily up through the forests on the lower slopes which led us out finally on to the open mountain. That first night was spent in the lea of the station at the top of the *téléférique*. Early the next morning we had our first taste of Alpine bad weather, when at 13,000 feet we met with almost white-out conditions and were forced to descend back into the valley. It was a desperate day, all tracks fast disappearing, giving us a really hard time finding our way down. But it was a useful lesson to learn, never to underestimate the speed at which a storm can roll in. One minute it was clear, and the next we were in a raging blizzard. We were lucky to have got down as quickly as we did. It had shown us, too, that some of our clothing was suspect and that heavy Army sleeping bags were far from being warm enough high on a mountain. I made up my mind that day to save up and some day own a lightweight duck-down bag, such as I had seen the 'posh' climbers using. The next few days were spent festering in town as the storm continued to rage all around us. Listening to the weather forecast in the pub on the fourth night, we learned that things were much brighter on the Italian side of the Alps, and decided to move there the next day.

Matterhorn, Matterhorn, Matterhorn! It was on all our lips. If we were going to Italy, then we were going to climb the Matterhorn! Ever since, as a child, I had read books about Whymper climbing this mountain, I had a yearning to climb it for myself.

We set up camp in Cervinia, where it was decided to split the party into two, and the next day to climb up as far as the vicinity of the Savoia hut. We would spend one night there and go for the top the next day. This, then, gave us the rest of the afternoon to prepare ourselves. It was interesting to see how people went about this: mostly we spent about an hour stuffing kit into our sacks, and then repaired to the tavern. I had been placed in Alex's team, along with Dick, Mac 'Nay-Sweat' (we called him this because his standard reply to any request was 'Nay-Sweat') and Johnny Creasey. Johnny was a Yorkshireman, and had done a bit more climbing than I had, so I chose to rope up with him since Bronco was off with the other party.

Alex outlined his plan to us in the bar.

'We will just meander up the hill,' he said, 'climb onto this ridge, here . . .' (he had bought a postcard by way of a guide) '. . . and follow it to the top. Nothing to it!'

Johnny cast a sceptical look in my direction. I drank up my beer and went off to find a map. My pocket money did not stretch to actually buying the map, just having a look at it. As things turned out, I would have done better to lay out on that rather than the beer.

As I was coming back to the tent site, dreamily gazing up at the hill and wondering what it would be like to be looking down here from the top, I heard a startled cry coming from the direction of our big tent and quickened my pace to see what the problem was.

'Turn him over, turn him over! He's bleeding to death!'

Throwing open the flap of the tent I rushed inside to see Henry crouching anxiously over the body of Norman, one of the other troop members, who was spread-eagled on the floor, with a river of red flowing from his gaping mouth. Henry was doing his best to staunch the flow with a large piece of cloth. I quickly realised that things were not quite what they seemed, and trying not to laugh, said, 'It's red wine. He's had too much and he's throwing up.'

'Red wine, red wine,' chanted the Major, relieved that Norman wasn't about to die on him, but hopping mad to have been made so agitated. 'He's bloody drunk, he's bloody drunk,' he went on. 'Throw him in the river!' His moustache was bristling and he was repeating himself as he always did when he got excited.

Grabbing Norman by the scruff of the neck, he started to drag him towards the river. It took us all our time to convince him, between bouts of laughter, that throwing him into the icy cold, fast-flowing waters was not likely to do anything other than give us more problems than we had already. Instead, we cleaned Norman up, covered him with his sleeping bag and left him to sleep it off while we settled down for a good night's rest ourselves. But every time I closed my eyes, I would see the look on Henry's face as he ministered to the prostrate body of Norman, and burst into giggles. Sleep did not come easily that night.

Waking early and stuffing gear into our packs, the five of us set off up through the meadows towards the mountain. It was a cold morning with just a few clouds flying high in the sky. The majestic outline of the Matterhorn seemed almost a shadow in the early morning light. Cows skitted to one side, their bells clanging, as we disturbed their sleepy munching. We had eaten a hasty breakfast before setting out, and filled our flasks, and we now walked for about three hours, though we stopped frequently to sit and view the surrounding countryside. Gradually we were making height, and at last we reached the top of the cableway where there was a large concrete blockhouse. In winter when the place is covered with snow, it probably looks all right to the skiers, but now, sitting as it does in the flower-filled pastures, it was positively ugly.

From here, the track forked, and checking with the postcard he still carried, Alex announced that we needed to take the left-hand fork. We still seemed to be some way from the mountain, but Alex assured us that we could get on to it by the ridge to our left, and then all we had to do was follow it to the top.

Soon the track petered out, but by this time we were underneath the ridge, and roping up, started to scramble up the easy-angled rocks. None of us had thought of doubting that Alex knew what he was doing, and it felt good to be climbing again.

After a short while, Dick decided he was not feeling too well and wanted to go back. Some way below us we could hear the cries of the other party, who were by now nearing the blockhouse. They were shouting and waving and pointing up the mountain.

'I think they're trying to tell us that we should have taken the other track,' said Johnny to Alex.

'We're too high to go back now,' he replied irritably, knowing we were off route. 'We might as well carry on and meet them at the hut by the Col du Lion.'

Pressing on, we found ourselves on a particularly steep bit of rock. Alex, who was quite a competent climber, led off up this pitch and called down that he was almost on top of the ridge. I was glad, for that meant that the climbing should become easier. The pitch he had just climbed was about a Grade 5, and I was sure this was not the sort of route we ought to be doing on something as big as the Matterhorn. Besides, the cloud had already started to thicken above us and throw down a light dusting of snow. Gaining the ridge proper, the weather closed in still further, and we soon lost sight of the other party who were by now following the other track far below us. One good thing was that we had already seen Dick arrive at the building, so we did not need to feel concerned for his safety.

The route along the ridge was rather ill-defined and craggy in places, but by no means difficult. The problem was that because of the cloud and snow, which had seriously closed in on us, we were travelling very slowly and getting quite cold. It became obvious to us that between where we were and the Col du Lion was another great lump of rock (I afterwards learned it was called the Tête du Lion), and that we would not be able to make the hut before nightfall. Nonetheless, we decided to press on and as luck would have it, just as it was getting dark, we stumbled upon an old tin shed perched among the rocks. It was the most welcome thing I had seen in a long time. By now we were all wet, very cold and tired, and during the last hour an icy wind had boosted the snowstorm. By the time the last man arrived at the hut, which was padlocked, Johnnie had put his axe to good use and forced an entry.

It was empty and had been unused for some time, but for us, it was a godsend. Half an hour later, from the warmth of the stove and with a hot drink inside us, we stopped shivering. Putting on all our extra clothing, we crawled into our sleeping bags and set about cooking the dinner. Outside the storm raged, and I tried not to think what might have happened had we not found this old hut. The plan now was to move around to the Savoia the next day, meet up with the other party and go for the top the day after that. We slept snugly that night in the welcome warmth of the little hut.

Next morning I roped up with Mac and set off along the ridge. It was quite late when we got away as we had waited for the worst of the snow to stop falling. Looking at my army watch, I noticed that it was almost 11.30.

I really enjoyed climbing with Mac. He was a jovial character, who never let anything get him down. Whenever we were together, there was usually a smile on our faces, but the smile drained away pretty smartly when we were traversing around the righthand side of the Tête du Lion on a very unstable snowfield and heard a loud crack. This was followed by a grumbling sound as the snow beneath our feet began to move. The whole thing was sliding downhill with us struggling to keep upright on top of it. We travelled for about fifty feet, before the raft of snow ground shakily to a stop. Like mice creeping across a frozen pond, we tiptoed on crampons to the other side, fearing at every step that we might trigger off another slide. We were both shaken, and looked up to where Alex and Johnnie were grinning from the safety of the rocks above. They were going to have to cross the same spot; that should wipe the smiles off their faces, we thought.

Shortly after they too were safely across beside us, the sound of thunder could be heard rumbling down the valley, and there were occasional streaks of lightning. The sky was an eerie green. I had never experienced weather like this before – it was snowing, hailing, and throwing thunder and lightning at us, all at the same time. It did not take much discussion to reach the decision to abandon our idea of traversing around the col, and make as swift a descent as possible. Looping the rope over a finger of rock, I threw the two ends down a couloir and started to abseil down it as fast as I could. The other three promptly followed, anchored the other rope to a piton that Mac hammered into the rock, and continued past me as I retrieved our rope. We continued manoeuvring like this, rotating the ropes, for about a thousand feet until the couloir ran out at the top of a steep rockface. We made our way along to the right until we found another snow runnel and resumed our descent. The sky was now black and the snow had long since turned to wet hail. Thunder was roaring directly above us and fingers of lightning started to strike the rock and crackle all around us. It was terrifyingly obvious that we were now in the eye of the storm. If we did not get ourselves off this mountain soon, one of us was likely to be struck – if not by the lightning, then by some of the stones that were now steadily crashing down the couloir.

Someone noticed a small cave-like shelter just off to the side and we quickly made for its safety. It was just about big enough to fit the four of us with our packs, and being situated on a small platform underneath a large overhang, was dry and safe from falling rocks.

The lightning got steadily worse, if anything, and it was almost like bullets ricocheting off the rock as fluorescent, jagged fingers snaked out of the sky and lit up the whole area around us. Settling into our relatively protected recess, we prepared to spend the night out. This was to be my first unplanned bivouac and I was not looking forward to it at all. I couldn't imagine what I was doing here. Where had all the fun gone? I was bloody scared, but not wanting to alarm the others or appear a coward, I kept my thoughts to myself, and settled down into my sleeping bag for a long, cold and sleepless night. To top it all, Mac had dropped his fag-tin, and my cigaretes were all soaking wet. Bloody mountains! All I wanted was to get off this one – alive!

The next morning Johnnie voiced the opinion of all of us when he said, 'At one stage last night, I didn't think we were going to see this morning.' It did my self-confidence the world of good to know that I was not the only one who had felt apprehensive about the situation. The storm had blown itself out and after brewing up the last of our tea and finishing off the remnants of food, we resumed the slow descent to the valley. Small avalanches cascaded around us, and after two hours of wading through soft snow, we finally met up with the other party at the top of the cable-car lift. Describing our epic to Bronco – and smoking his cigarettes – I felt relief at being safely off the hill, but strangely excited that we had been in such a potentially dangerous situation, yet had got ourselves down all in one piece. The others had made it to the Savoia hut and been snowed in there for two days, unable to move up or down.

When we were all safely back at the tent, fed and dried off, and had heard each other's stories, the decision was taken to move back to Chamonix for one last quick go at Mont Blanc before going home. But Mac 'Nay-Sweat' and I decided that we would stay on in Cervinia for a day or two and try the Matterhorn once more. I tried to get Bronco to join us on the Matt, but his sights were set on getting up the Blanc.

Three days later, Mac and I had to follow the rest of the team to Chamonix. We had still not been to the top of the Matterhorn. Climbing above the Savoia Hut, we reached a point just short of Pic Tyndall when again we were forced back by bad weather. At least this time, though, we had followed the correct route, and experienced the thrill of climbing high on the mountain. We had been on fixed ropes and had had no epics, but it had been really enjoyable, nonetheless. I could now call myself a proper mountaineer, I thought, since I'd been high. If we hadn't reached the top, it didn't really matter. The mountain wasn't going to go anywhere, and one day I would be back.

Back To the Jungle

SOME OF the nicest times I can remember have been in jungles; some of the most tragic ones, too. One particular operation I will always remember with affection occurred when I was sent to British Guiana; the whole trip was a delight. For five days after our arrival in Georgetown, the capital, we were constantly on the move, getting to know our hosts from the local Army unit, training and socialising with them. The unit was made up of tribesmen from different areas of the country, and for many of them, this was their first time in the city. It meant that when they went on the town for a drink, it must have been like Christmas to them. They went wild.

Such was the case with 'George', a small Amerindian we befriended. We called him George because none of us could get our tongue around his real name – one of those Indian names that seem to go on for ever – but he seemed to like it, so George it was. Big Alf, one of the squadron sergeants, a down-to-earth Geordie with no frills, took a shine to George and looked after him in the wicked city, bringing him along on our frequent forays to the bar. It was during one of these sessions that poor old George, like the rest of us, had a little too much to drink and started to fret about how we were going to get back to the barracks in time to move into the jungle later in the day. He was to be our guide. Alf told him not to worry and bought another round of drinks. By now it was 5.30 in the morning and we were some fifteen miles from camp. We had to be back by eight o'clock, ready for muster. (This was a daily check to ensure that no one had got 'lost' during the night. The local gangs had a habit of turning people over for their valuables.)

Taking off into the new day, Alf informed us that he was going to get some transport. True to his word, fifteen minutes later he was back.

'The carriage awaits,' he announced from the door, looking at the bodies sprawled in front of the bar. No one moved, everyone lay fast asleep.

'Give us a hand, young 'un,' he said to me, and started to pick up the booze-numbed forms and carry them outside. Bleary eyed, I staggered to help him.

'Ahhh, my head!' I had drunk far too much and wished I could just flop down beside the rest of them and go to sleep too. Eventually, we got everyone out to the vehicle and were on our way along the dusty road. As we swung through the main gates of the garrison, I could see the rest of the squadron outside the accommodation block. They were all pointing our way and laughing. It was only then that I realised what a sight we must have presented. Our transport was a horse-drawn, flat bed, rickety old wagon, piloted by a toothless old man in a straw hat and smoking a pipe, and co-piloted by George, astride the horse, head bowed and swaying unsteadily from side to side. We looked like something out of a Spaghetti Western. Bodies were piled on the cart, legs and arms dangling over the sides, and we were all struggling to open our eyes to see what the hilarity was about, blinking against the cruel daylight. The squadron commander shook his head in disbelief and walked off, leaving the RSM to sort us out.

'Don't you know it's against the law to give liquor to the Indians, Alf?' he asked. 'Come on, you lot, get yourselves showered and shaved. We move out in an hour.'

With that our mighty Amerindian fell to the floor from the back of the steaming horse.

There is something magic about travelling up a fast-flowing river with the jungle sweeping by: birds screeching and flying before you, warning the rest of the forest of your approach; fish jumping on all sides of your boats as you cut swiftly through the water. Every so often you pass a small village on the muddy banks with naked children splashing about, laughing and waving excitedly as your armada weaves its way through their fathers' fishing nets; the sun-tanned bodies of bare-breasted girls flash in the sunlight as they make their escape from washing pools, squealing and giggling at being disturbed. But I have to say that on this particular day, most of the beauty was lost on me as I dropped in the bottom of the boat feeling as sick as a dog. The sun beat mercilessly down, compounding the effects of my king-size hangover.

We chugged on upriver, low in the water from the weight of heavy packs, the villages becoming less frequent the further upstream we went. I was rocked into consciousness as the boat bumped against the riverbank just above one small village, where we stopped to have a brew and something to eat. By now I was feeling a little more refreshed. Throwing some river water over my head and face, I picked up my rifle, buckled on the belt which carried all the spare magazines for my weapon, my water bottle, emergency pouch and compass, and headed off to help with the cooking. George was chattering away with the headman of the village and people milled around, all talking at once and pointing to the village centre. The excitement, George told us, was because one of the village dogs had been eaten by a reptile during the night; the villagers had caught the offender and held it in the village. Perhaps we would care to take a look? My eyes widened as I watched one of the men cut open a very large boa constrictor and drag out the remains of the unfortunate pooch from its stomach. The sight and smell of this little lot was all that I needed on top of the beer I had drunk the night before, and I slipped off into the trees to one side of the rough-built houses to unload my stomach too.

Returning to the scene, I stared in amazement at the length of the snake. It must have been over twenty feet. I had seen snakes before, but never as long as this, and the thought of meeting a giant like this in my hammock one dark night was not something I cared to contemplate. One of the blokes told me he had seen a stuffed specimen in Georgetown Museum that measured twenty-seven feet. Ugh! How I hated snakes! During the few hours we spent in the village, the reptile was cut up and cooked for us to eat. It was not something I could face and I settled instead for tea and a hard-tack biscuit.

Climbing back into the boats we then moved off for two more days travelling upriver, stopping at night to sleep in hammocks slung between trees on the riverbank. It was a pleasant couple of days, which enabled me to get the alcohol out of my system and tune in to the jungle smells and sounds. I began to enjoy being back in this environment.

Contrary to what many people believe, the jungle is a very

clean, fresh place to be. It rains almost every day with monotonous regularity, mostly in the afternoon, and the air is continually, therefore, being cleared. Except in the swamps, the steaming jungle, as it is depicted in most films, is brought about simply by the rays of the sun evaporating the moisture from the leaf canopy and the vegetation of the jungle floor. There is always something new to see and learn in the rainforest – or *Ulu* as we learned to refer to this kind of country. (It is a Malay word meaning jungle headwaters, or deep jungle interior.) Although they are there, of course, you do not see many animals, because most of them hear the sounds of movement or smell your presence long before you reach them. It is a measure of how well attuned you are to jungle life, if you can approach an animal before he senses you are close.

On the third day we reached the small village of Tamataria, which was way up in the interior. Here we left our boats and the waters of the Essequibo river to set up a squadron base on the other side of the village, from where we would make training forays into the jungle. Village life centred around a longhouse, built on short stilts, which served as general store, bar and main meeting house. We quickly learned that this was also the jumping-off point for the 'Pork Knockers', colourful characters who were the Guyanian equivalent of North American goldminers. Being 'grubstaked' by the owner of the longhouse, given tools, food and a mule, they would push off into the jungle to pan for gold and diamonds, or as they put it, 'We goin' up de river, in de krick, and look for de gold, man.' With their mules loaded to the gunwales, they would prospect until all the food was eaten (mostly dried pig, hence the name 'Pork-knockers'), then butcher the mule and live off that for a while, only returning when all was gone or they had made a lucky 'strike'. If it were the latter, they would get paid off by the 'grubstaker' when they got back. We were fortunate enough to be present when one of these pioneering old gentlemen returned from a trip. He had been 'in de krick' for two months and had made a big find of gold dust and a few small diamonds. This was what life must have been like in the days of Klondike. Drinks were bought 'all round' and the hootin' and hollerin' went on late into the night. These old boys certainly knew how to live it up.

Sitting chatting to the old Pork-knocker after things had quieted down, we learned that there was quite a bit of gold to be found in this area. Guardedly, he told us that they did not always bring back all the gold or diamonds they found for the grubstaker, but would stash away a small amount for the 'sittin' days' when they would be able to retire and buy a small shack in the city.

All this talk sent a ripple of gold fever through the camp, and pretty soon everyone had got hold of an old tin plate or a scooped out bowl and was off 'up de river' with dreams of easy pickin's. None more so than the Squadron Quartermaster, a bloke we called Gypsy, who did indeed manage to pull out some diamonds at his first try. After that, the sign on his door used almost permanently to read: 'Closed – gone up de river and in de krick, man.'

After four weeks' training here, we set off for our final exercise, splitting down into four-man patrols, each consisting of the patrol commander, a signaller, medic and lead scout. I was to be lead scout in Pete Mcleese's patrol, with two Welshmen completing the party. To avoid any confusion, one of them retained the nickname 'Taff', while the other was known as 'Legs', because he was so tall. The first part of our task was to raft downstream with several other patrols to our drop-off point, move along a track and then cut into the jungle and cover a distance of about thirty miles before meeting up with the rest of the squadron. The other patrols would all be making similar approaches, and together at the end, we would stage a mock attack on a camp.

Rafting downriver made a pleasant interlude, because the exercise did not start until we were dropped off. Some of the time was spent swimming alongside the craft, but this pastime ground to a rather fast halt when we noticed the carcase of a dead bird floating by, and seconds later the water around it appearing to boil as the feathery mass was pushed first left, then right in the current. Our Amerindian pilot was shouting for us to get out of the river, jabbering so fast that we could not understand a word he was saying, but his gesticulations left us in no doubt that we should do what he said, and quickly. When we finally did make out one of the words he kept repeating, we realised the reason for his agitation. 'Pira . . . Pira . . . *Piranha!*' The river was apparently a breeding ground for the fish, which could grow to quite a large size, he told us.

Mid-afternoon found us pulling in to a small jetty made of bamboo beside a village of five houses. It was a hunting camp which was now little used. This was to be our jump-off spot and we gathered up our equipment and moved off along the muddy track. After a few hours' walk, we came across a small tin hut, where we stopped and checked our maps. By now we were miles from anywhere and it seemed strange to hit a metal hut this far out when everything else we had passed had been made of wood and bamboo. Voices and laughter were coming from inside and we crept up quietly to try and see what was going on. Just then, the door was flung open and out strode a wizened old Guyanian, a look of total surprise invading his face as he caught sight of the four of us. Shaking his head, he staggered off to relieve himself in the bushes, while we went inside. The shack was stocked with all sorts of goods and served as general store and bar for the loggers who, we learned from the wrinkle-faced man when he returned, sometimes worked this forest track. They invited us to sample some of their prized local grog. It was called XM Rum, and almost burnt out the back of our throats; we quickly dubbed it 'Fireball XM5' since it seemed indistinguishable from rocket fuel to us. Enthralled by the many stories told by the shack's clientele, we decided the exercise could wait another day; we would put up our hammocks and shelters here for the night. It was a bad move. I just knew we were going to end up with thick heads again in the morning. And we did.

Before the light of the new day, Pete was shaking us all awake. We packed and started to move off. The routine had started. From now on we would become tactical: up and packed before it was light, move for an hour, then stop for a brew and to make the morning signals call to base. Taff, who was the signaller would tap out the coded message, one of us would make the tea, while the other two lay watching and listening for signs of 'enemy' movement. Two hundred troops of the Guyanian Army had been deployed in the area to act as enemy and add a bit of realism to the exercise. We would be moving in single file through the *Ulu*, trying as far as possible not to cut down any vegetation or leave signs of our passage. We would walk for most of the day, only *basha-ing* down after it was dark. This would cut down on the risk of being caught. We had to accept that we would get wet every afternoon as the torrents of rain fell roaring from the sky, and drumming on the elephant leaves. This rain, although uncomfortable, was a help in that it masked the sound of our movement from anyone close by, and came down with such force that it covered most of our tell-tale tracks. All the niceties of life had to be done away with in order to move comfortably, since we had to carry everything on our backs. We would never wash with soap in the jungle anyway, because of the smell. Apart from the possibility of this giving us away to an enemy, a sweet-smelling body tended to attract all sorts of biting insects. Toothpaste was also done away with for the same reason, and salt was used as a substitute. It was no picnic off the beaten track, but it did enable us to see the jungle at close quarters.

After we had left the hut that morning, we quickly moved along the track for a mile or so, then faded off, one by one, into the trees, so as to leave less sign of exactly where we had entered. Laying a couple of false trails – just in case – we set off towards our destination. On the third day we started to descend into a large valley. The maps we were using were not very good anyway as most of this was uncharted jungle; nevertheless, we were concerned by the fact that we appeared to be slowly moving into a large area of swamp. At first it only covered the ankles, but later it began to creep above our knees. After an hour's travel, I was up to my waist in mud and water. Swamps always give off nauseating smells and this one was no exception; the only thing that was conspicuous by its absence was any form of bird life. An eerie silence hung over the place. As lead scout, I was naturally out in front, with Pete directly behind me and the two Taffs bringing up the rear. Being only five foot five inches tall meant that the oozy swamp was soon licking around my chest and Pete was in much the same predicament, though on the taller Welshmen, it only reached just above their waists. I was not a happy man.

'Come on Pete, this is like being on the films. The only thing we don't have is the African Queen to pull behind us.'

We certainly had the leeches, because I could feel them pinching as they gorged on my blood. Looking round, I had to laugh at the sight of Pete, chest-deep in the quagmire, his rifle held above his head to keep it clean, and saying in his best Cagney accent, 'We're coming to get ya, Gypsy – you can't buy us off with your diamonds.' Then more seriously, 'It's getting deeper, ain't it?'

We all knew that if we didn't start to climb out soon, we were going to have to turn back. The decision was made for us when gliding across the top of the swamp and advancing rapidly towards us, was a rather large water snake. Splashing water at it with my rifle butt, I took off one way and the snake, luckily, headed in the opposite direction. The others were almost overtaking me as I made swiftly for higher ground off to our left. On *terra firma* once more, we fell about laughing at ourselves. Four brave SAS men, armed to the teeth, ready to take on a whole army if necessary, but running away at the first sign of danger from an overgrown worm. What is it about snakes?

After brewing up and eating some cheese and biscuits, we moved off to find a different route around the swamp. We now stuck to the drier ground of the ridges. At least we now carried a more authentic jungle smell and were able on more than one occasion to get quite close to some wild pigs and monkeys!

Settling down in my hammock that night, I found it hard to get off to sleep as I had started to itch all over. I could feel lots of little bumps all up my arms and thought that I must have been bitten by ants or something. Some time after midnight I could stand the irritation no longer, and jumped out of my sleeping bag, a lightweight thing made of parachute silk, to put on a brew. It occurred to me that I might be experiencing an allergic reaction to the silk. By the light of my candle I examined one of the tiny bumps more closely, giving it a gentle squeeze. To my absolute amazement and horror, I saw a little white maggot wriggling half in and half out of my arm. My confused brain refused at first to register the enormity of what was happening to me. But it couldn't be ignored. My whole body was covered in these bumps, which meant that I must literally be crawling with maggots. I was being eaten alive! It definitely made we feel worse to think about it. I moved my shoulders and limbs, as if to make it all disappear, hoping against hope it was all just a bad dream, that I would soon wake up and everything would be fine, but all the time I knew that I wouldn't. With a final shudder, I woke up 'Legs', who was the patrol medic, and explained the problem. Instead of giving me some wonder drug that would rid my body of these vermin, he let out a yelp of delight and woke up the others, saying, 'Maggots! Maggots! He's got maggots! Come and have a look at this!'

They gathered round where I sat feeling absolutely wretched, staring in disbelief at the thousands of bumps on my body, all shouting with glee as I squeezed out another tiny maggot for their benefit. After feeding me a couple of Piriton tablets, the rest of the night was spent on the radio back to base, asking the doctor what drug to use to kill these things, and listening to the three of them making wisecracks about what a good bloke I was to have along on a fishing trip, a walking bait tin. I was not amused.

Base informed us that the doctor there was as baffled as we were, and that we should make for a helicopter landing site a day's march away, from where I could be picked up. The next thirty-six hours seemed to drag by as we made our way to the rendezvous, and it was with considerable relief that I clambered aboard the aircraft. At last I would be treated by someone who knew what he was doing. The whole thing should be cleared up within twenty-four hours, or so I fondly thought. I was in for a shock.

The chopper flew me straight back to the hospital in Georgetown. With two and a half weeks growth of beard, my clothes covered in murk and slime from the swamps and smelling like one of the wild pigs we had met on the ridge track, I was not a pretty sight. I hadn't washed for weeks, and to top it all off was covered from head to foot with these angry red bumps. It was no wonder that the nurses in their starched white and blue uniforms reeled back in disgust as I strode along the corridors of the hospital on my way to see the tropical diseases specialist.

Ater examining me, taking blood samples, shoving thermometers into every orifice he could find, I was finally allowed to take a bath. The water turned black, but not nearly as black as my mood when I was informed that my case was unique. I had been bitten by a pig fly that had planted its eggs into my body, the warmth of my blood was now incubating them, so that they were hatching out under my skin. It had never been known to occur in a white man before, and they intended to keep me in a room at constant temperature until I could be flown to London, where I could be observed by the top specialists in tropical medicine. It was all very exciting, the doctor said, a marvellous opportunity for science.

I had had it up to the neck, what with pigs and pig flies, and threw a wobbler. 'Forget it!' I raged. 'All I want is to get these things killed off and out of my system as soon as possible. I'm not going to be a bloody guinea pig for anyone!'

Realising I meant it, they disappointedly pumped me full of antibiotics and a few other things I didn't recognise the names of, and allowed me out. The medic came in for the sharp end of my tongue, too, when he arrived to drive me back to the barracks with the words, 'Come on then, Maggot, let's go home.'

Jungles of quite another type are to be found in Jamaica. Apart from a totally different range of animals in the forest, there are wild animals to contend with in the concrete jungles of the cities, too – of the two-legged variety. I was to meet a couple of these species while training the Jamaican Defence Force in 1978. In those days I had a habit of disappearing down back alleys and into the more sleazy bars, hoping for a glimpse of how the real Jamaicans lived in the evenings after work. One night I bit off more than I could chew, when I ended up in a cellar dive surrounded by a nasty looking gang of drug pushers, brandishing knives and pistols. Mine was the only white face in the place, and the regulars were making it increasingly obvious that I had entered uninvited and was unwelcome. I attempted to leave. The way up the stone steps to street level had been blocked by three hefty thugs who were making no secret of their dislike for Europeans. It looked increasingly as though I might end up floating in the dock with my throat cut. I needed to do something fast. There was no way that I could get up the steps past the three gorillas, and I had noticed no other exit.

'What yo doin' in dis place, white man?' asked a smaller man of about thirty, standing next to me. He had a pistol in his hand.

'I've come to sell you some better models than that thing, there,' I said, indicating the gun which was pointing at my stomach, and pushing it aside with a show of confidence that I certainly did not feel.

'Do I get a drink in here, or not?' I demanded, pressing the advantage, my mind racing for an idea of what to say next and to work out a plan that would get me out of the place fast.

The next hour was spent lying through my teeth about how I could supply them with fifty brand new Browning Automatics – for a price, and the guarantee that they would assist me to hide out for a while after I had stolen them from the military. With a wicked grin crossing his face, the small man, clearly the leader of this little band of small time crooks, satisfied himself that I was indeed a soldier by rifling through my wallet and finding my ID card. He agreed to the deal, but insisted that two of his men go with me and the job be done that very night.

It would appear that my bluff had been called, but I nodded, finished my rum and coke, and headed for the door with his two men at my heels. Two steps from the top, I lashed out with my foot into the head of the first of the followers, and as he started to topple backwards, snatched open the door, slammed it behind me and made like a sprinter through the darkened back streets, heading for the lights of the main road. My heart was pounding as I pressed on with the shouts of my pursuers diminishing behind me. I managed to jump into a taxi and within a short while was rolling up at the entrance to the camp where we were staying with the Defence Force. There and then I made up my mind that perhaps it was not such a good idea to do my sight-seeing in the back streets on my own, and that gun-running was definitely not for me.

While training the Jamaican Defence Force in 1978, I joined the troop for an exercise, the first part of which was to make a traverse of the magnificent Blue Mountains which lie in the northern part of the island, an area in which the local forces rarely trained. When we arrived there by vehicle and started to climb up into the jungle-covered hills, it was easy to see why it was not a popular area. The ridges were ill-defined and there was very little water. These were the thickest, dirtiest woods I had ever travelled through. The undergrowth was so intertwined with roots and vines that in places it was impossible to walk on the ground and we had to step from root to root. This made the going extremely slow and difficult, and the chance of twisting an ankle very real. Out of necessity, we stopped much earlier in the day so that we could erect shelters from our lightweight ponchos, stretched in such a way as to collect some drinking water. On the afternoons when it didn't rain we had to rely on emptying the greyish, foul-tasting liquid from the inside of what became known as 'water-bowser plants', hollow vase-like bromeliads that collected and stored rainwater for two or three days at a time. Mixed in with this water were all sorts of tiny bugs and parasites, and it mostly produced a purple-looking tea with hundreds of small flies and things floating about on top, but when you have nothing else, even this tastes good.

Having struggled through this terrain for five days we were more than surprised when we descended into a clearing at the end of one of the never-ending ridges to be confronted with a small hamlet made of bamboo and straw, which would not have been out of place in a Li'l Abner cartoon strip. The sun was shining through the branches of the taller trees on to a large, fat lady, who sat outside one of the small huts in a rocking chair. Her hands were busy knitting and she was humming a tune as she worked. When we walked into the clearing, she rocked to an abrupt halt and stared at us in surprise. We were well bearded and dishevelled by this time, covered in mud, wearing enormous packs and bristling with weapons. A pretty gruesome spectacle.

She slowly shook her head. 'My, my,' she said, 'look at deese white men – a whole heap o' dem, too.'

We closed the gap between us as she asked, 'Where you bin, white man?' We told her of our crossing of the Blue Mountains.

'Why yo done go up in dem mountains, man, ain' nobody goes up dere. Ain' no wimmin and rum in dem mountains – look at yo, man, all covered in dirt. Yo cum into my house diss minnit.'

It was no use protesting that our boots were too muddy to go inside and that we would be OK sat out here in the sunshine; we caught the short end of her tongue as we were ushered inside for tea. The rest of the day was spent in the company of this grand lady and her family, learning about the way they lived. They did not possess much in the way of wordly goods, were good at making do, and obviously worked the land hard. As we said goodbye, we left a few sweets, chocolate and chewing gum for the children, some candles for the house and a packet of cigarettes for the old man. In the back of my mind I felt a little envious of their lifestyle and thought how marvellous it would be to settle down some day to something as peaceful as this.

Once down off the mountain, we met up with the rest of the squadron and prepared for the next stage of the exercise, the crossing of the Cockpit Country. This was an area of chequered history – a vast tract of empty jungle, the outer perimeter of which had been settled by some of the first missionaries to arrive in the country. In some of the remoter villages, you could still find high-collared school-marms in the billowy black gowns of an earlier era. The 'interior' had been the Badlands, where rogues, ruffians, pirates and thieves holed out whenever they were pursued by Government forces. The area still held attractions for modern-day smugglers and drug pushers, and our maps showed places with expressive names, like 'Me no sen – You no cum'. None of the locals we found out would enter this part of the jungle, and the police advised us that we went in 'at our own risk'. They resisted the offer to join us.

Our commander, Big John Slim, decided to explode this myth for once and all and so we made our way across this little-known area. By the time we came out the other side, we knew why the locals did not venture into this part of the jungle. Made up of a pocked volcanic-looking rock that held stagnant water, it was ideal breeding ground for mosquitos. The whole area was alive with them and whenever we put our foot into a pool and disturbed them, we would be attacked by swarms of whining dive-bombers, bent on helping themselves to our blood. It would be a brave villain or pirate who lived there for any length of time.

Of all the jungles I have visited, I think perhaps the one I like best is in Malaya. You normally approach it from Singapore, driving across the causeway from there to mainland Malaya and then travelling on small, winding roads through a constantly changing landscape up towards the border with Thailand in the north. This route enables you to see paddy fields being worked, rubber plantations with their miles of tall, regimented trees and the tappers flitting from trunk to trunk like bees collecting honey. Villages in the various districts differ in size and character according to whether they are predominantly Chinese or Malay. Each has a face of its own, but all have the common sounds and smells of *kampong* life – children and chickens running everywhere and the ever-present odour of inadequate sanitation. The overriding sound is that of laughter. Further north, where the jungle has been repeatedly burned off for cultivation, it can be seen slowly returning to its wild, overgrown state. It is here that the terrain becomes more mountainous as great peaks and craggy rocks tower above the trees, riddled with inaccessible caves that provide sanctuary for hundreds of birds and bats. Day and night you can see them dive in and out of the dark entrances.

Twisting and turning round bend after bend, crossing rickety old wooden bridges, vehicles labour up through jungle-tangled hills that appear, to the untrained eye, to be completely impenetrable. Finally, almost with a sigh of relief, the engine strains no more as you arrive in the rolling hill country of the Cameron Highlands and the border country. Here life revolves mainly around the tea plantations – huge valleys denuded of big trees and now covered with low tea-leaf bearing bushes that are tended by sarong-clad women with baskets on their backs. It is easy on the eye to be able to see once again further than the wall of green, which is the jungle.

On one of my many trips to this area, I found myself working out of the village of Grik, which was a small border outpost of about forty houses. The squadron had various training exercises planned and I became involved in all sorts of different activities, some of which proved interesting, some amusing and some, as it turned out, rather tragic.

Having been lead scout for patrols since my early Borneo days, I always felt relaxed and at home in the jungle; the next stage of learning to live and work in the trees was to become a tracker. I had operated with tracker dogs and Iban trackers in Borneo, so had a fair idea of what was required. I had no idea I would enjoy it as much as I did, nor could I have envisaged that it would bear fruit so quickly.

Ten weeks before arriving in Malaya, we had been given a thorough grounding in the art of locating and following human tracks, taught ways to relocate the sign when it was lost, and some of the deception tactics that might be practised by an enemy to put people off his trail, along with a host of other skills. This training had been given to us by a New Zealand Maori, who was attached to the Regiment. Through his contacts with the New Zealand Military, we were allocated a team of Kiwi trackers, a tremendous bunch of blokes, who spent the next six weeks reinforcing and putting into practice all the theory that we had learned to date. They welcomed us warmly with a Maori dance, followed by a Hangi dinner and a dustbin full of beer, which was to be our last alcohol for the duration of the course.

During the second week when we were following signs which had been left for us by a 'track-laying party', events turned quite unexpectedly into the real thing. We had located fresh footprints of between twenty-five and thirty people, and by the amount of foliage disturbance and obvious ground sign we knew that they had been moving rather quickly. They appeared to be heading towards the border. We knew that the party laying tracks for us numbered only four, and could in fact see their tracks at right-angles to this larger set, so it did not take us long to cotton on to the fact that we were on to something 'live'.

Sending three men off to let our four track-layers know of our discovery, we set off after the larger party. There was an urgency about the whole thing now, we felt somehow that this was not just 'exercise tracking' any more; it had the feel of danger about it. To a man, we switched on. Blank ammunition was replaced by live bullets. If it was a band of Communist terrorists we had discovered and we managed to catch up with them before they got to the border, we could be in for a scrap.

We started to track faster, sacrificing stealth for speed in the hope that at the end of the day we might have a few 'kills' under our belts. We were aware that there had been reports of CTs crossing the border not far from here and that also during our training period, all routine police and military movement in the area had been called off. There could be no doubt that we were on to a good one. Before the day was over, we had tracked the group right up to the Thai border, from where we radioed back to report our findings, and were ordered to go no further for fear of causing an international incident. Disappointed, not to be getting our shoot-out after all, we backtracked to our start point and decided to follow the trail the other way to find out where it had come from.

An hour and a half later, we had come across, and were checking out, a complete bunker system. Within a perimeter of nearly 1,000 yards, it housed sleeping huts, storerooms, a teaching area and a command centre – the whole lot underground. It must have taken months of hard work for those we had just followed to prepare and was obviously intended as a training camp for local communist sympathisers.

Planning where best we could lay an ambush against their return, we made another report later that day, only to be told that we would have to go and train somewhere else. This was not our war and we could not be allowed to get mixed up in it. The job was taken over by a local unit of the police. Once more, we had missed out on the action!

A different trip to the same area, this time with my own squadron, was made memorable by a series of incidents, the first of which took place during a freefall parachute demonstration. This had been put on for the benefit of the locals (another demonstration of the Hearts and Minds Campaign at work, attempting to win the confidence of the inhabitants). The idea was that several of the squadron, who were freefall-trained, would descend from helicopters and land in an open area outside the small schoolhouse. All went well as they launched themselves from the chopper which had climbed to 10,000 feet in the clear blue Malayan Sky. Tiny dots could be seen falling to earth, changing direction to enable themselves to link up and form a circle, and maintaining this formation for a few seconds before breaking off and deploying parachutes. As the men spiralled slowly to the ground, they each triggered off coloured smoke canisters attached to their ankles. Yellow, red and blue trails criss-crossed to make patterns in the sky, giving a carnival atmosphere to the scene. The village children, chaperoned by their teachers, were screeching and clapping with delight, craning back their tiny heads in order to get a better view. The applause went wild as each member landed, but stopped abruptly as the last man was seen gently floating down to earth about half a mile from where he should have been.

I piled into a Land Rover with some of the other lads and we raced off towards the spot, screaming to a halt when we saw the parachute entangled in the branches of a rather large tree, and a body dangling below it. Being only feet from the side of the main track, a crowd had gathered around the base of the tree, most of them children, who from their laughter were finding the situation quite amusing. A military staff car had arrived just before us, we noticed, flying a red flag which denoted that there was a General on board. We had been expecting a visit from this gentleman for a few days and his timing could not have been better. This was the only thing to have gone wrong on our whole trip, and he had to choose this moment to show up!

It was a slightly comic scene as the General stood looking up at the smiling face of Mac 'Nay-Sweat' as he dangled uncomfortably in his harness twenty feet above the ground. With his usual broad grin and a cigarette stuck in the corner of his mouth, Mac was gaily chatting away with the senior officer. As we approached, we heard him say, 'Noo, sir, I dinna mak' a habit oot o' hangin' aboot in trees. Mind you, yer never alone wi' a Strand,' indicating his cigarette, and adding, 'Ye wouldna hae' a light, would ye, sir?'

Throwing up his lighter, the General let out a groan as Mac reached to catch the flying object and in so doing, dislodged his parachute from the branch above. Mac crashed down on top of the General and both men rolled to the ground. The audience erupted, but we held our breath until it was clear that the General, too, had some sense of humour. He picked himself up, dusted himself down and remarked to Mac, 'You don't hang around for long, you people, do you?' We all left, laughing.

Several days later, the squadron was practising abseiling into the jungle from helicopters. Some of the trees were over 150 feet tall and a special system had to be devised. It was feasible to parachute into the trees – rather like Mac had done inadvertently

– but this frequently stranded people high above the ground, as it had him, with their parachutes stuck fast in the foliage of the treetops. The procedure then was to attach a 200 foot roll of tape to the parachute harness with a karabiner, drop the roll to the forest floor, clip into a descendeur and abseil down. It all sounded quite simple and straightforward, but was in fact rather a tricky operation to carry out. It was decided that we all ought to practise ordinary abseiling from helicopters using this tape, so that everyone was familiar with the system and the equipment involved.

Splitting down into 'sticks' of four, we were issued with our harnesses and an order of descent. I was given the Number Two slot and made my way with the other three towards the helicopter on the school football field, where the sergeant in charge of 'dispatching' was waiting. The rest of the squadron sat or lay about, basking in the morning sunshine on the short grass off to the side of the field; their turn would come later. The sergeant herded us aboard and positioned us in our respective places inside the Wessex helicopter, and the pilot started up the engines. Slowly at first, the huge blades rotated past the open doorway with a whoosh, then as the noise of the turbos built up to a scream, swung round faster and faster until they became a blur of silver above us. The machine rocked with the vibration of power being generated and we lifted off the grass into the air.

As we gained height and started to circle higher, 'Ollie', who was to descend first, leaned towards me and over the noise of the engine asked if I would mind going out first, so that he could watch one more time how to exit from the lip of the doorway. This was all right with me; as a member of the Mountain Troop, I quite enjoyed abseiling, and I cleared it with the dispatcher. Once rigged up and with my equipment checked to ensure that I had fitted it correctly, the tape was thrown to the ground and I was given the signal to go.

Holding the tape below me with my right hand, I edged my way over and off the lip of the heli, and started my descent, controlling my speed with small movements of my hand and arm. Once clear of the chopper, the noise was not so great and I started to enjoy the view over the treetops and the slashes of clear areas gouged out by the rivers as they wound their snake-like paths southwards, towards Singapore.

Descending the 200-foot tape, I was slowly rotating, taking in all these sights on my way to the ground. All too soon, my feet were back on green grass and I was quickly unhooking myself and signalling up to the dispatcher that the tape was clear for the next person. I began making my way towards the rest of the squadron, congratulating myself on how well I had carried out the descent, and glancing up once to watch the next abseiler leave the cabin of the hovering machine. Before I had covered a quarter of the distance to the others, I was alarmed by the look of horror spreading across their faces, as they stood and gesticulated upwards with cries of anguish. They were indicating something over my shoulder and up in the sky. I turned just in time to see the body of the second abseiler falling rapidly to the ground. Something had gone wrong; the tape had snapped. We raced back to the spot where Ollie had hit the ground. It was obvious to me, looking at the extent of his injuries, that Ollie was already dead, but out of routine as much as anything else I opened his mouth to clear his airway. The squadron medic arrived by Land Rover and eased me to one side. I felt sick, knowing in my guts that it was too late. Even so, the medic worked hard at trying to revive him and I attempted to assist by blowing air into the by-now empty lungs. Ollie was rushed by helicopter to the nearest hospital, but it was too late.

My face was white and I was shaking with shock as I walked off behind a building to be on my own. Tears welled into my eyes and a great lump blocked my throat. My stomach felt hard as I sat down, put my head and arms on my knees, and cried for ages. My tears were for Ollie, whom I had only known a short time and who I would never see again, but they were also for myself – tears of relief, as I realised that if we had not changed places it would have been me lying out there and not him.

I sat and sobbed for ages, left alone by the rest of the men who realised that sometimes people need to be alone for a while. SAS soldiers cry and hurt just as much as anyone else when they lose friends or relatives, and the hard SAS macho-image seemed totally out of place now as the Squadron sergeant-major came across to console me. He sat down beside me and passed me a cigarette, speaking gently. I remarked to him that I must surely be the luckiest man alive today, and he listened compassionately, nodding agreement before escorting me back to his office for a brew. I gained even more respect for the man when I realised that the job of explaining the day's events to Ollie's parents would fall on his shoulders, too.

That night I got drunk, and was glad when a week later we moved to Brunei for further exercises. It is somehow easier to live with some things when you are not constantly reminded of them.

Hospital Attachment

I T IS a fact of military life – or of any adventurous life for that
matter – that as risks increase, the further you find yourself
from conventional assistance. In the Arctic, in deserts, mountains, jungles, in battle or in any unfamiliar surroundings, the
chances of accident or sickness increase dramatically, but
doctors and hospitals can be days or weeks away; it is important
for everyone involved to have a basic knowledge of practical first
aid and for someone in the party to be able to cope with real
medical emergency. The best way to ensure there was always
someone around to help me or my team mates if we got into
trouble, I decided, was for me to know what to do, and I signed up
for a paramedic course. After six weeks of intensive training in
Hereford I was sent to a hospital in Bradford to gain practical
experience.

Driving along the motorway my mind was racing over all the
things we had just been taught: I now knew the names of every
bone in the body and the function of every organ. I knew what
could go wrong with those bones and organs, and could, in theory
at least, set broken limbs, diagnose disorders, stop bleeding,
suture wounds and treat for shock. Now that I was about to put all
this knowledge into practice, however, I was more than a little
apprehensive. How would I fare? What would the regular staff
think of me? It took years to train a doctor or nurse, but here I was
invading their territory after only a few short weeks.

'Just don't get over-enthusiastic,' I told myself. 'Wait and see
what's what before jumping in with both feet.' I was remembering
a cautionary story my instructor had told of the day when he
happened upon a road accident. Two cars had been in collision
and when he pulled up a crowd was already forming around a

couple of people lying inert and bleeding in the road. He switched on his four-way warning lights and jumped out, grabbing as he did so the medical bag he always carried in his car. Pushing through the crowd, he rushed up to the casualties and announced to a man kneeling at the side of one of them that he was a medic and would take over the situation. Seeing the potential danger of being hit by further traffic, he then posted people up and down the road to direct traffic and dispatched a lady to a nearby house to telephone for an ambulance. Telling the crowd to stand well back, he opened his medical bag. Just then, the man who had been kneeling in the road said in a quiet voice, 'When you get to the bit about "Send for a doctor!" I am already here!'

That was one trap I would not fall into, but what others would there be? This was all very much of an adventure. Most of my adult life had been spent in the company of soldiers and now, suddenly, wrenched from a fairly organised lifestyle, I was to be thrust into the day-to-day workings of a civilian hospital. Some of my apprehension dissolved when I reported to the matron. Instead of the old dragon I had expected, scowling a starchy look of disapproval, I was confronted with the friendly smile and cheery greeting of a young and pretty woman, who instantly made me feel at home. She was always pleased to see helpers from the Regiment, she assured me, having only good words for most of my predecessors who had been assigned to her care. She hoped I would benefit from my stay, but I would find there was little to be gained from working on the wards; better, she said, that I assist the duty doctors in the Casualty Department. That way I could obtain maximum exposure to 'live' casualties. For the same reason she also recommended that I spend time on the road with the ambulance crew. It was up to me to ask questions and pick up as much as I could. The operating theatre, the morgue, the maternity unit were all departments I should make a point of visiting. Matron then handed me a list of names and addresses of people who might be able to help with accommodation and sent me off to get myself organised.

Deciding that the more time I spent at the hospital, the more I was likely to pick up, I reported back at six o'clock the same night. Walking through the doors of the main entrance I could hear the alarm bells of an ambulance approaching. By the time I had introduced myself to the sister in charge of Casualty, been issued with my white coat and met the duty doctor, the ambulancemen were wheeling in two stretchers containing a man and a boy who had been involved in an RTA, a road traffic accident. They were both badly injured, and not really knowing what, if anything, was expected of me, I stook back out of the way to let the doctor and nurses go about the job of stopping their two patients from bleeding to death and assessing the extent of damage. However, I soon found myself caught up in the general flow of events and began to assist.

When the man's blood-soaked trouser-leg was cut away, I was horrified to see a gaping, jagged wound running all the way from his knee to his ankle. The doctor, whose name was Alan, was busy working on the boy who had sustained a head wound, and he nodded across to me.

'Take care of that leg, can you, Brummie?'

All our practice so far had been on oranges or rubber substitute flesh. This would be my first 'live' suture and my heart was hammering away at the prospect. It was hard to control the trembling in my fingers, but I told myself to take it slow and do it right, at the same time endeavouring to look bright and confident.

'Three O,' I said to the nurse who was assisting me, indicating the size of needle and thread that I would require. Within seconds she had produced a tray laid out with all the instruments necessary for the task. Scrubbing my hands again, I mentally took time to reorganise myself and think out my plan of action. The patient was conscious and I sought to reassure him by explaining that I would freeze his leg so that I could stitch the wound without his knowing too much about it. He nodded, white faced, and I could almost read his mind saying, 'Looks a bit young to be a doctor, this lad!'

I smiled at the nurse from behind my face mask and set about repairing the damaged leg. By the time I had inserted the Lignocaine to freeze the area, I had settled down considerably and was able to concentrate properly. Pushing the needle through the two flaps of skin and flesh nearest to the man's knee, I drew both ends together and made a tight knot, exactly as I had been taught in Hereford. The jagged edges of the wound came together like a jigsaw puzzle. I was amazed: it was actually working and it was me that was making it work! The next suture was placed at the ankle-end of the leg and I continued to alternate between knee and ankle until the sutures met in the middle and the wound was completely sealed. Smiling up at me, the nurse began tidying up the tray of instruments, all by now blood-stained, and counting the number of sutures I had inserted.

'Twenty-seven,' she announced and looked at the doctor who was standing by my side inspecting my handiwork.

'Neat job,' he said with a grin. I had been so wrapped up in my work that I had no idea how time had passed until I looked around and noticed that the boy had been attended to and wheeled off to the ward. The clock told me I had been engrossed in the man's leg for three-quarters of an hour.

Alan told the nurse to dress the wound and give the man an anti-tetanus injection and then he led me off to the staffroom for a cup of tea. Flushed with excitement, I confessed that was the first time I had ever sutured anyone in my life. I felt so proud, I could have screamed from the top of the hospital to anyone who would listen. Here was I, Hamstead-lad Brummie Stokes, doing what doctors, real doctors, do! It was tremendous. As far as I was concerned, I had just performed major surgery, although during the next few hours I was to learn that suturing cuts was no big deal. Following Alan around like a lap dog, I was to be involved in two more RTAs that night, and watched intently as he set broken bones, stitched up several wounds, sorted out two drug addicts who burst in demanding a fix and calmed down a couple of drunks who had been brought in by the local police after a pub brawl had left both of them with badly cut faces.

By the end of the second week I had put so many sutures into torn flesh that I had lost count, and had assisted in setting broken bones, applying plaster casts to legs and arms, as well as being present at the birth of a baby, an experience which moved me deeply. I had acted as bouncer in the waiting-room late at night after the pubs closed and the drunks rolled in, bloodied and swearing, and one occasion I was called to assist a Sister who found herself in trouble with a drug case.

The ambulancemen had brought in a rather hefty woman in her early thirties who had taken an overdose of pills. It turned out that this woman was a regular visitor and had a reputation for violence. The doctors accordingly ordered that she be strapped on to a bed to stop her from punching everyone in sight while her stomach was pumped out. Swearing vengeance, she then raged and ranted for half an hour before beginning to calm down. Sister, seeing her rational and quiet at last, took pity and released the straps from her hands and arms. Immediately the woman's personality changed once more and she again began screaming obscenities and lashing about.

Sister was no match for her in size and was caught off-guard when the woman made a lunge at her with all her strength. I had left the room and was half-way down the corridor when a scream stopped me dead in my tracks; it was one of those screams that make the hairs stand up on the back of your neck. I raced back towards the recovery room where a young nurse was staring in disbelief at what has happening. The woman who had taken the pills was sitting bolt upright on the stretcher-bed, her legs and upper thighs still firmly strapped down. Her face wore an ugly, distorted look and her tongue was out, saliva dribbling from her mouth. The woman's hands – huge hands they were – were locked firmly around Sister's neck, and Sister, helpless and alarmingly limp, was sprawled across the women's bed. From her ashen face I couldn't be sure whether Sister was alive or dead.

I bounded across the room and tried to prise the woman's hands and fingers apart, but without success. She seemed to be in some sort of trance which gave her unnatural strength and her eyes were glazed over. She was exuding a nauseous reek of sweat and sick. Try as I might, I could not get her to release her grip and it was at this point that instinct too over: I found myself grabbing a handful of her hair in my left hand, jerking it sharply back and forcing the woman's head upwards while I drove my right fist as hard as I could into her face. I cannot ever remember hitting a man with as much force as I hit that girl. She became unconscious immediately, relaxed her grip and fell back on to the bed. Sister slumped to the floor.

'Get this woman strapped down!' I shouted at the startled young nurse who was still by the door, riveted to the spot, and I bent down to pick up the Sister.

I was relieved to discover she was still alive, wheezing to draw breath and trembling all over.

'Thank God you came in when you did,' she managed to whisper at last.

Soon she was sobbing violently, clutching tight hold of me and I was beginning to feel embarrassed. Emotional situations always make me uncomfortable, so I was relieved when other nurses and a policeman came in and took over the responsibility of returning things to normal. I made an excuse to leave early that night, went out, downed a few pints and reflected on the rough deal medical staff get. I was badly shaken; I had never struck a woman before.

The next morning the incident was the talk of Casualty and I was constantly being thanked wherever I went. To escape it all I asked Alan if I could have a look at another department and he promised to arrange for me to experience something different.

At three o'clock that afternoon, with my book of notes in my hand, I crossed the yard at the back of the hospital and, as instructed, reported to a small brick building with a green door. Receiving no reply to repeated knocking, I turned the handle, pushed open the door and peered inside.

A large tiled room was dominated by a marble slab in the centre of the floor, and on the slab lay the naked body of an elderly woman. There was a pungent smell of death in the air. On a wooden chair next to the body sat a man in a white coat, legs crossed, reading. The book, I noticed, was called *Man, Myth and Magic*. He lowered it slowly revealing a mop of flame-coloured hair and a moustache to match.

'Ah, hello, young man.' The book was set aside, as the white-coated gentleman stood up and seized my hand. 'Welcome to the morgue. You want to see what the inside of someone is really like? Is that it? Well, you've come to the right place.'

The rest of the afternoon was spent watching the grisly business of a post-mortem. It doesn't matter how well you have memorised diagrams of what organs look like inside a body, seeing them exposed in reality comes as a rude shock. I stared in disbelief as bits were dissected and checked for disease before all being neatly sewn back into the stomach cavity, regardless of their original position. I had learned a lot, thanked him and left as quickly as I could, glad to get out into the fresh air. I did not eat that night, and to this day will still not touch a meal of liver.

Later that week, I had the opportunity of witnessing major surgery in the operating theatre. Before I went in, one of the nurses from Casualty came and wished me luck. When I asked her why I should need luck, she informed me that the house surgeon had a reputation for being a bit of a tyrant. He could be very gruff and short-tempered during an operation. I would be advised to keep well clear of him in the theatre. Me being me, such advice was like red rag to a bull. We were set on a collision course.

I soon learned that I was not to be the sole spectator that day. A group of student doctors were also there to watch the master at work. When we had all scrubbed up and put on green overalls, boots, mask and gloves, we were ushered into the theatre by a Sister who had prepared a two-tier set of benches on which we could stand. This would ensure that we all got a clear, ringside view.

'Right, gentlemen,' said the house surgeon, standing next to a patient who was almost completely covered in green sheets. 'I recognise most of you, but not all.' This was addressed in my direction and feeling that something was expected of me, I introduced myself.

'Stokes, Sir,' I said. 'From Hereford.'

His eyes widened. 'Ahh. So *you're* our doctor from the SAS are you, Mr Stokes?'

I corrected him. 'A paramedic, sir, here for familiarisation.'

'Don't quibble, Mr Stokes,' he retorted irritably. 'If I say doctor, then doctor it is. Now, if you don't mind, we shall proceed with today's business.'

I opened my mouth to say more, but thought better of it and remained silent. He went on to explain that he was about to perform a Trochanterectomy, 'which in *laymen's* terms' (another glance in my direction) 'means a replacement of the head of the femur,' adding for good measure, 'the ball and socket joint of the hip.' It is an operation quite commonly required by older people.

Situated in the corner of the room was a TV screen suspended from the ceiling, which relayed a moving, live, X-ray picture of the patient's hip.

'We must first get at the affected part,' he said, and made an incision about twelve inches long from the top of the hip to the side of the leg. Clamping off arteries and pinning back flesh, he exposed the bone.

'Now we must dislodge the head of the femur from its socket.' His assistant rotated the leg and out popped the bone. The patient's leg was now disconnected from the hip. We could see this clearly on the X-ray.

'This is where it becomes like the woodwork class,' he informed us, and taking a steel saw, proceeded to cut through the top of the femur. The sawn-off section was discarded into a receptacle at his side. He was now working very quickly. Holding up a pre-fabricated part that exactly resembled the piece he had cut away except that it had a six-inch pointed extension, he positioned it against the inner core of the femur and hammered it home. I felt decidedly queasy. The TV screen confirmed that the extension was firmly embedded into the bone of the patient's thigh.

Just then, the assistant accidentally knocked one of the green sheets covering the patient to the floor and bent to pick it up. The mood of the surgeon was black.

'Don't touch that!' he screamed. But it was too late. The sheet had been retrieved.

'Get out! Get out!' he thundered. The assistant left immediately while a fresh sheet was put into place by the theatre sister. We all stood stock still, holding our breath and wondering what would happen next. What did took me totally by surprise.

'Do you know the difference between lateral and medial, Mr Stokes?'

I could hardly believe I heard the surgeon's voice right. How could he be talking to me at a time like this? Dazed, I stammered, 'Yes, sir. Lateral relates to the outside of the body, and medial to the centre.' His next question shocked me even further.

'Are you scrubbed up?' he demanded.

'Yes, sir.'

'Then perhaps you would be kind enough to assist me?' It was a command, not a question.

Gingerly I stepped from my perch and moved forward. I was thinking, 'Is he trying to make me look foolish in front of these real medical students, just because I spoke out at the beginning?'

He instructed me to take hold of the ankle and knee and rotate them medially when he gave me the word. He adusted the top half of the patient's leg and lined it up with the hip socket. I could see this happening on the screen.

'Very gently, rotate it – now!' he commanded. I did, and could feel the leg resisting.

'A little harder.' I heard and felt the new plastic hip joint click into place.

'Turn it back slightly and hold it there,' he said, and set to work with the Sister, suturing the wound. When he had finished he turned to the student doctors and said, 'Well, there you are. It's all just butchery and joinery, which even a *paramedic* can do.' Turning round to me he winked and thanked me.

After we had washed and changed, I was shown into the great surgeon's office where he explained that it did wonders for the confidence of his young doctors to learn that it does not require years of training to assist in an operation like that. Just common sense.

'You could probably perform that same operation yourself in the middle of a jungle if it was a case of life or death now, couldn't you?' His manner had softened and I knew that he was just being kind. He went on, 'Anyway, I hope that you learned something from it yourself.'

I assured him that I had, thanked him and left. He would never know just how much I had learned this day, nor the amount of confidence he had instilled in me. I had also learned quite a bit about human behaviour.

Two weeks before the end of my time at the hospital, I found myself back in Casualty late one Friday night. I was sitting in the rest room drinking tea when Alan came in and told me he had a suture job for me to do, adding, mysteriously, that he thought it might appeal to my sense of humour. He led me into a side room where a pretty young girl of about seventeen was lying face-down on top of the treatment trolley. She was covered by a sheet from midway down her back to her ankles. Looking up at us as we walked in, I saw that her face was flushed with embarrassment, but could not see the reason why until Alan pulled the sheet away. The lady's posterior sported a large transverse gash from one side to the other. Perhaps she would like to explain to me what had happened, Alan suggested, as I stitch her up? In an agonised whisper the unfortunate girl told me how she and her boyfriend had taken shelter in a shop doorway while waiting for a bus in the rain. Being sweethearts, not unnaturally they had begun to kiss and cuddle. The kisses and cuddles became quite passionate and the lady found herself pressed firmly against the glass-fronted doorway. Something had to give, and it turned out to be the door. Her bottom crashed through the glass, causing the injury I was now patching up. I could hardly suppress a grin as I worked fast to save her further embarrassment. She was relieved to be allowed home afterwards, but I doubted if she would sit down in comfort for the next week or so.

Just before returning to Hereford at the end of my six weeks' attachment, I was again to see a little girl to whom I had completely lost my heart. She was six years old and had been my youngest and proudest suture case. Her mother had rushed her into Casualty during my second week there. It was a day that will remain in my mind for ever. Her cries of pain and fright resounded along the corridor as Sister wrapped her in a blanket and carried her into the suture room with blood dripping from a ragged cut on her little face. Her bright blue eyes flitted everywhere, taking in every detail as she was gently placed upon the table. The duty doctor had sent her for X-rays to see if any of the glass she had fallen on was still embedded in her cheek, but finding that it was a clean cut he asked me if I would mind suturing it. At first I declined as I was afraid of leaving her 'scarred for life'. He persuaded me to change my mind by asking me how many stitches I would put in to close the wound. I looked at the cut, which stretched in a jagged, ugly line from the corner of the girl's left eye down to the side of her chin. Her wide, scared eyes seemed to beg, 'Please don't hurt me, mister.' I smiled to reassure her and asked if she was going to be a brave girl for me. Turning to the doctor, I told him that I would insert approximately thirty very fine sutures close together, so as not to leave too much of a scar.

'There you are, then,' he said. 'You will do a better job than I. I don't have time to put in as many as that. I have too many other patients to attend to.'

I realised that what he said was the truth. His workload was never-ending, so I agreed and resolved to do the finest job I could on this little beauty. With her mother sitting at her head, holding her hand and talking gently to her, the next hour was spent working with the assistance of a young nurse on what was, for me, the most important suture case in the whole world. During that time I was to learn everything there was to know about this little six-year-old, her likes, her dislikes, Mum, Dad, friends, teachers, but most of all I was touched by the absolute trust that she placed in my abilities as she continued to stare at me with unblinking, china-blue eyes. I was in love. She was a little smasher. I sent her away smiling and, as I thought, mended, but shortly afterwards when she came back to have the stitches removed, bravely counting out all twenty-eight of them, the line that was left looked red and angry and I was bitterly disappointed with the result of my handiwork.

'Ask her to return in two weeks, so you can see the results before you go back to Hereford,' Alan advised. 'That's as good a job as I have seen in a long while.' I was convinced he was only saying that to make me feel better.

The last weeks seemed to fly by and soon she was back again on my very last day. She had brought me a present of a packet of sweets as a thank-you. Tears sprang to my eyes. 'Big, hard SAS soldier, eh?' I muttered to myself. I knew there was no such thing. Kids were an important factor in the life of most SAS men, probably because we see so many of them living in harsh conditions when we travel abroad. Now here was this one giving me sweets. The scar on her face had softened to a thin, pale line which Alan assured me would grow smaller as the years moved on and would easily be covered by make-up when she reached her teens. With a glow of pride, I said my goodbyes to my bright-eyed beauty and to Alan, the doctor who had taught me so much during my stay at the hospital, and to Matron and the rest of the staff, who had all been so understanding.

It was with mixed feelings that I started the long drive back to begin the next stage of my life.

The Dhofar War

AFTER COMPLETING a Bodyguard Course in Hereford, I was lucky enough to be picked for a 'Team Job' in the Oman. I did not know where the Oman was, but it was abroad – that's what mattered. Six of us were to go to the Middle East and train the personal bodyguard of the Sultan of Muscat and Oman. We would first have to select suitable men from among local troops, then teach them all about weapons and protection work. This sounded like a good trip to me, but the crunch came when I learned it all had to be conducted in Arabic! An Army Language Aptitude Test some time before had indicated that I could not speak English properly, so how on earth was I going to master Arabic?

Six weeks' intensive training at the Army Language Wing in Beaconsfield sorted that one out, and I found that I took to it fairly naturally, if not as quickly as some of the others. I usually had to burn the midnight candle in order to memorise words required for the next day. My grammar was lousy, but then, I was not intending to converse with bank managers or academics.

When we arrived in Muscat, my first thought as the door of the aircraft swung open to reveal barren desert with hills in the distance, was 'I wonder if there's any climbing to be had up there?' The dry heat hit us like a wall as we stepped out into the blinding sunshine; at least it should be cooler in the mountains. We were picked up by the police and driven into the desert to an old outpost called Seeb. It has since become an international airport, but in those days consisted of a crumbling fort, which served as the armoury, and a fairly new mess and accommodation building for the British ex-patriot police officers. Standing neatly in a row to one side were four two-man tents. They were obviously meant for us – no mixing with the resident colonial types! It seemed to me that no matter where the SAS went, it always ended up sitting on the outside of luxury. How come we were roughing it in tents, anyway: what happened to the palace we were supposed to be working in?

Despite this, the next three months were enjoyable ones. We would teach the Arabs the techniques involved in looking after a VIP: car drills, ambush drills, weapon training, emergency medical skills and signal training. The flowing robes of the trainees frequently tripped them up as they tried to master the unfamiliar routines. One exercise, designed to simulate a method of extricating a VIP from an ambush, involved diving out of a moving car, while drawing a pistol and firing at targets, and this always seemed to tangle them up until they got the hang of it. For our part, it took us a while to get used to their religious priorities. Half-way through a drill, one of them would give a signal and, suddenly, they would all be off in a long line, prostrating themselves towards Mecca. I used to pray with them, but my prayer was that the poor Sultan would never get involved in a real life-or-death situation and have to rely on his bodyguard – certainly not at prayer time!

Fridays and Saturdays were free days, and this gave us the opportunity of going up into the hills, or exploring along the coast. Daily my Arabic improved. Just before the end of the tour, I went down with malaria and had to be flown to Sharjah, the nearest place with an Army Hospital. For several days I was delirious and could remember nothing afterwards except having nightmares about ambushes and air attacks. When I finally came round, I was told that the Sultan had overthrown his father in the province of Dhofar and that a squadron of SAS had been flown in to help out with a war in the hills.

Being single and not really wanting to return home for Christmas, I volunteered to relieve one of the married men as soon as I was fit enough. It seemed time to get stuck into a bit of battle: after all, that was what I had joined the SAS for!

Moving into Salalah was like going back three hundred years in history. The buildings were mostly adobe hovels, indescribably poor and dirty. Life moved very slowly, if at all, and the hot, sticky weather sapped every ounce of energy. The old Sultan, the deposed ruler, had been a despot, renowned only for his inflexible strictness. Women were kept in deep purdah, obliged to wear face masks at all times, and no one was allowed on to the streets after dark without the Sultan's express permission. Even then, only if he was carrying a lantern in his hand. The Sultan had not allowed any schools to be built within the province, nor hospitals, nor roads, and this notwithstanding his own numerous brand-new Rolls Royes, Morgan sports cars and other Western goodies. There were warehouses full of radios, hi-fis and other electrical gadgetry reserved for his own use, but the people were not allowed anything from the outside world.

A delegation had been sent to the palace, petitioning for money to start a social building programme. On being told 'No!' the dissidents immediately decamped into the hills with their families and whatever weapons they could lay their hands on to wage war against him. They were proving to be very good guerrilla fighters and enjoyed considerable military success. Most had moved across the border into Hauf and were being trained by Chinese instructors. One had even been taken to China for special tuition. 'Peking Pete' was a name I was to come to know very well over the next eight years.

Seeing what was happening to the country, Prince Quaboos, with the connivance of certain 'friendly forces', succeeded in overthrowing his father to become the new and respected Sultan. With a British military background, it was inevitable that he should request assistance from the British Army, hence the presence of the SAS. No sooner had this young Sultan taken over, than he launched into a programme of road building along the coastal plain, and schools and hospitals began springing up all over the place. The local populace was at last enjoying what it had been requesting for many years – a culture that was catching up with the twentieth century.

Moving to the inevitable tented camp just outside the city limits, I was soon to find what life must be like for a bedouin, living amongst the sand. Flies were into everything, sandstorms blew up daily, and the sun struck the back of your head with all the force of a blunt instrument. Like everyone else, I soon adopted the *shemagh*, or Arab head-dress, and shorts as everyday wear. Water was scarce, so razors and shaving quickly went by the board. I remember thinking that with our unkempt beards, and bristling with guns and ammunition, we must look like *commanceros*. We were certainly a mean and motley bunch.

The Squadron Commander informed me that I would be teaming up with Big Jim Vak, a Fijian, and was to move into the ill-fated coastal town of Marbat.

Within two days of arriving in Dhofar, I was on an old Arab dhow sailing slowly along the coast towards the small town of Marbat to join Jim, who was quite literally 'holding the fort'. The town was a cluster of mud and clay houses lining the beach at the foot of Jebal Ali and dominated by an old fortress 200 yards distant. The whole scene was reminiscent of a sleepy old Mexican border village and absorbing the atmosphere, we gave ourselves nicknames from characters out of movies about the Old West. Our base had been set up in what we came to call 'The Alamo', although just how apt this was as a name only became apparent some years later when the whole town was overrun in a mass attack. After a running battle which lasted all day, in which one of our mates was killed, it was only thanks to the timely arrival of a second Squadron of SAS, in the area purely by chance, that the town was held.

We were not in Dhofar officially as SAS and so had gone under the title of BATT (British Army Training Teams). To confuse the issue still further, we then broke down into small six- to ten-man units, of which our little team was one, and these were called CATs (Civil Aid Teams). The SAS had long ago recognised the importance of winning over the hearts and minds of the local people in any new area of conflict. This was one of the functions of the CATs. We had orders to set up small business deals in the area in order to initiate commerce. Money had to circulate and we had to think of ideas of how to achieve this. Many and varied were the ideas we came up with. 'Set up a fishmarket,' said one; 'Start a brothel,' another. Finally, it was decided to build a set of corrals and to encourage the locals to sell us their goats at our weekly market. The goats could then be sold on to the military for meat. The main reason for this was to attract the *Jebali* (hill tribesmen) down from the Jebal, gain their confidence and hope to extract information about the Adoo (the enemy). Needless to say, that soon opened up a further outlet for cash to change hands. Jim, whose Arabic was far superior to mine, was not long in setting up his own spy in the *souk*. Earning only £15 a week as soldiers, handling such vast sums was a hard task to cope with. Mostly we did, but our NAAFI bills were always very low.

After we had been there for a few weeks a propaganda wing was established and leaflets sent to us for distribution among the Jebalis. These told of all the good things that the new Sultan was doing. They invited the Adoo to come down out of the hills and defect back to our side. Faithfully, the hill tribesmen who had come down to sell us goats and gain information, would carry the paper slogans back up to the Adoo. Gradually, they started to defect, bringing with them their weapons and, more importantly, up-to-date information on the whereabouts of camps, stores etc.

It was not long before a dhow loaded with defectors was dispatched to our unit. Over the small walkie-talkie radio I heard Don say that he had thirty 'friends' for us to look after. Jim and I quickly paid a visit to the *waali* of the town to request he provide accommodation and food for the newcomers, whom we would re-train and with whom we would eventually return to the hills.

'Al Hamdulli-la,' said the waali, 'Praise God!' A conniving old rogue with thoughts only for his own safety, he continued, 'We would just love to be able to put them all up, but we have so very little. As you see, we are a poor people.'

A wave of his hand, heavy with gold rings, indicated his *small* fort on the hillside. There must have been at least sixty rooms in it.

'We will get the people of the village to feed them, but it would be best if they stayed with you in the CAT house. After all, they are soldiers, just like you, aren't they?'

'The crafty old bugger! He's turned the tables on us, Brum,' said Jim with a frown.

We both knew that we would have to watch this bunch very closely indeed. What better way to take out a town than by pretending to be defectors, entering as friends and then malleting everyone and everything from within? They were going to have to live with us, no matter how pushed we were, so Jim and I quickly made the plan.

While I was down on the shore, waiting for the dhow to land, Jim was rearranging The Alamo. Constructed of adobe brick and clay, the building had only one entrance which led into the cellar where we kept all our ammunition. You climbed a rickety old ladder to reach a narrow open corridor with rooms along the outside edge. Above the rooms was a flat roof with walls reminiscent of a fortress, on which we used to perform our sentry duties at night. The inside of the building was a hollow square, like an American cavalry fort.

By the time I brought our 'friends' into the building, Jim and the other four had moved all our kit and bedding up onto the roof, leaving the rooms for our guests. The crowning touch to ensure our safety was that the General Purpose Machine Gun (GPMG) which normally pointed at the Jebel was now strategically placed in a hastily-erected, sand-bagged position, which we hoped looked innocent enough but in reality concealed the fact that it was aimed just a few feet above the accommodation of the defectors. The toothy grin that Jim flashed as a welcome to the Arabs belied his pragmatic stance of 'when outnumbered four-to-one by a potential enemy in your own house, it always pays to hedge your bets.'

The night passed uneventfully, but with very little sleep for us. When I did finally drop off, my dream was one of wooden horses being wheeled into town as gifts from the Greeks.

As it turned out, we had absolutely no reason to be concerned, and during the next few weeks great friendships and respect grew between us as we trained what was the start of the 'Firqat', a 'fighting force that proved itself many times during the ensuing years.

It was on this 'trip' that I learned that the Jebali Arabs of Dhofar, the Dhofaris, were far superior fighters to their cousins from the north, and extremely loyal to people they accepted. We, of course, were all 'infidels' because we were not of the muslim faith but, that apart, appeared all right in their eyes; they mucked in with the rest of us and were not slow in picking out the mistakes of some of our Ruperts. I can remember how some of them walked out, shaking their heads in disbelief, when one of our young captains was unfolding a plan to walk to the foot of the Jebal in broad daylight to check a *wadi* bottom for signs of the Adoo. One of the most basic rules of Middle East warfare (or any other, for that matter) is never to allow the enemy to dominate the high ground while you are below. Needless to say, he was taken to one side for the error of his ways to be pointed out to him.

One of the problems of the SAS system is that whereas a 'Trog', once he passes selection, normally remains with the Regiment for the rest of his service, a 'Rupert' will initially stay for two or three years and then move on; perhaps to return some years later as a Squadron Commander. This means that by the time you have re-educated a young subaltern into the ways of SAS soldiering, and he is just about ready to hack it, he disappears to another unit and you have to start from Lesson One all over again with a new raw officer. The ones who are good are normally the ones who have the good sense to learn from old hands who have done and seen a bit. During my time with the Regiment I was to meet a fair share of both good and bad.

From our base in Marbat we were quite safe from the bigger weapons and mortars of the Adoo in the hills, but would periodically be subjected to small arms attacks from Jebal Ali, a small hillock some 600 metres from the city. We would sometimes lay ambushes on Ali in the hopes of getting to close grips with the enemy. None of these encounters, however, ever came to very much.

One of the first pushes up on to the hill started when the squadron I was with moved by dhow in an overnight raid north along the coast to attack the village of Sudh. Intelligence had indicated that this was an Adoo-held position where hundreds were massing for an all-out attack on Marbat. We had orders to forestall the attack. Being an Arabist, I was with the Firqat as we went over the side of the dhow once it had got close enough to the shore. Moving up the beach as quickly and as quietly as we could, we soon arrived at the edge of the town to be greeted by an angry whining above our heads accompanied by the unmistakable crack of bullets. The opposition was not as great as we had been led to expect and after lobbing in a couple of grenades there followed a quick skirmish as we fired rifles at muzzle flashes in the early-morning gloom, after which fleeing figures could be seen retreating towards the hills. We had taken the town with no significant casualties. So much for the intelligence reports of massing hundreds! We later qualified that type of information as 'G6-info', which indicated to us that it must have been from a drunken Jebali.

Rather than stop there with nothing going on, the Squadron Commander held a meeting of troop sergeants during which the decision was taken to push on, chasing the enemy further up into the hills. The Jebal rose some 6,000 feet above sea level in this area and it took us all the following night to force our way up narrow goat tracks, known only to some of our Firqat guides. By dawn, we were ensconced on the top of a great escarpment, looking out to sea and along the coastal plain towards Marbat in the distance. The position also overlooked a small Adoo village of about ten *sukkoons* (small mud and brick huts), built in a circle for mutual protection. That afternoon we pushed on through the village with only minimal retaliation and captured positions on what we called the Eagle's Nest, the highest point in the area. This eyrie commanded views of the countryside all around. The Adoo were content to stand back and snipe at us from a distance. We had given them a bloody nose twice in as many days.

After a week the operation was called off. We had been supplied daily with food and water by helicopters flying in low and dropping underslung loads – hanging nets full of goodies. There should be no problem lifting us out from here, we thought. Four of us plus twenty of the Firqat were detailed as a rearguard, while the rest of the squadron withdrew from the Jebal in a constant toing-and-froing of helicopter lifts. Sod's Law decreed that by the time evening arrived the helicopters had run out of flying time, and we were informed that we would have to move down off the hill under cover of darkness – on foot. We estimated a walk of at least two days. Oh well, at least with four of us, we could share the carrying of the heavy kit, I thought.

Just before it got really black we received a message over the radio, telling us that a helicopter was on its way to pick up one of our number, Taff, who was required urgently for another job. 'Sorry, only room for one pax,' the signal read. The pilot and loadmaster must have got the shock of their lives when they finally landed on our torchlights, for we piled everything we didn't want to carry with us on to the chopper, taking no notice of their protests. We only just managed to squeeze Taff in on top of it all. The helicopter fell off the lip of the escarpment and swayed left and right as the pilot fought to keep it in the air before screaming off towards the Salahlah.

'Good blokes these contract pilots. Must remember to buy the guy a beer when we get back.'

When we get back! Seven hours later we stood at the foot of the Jebal, tired, hungry and in pretty low spirits. The rest of the Squadron would have been showered, fed and beered, and tucked into their sleeping bags long ago. We tried to cheer ourselves up with the thought that we only had about another twenty-five miles to go, and after a quick brew and a couple of hard-tack biscuits moved off in the direction of a waterhole that the Firqat knew.

We had each a gallon container of water brought with us just in case, and this proved to have been a wise move for when we arrived at the waterhole all I could hear was the excited chatter of our leading Firqat hill fighters.

'*Sho feek?*' I asked in Arabic. 'What's the matter?'

'The well is dry,' replied Salim, the leader. They did not look very happy and I knew from the way they were behaving that that wasn't all that was bothering them.

'What else is up?' I pressed.

'We have been informed by one of the local goat herders that there is a band of about twenty Adoo patrolling somewhere between us and Marbat,' he replied with a frown. This was worrying. Experience had taught me that if the Firqat were bothered, then we ought to sit up and take notice, too.

With the well dry, we were obliged to share our water with the Firqat for the rest of the day, so there was not much for any of us. To make matters worse, Ted, the patrol commander, was suffering from a bug he had picked up along the way, and was vomiting constantly. By late afternoon we were all feeling the effects of the blazing sun. I have never, before or since, seen Arabs suffering in the desert as they did then. I held a brief consultation with Geordie (who was carrying the machine-gun) and decided that if it was possible we should call in a helicopter with more water and get Ted out, even if this meant that we would be pinpointing our location to the Adoo. By the time the chopper arrived, Geordie, too, was in a bad way, and the pilot was persuaded to take them both as far as Marbat. Throwing out his extra fuel and three jerrycans of water for us, he just managed to lift off with the additional weight.

As always happens after a helicopter departs, taking all its business and noise with it, you feel the ensuing silence more acutely, especially in a desert where there are no other distractions. It was only then that it really hit me I was alone. The rule had always been that at least two 'white faces' should be employed with the Firqat for mutual safety and support.

'Oh heck!' I thought. 'What happens if they all decide to defect back over to the other side and take me with them?'

There wasn't much I could do if it came to that, except make a run for it or go down fighting. 'Not much of a choice,' I told myself glumly.

But by thinking such thoughts, I was doing the Arabs a great disservice. As we plodded on towards Marbat the next day, the sun rising higher and hotter in the sky, one of the Firqat, an older Jebali, stopped and sank slowly to the ground. The hairs stood up on the back of my neck and despite the heat I broke out into a cold sweat. I had been out front as lead scout too many times not to know what these signs meant. Then it came, first a single *crack* over our heads and then, a fraction of a second later, the *thump* from the direction of a small hillock some three hundred yards to our right. The *thump* at least told us where the enemy was, and the hundreds of *cracks* that followed spelt out that there were a lot of them.

The Firqat reacted perfectly, 'pepperpotting' forward using fire and movement tactics we reached a position which we could defend more easily and, more importantly, one which would afford us more cover from the fusillade of small arms fire that was still being rained upon us. All the same, it was not a position I would have recommended: middle of the day, low on water, exhibiting first signs of dehydration and exhaustion, hoping not to have picked up the same bug that floored Ted and Geordie, and caught up in the middle of a limited shooting war.

I had a quick conflab with Salim and got on the radio to base. Could we have immediate ground and air support? During the twenty-five minutes it took to get the pair of Strikemaster jets up and over us from Salahlah, we laid out a T of stones, pointing in the general direction of the Adoo. Salim then told me that he thought the leader of the band that we were fighting was a character known to us as Peking Pete, a man who commanded considerable respect as a fighter. Reputation or not, he took off with the rest of them when the first of the jets bore down upon them.

Shortly after all the excitement had died down, we pulled out and began moving towards Marbat again. By this time we had run out of water and I was definitely feeling the effects of hunger and thirst as I staggered about under the weight of the radio and all my kit and equipment. I thought I was hearing things when the sound of vehicles came to my ears.

'The wagons!' shouted one of the Firqat from the crest of a rocky outcrop. I sighed with relief. It had been a long old two days, and bouncing about in the back of the three-ton truck on the way to Marbat, I reflected on all that had happened, on the Adoo and the Firqat, both of whom had earned my respect. A closer bond, I knew, had been forged between Salim and myself and I would have absolutely no hesitation now in trusting him and the Firqat, whatever the circumstances.

By the time we arrived back at base my own squadron had begun to take over the operation and release D-squadron for home leave. It was then that I met the new Troop Rupert. This one was a classic. It soon became apparent to everyone that he was not from an infantry background as he knew very little about the fundamentals of field soldiering. The troop sergeant introduced him to me, then took me to one side and confided that the new man appeared to have a bit of a bee in his bonnet about 'being in charge'.

'So humour him a bit, Brum,' he urged. 'He will soon settle down.'

The sergeant knew I did not suffer fools easily. Alas, some fools never settle down and this was one of those. From the very start we all sensed we had a 'problem child' on our hands, and had the dissatisfaction of having our fears justified over the next two years. He was always known as 'Sir', never 'Boss', except when being wound up by the troop. Never once did he gain the respect and confidence of the Trogs – instead he was a source of much pain, sadness, ridicule, anger and laughter.

Returning to our new troop base on the coastal plain from a patrol to the foothills of the Jebal one morning, we received information from one of the locals that a small group of four Adoo were holed up in a cave, not far from where we were. The Firqat were excited and raring for action. Spike, the troop sergeant, had been instructed to get back to base to see the CO about an impending Big Op on the Jebal proper and his first reaction was to ingore this little band of four. I felt that the Firqat were straining to 'have a go' and asked Spike what he thought about letting me take a couple of the lads with the Arabs for a 'look-see' while he moved off back with the rest. He agreed.

As plans were being made with the Firqat – how to proceed, what to do in the event of ambush and such like – I could not help noticing that 'The Boy', Sir, was sulking in the background. He was upset because he had not been put in charge of this little jaunt. Mac grinned at me; he had noticed it as well. Oh well, not to worry, I thought, as we prepared to move out.

The lead scout of the Firqat stopped when we got close to the spot where the cave was reported to be. I moved forward to speak to him and to get a first hand look at the situation. Crawling up a small rise, we found ourselves looking along a small *wadi* towards a series of caves, half hidden in the wall of the Jebal. There were hundreds of goats milling around and a herdsman, but no sign of any Adoo. Just then a figure appeared at the entrance of one of the caves.

The Firqat lead scout immediately came into the aim with his rifle. Touching his shoulder with my elbow I stopped him from firing and motioned for him to follow us back to where the others were waiting.

Once everyone was together – six of us and ten Firqat – the plan was quickly laid. Dave, the signaller, together with a Firqat escort would contact base and inform them what was going on, suggesting they stand by the jets in case we stirred up a hornet's nest. Malc would man the machine-gun off to the left in the best position he could get, with 'Wildman' as his back up. The rest of the Firqat would take the right-hand side of Mac, 'The Boy' and me. The plan was a simple one, or so I thought. We would crawl quietly up to our positions on the lip of the rise and wait for the Firqat to identify the bad guys, whom by now we had nicknamed 'the Hole-in-the-Wall Gang'. No one was to open fire until the leader of the Firqat had identified who was who. Several times during the next twenty minutes or so people could be seen around the mouth of the cave, but none with weapons.

'The Boy' was getting very edgy, jumping about and saying, 'Come on, come on! Why don't we fire?'

'Shhhhh!' said Mac, who was an experienced soldier and hardly able to conceal his annoyance and disbelief at such impatience.

Five seconds later the peace was shattered with the sound of an explosion. Sitting slightly behind and to the side of me, 'The Boy' had started firing towards the caves. He had broken the rule, 'Recognise your enemy first!' All hell was let loose as the Firqat and the machine-gun opened up in answer to the initiation of the ambush.

The firing lasted about three minutes and then total silence. We went in to sort out the damage. One Adoo and one civilian goat-minder were wounded and about three Adoo had escaped through a connecting cave system back into the hills. If only we had waited, we could have had the lot! We considered the whole action a shambles, not only had we missed the majority of the Adoo, but we had lost a lot of credibility by hitting a civilian. 'The Boy', however, thought he had done really well and duly made a report to that effect. We knew better. On his first initiation to gun-fire, he had been found lacking. He was not stable, not to be trusted. When a man loses the confidence of an SAS Trog, it remains lost a long time.

Some time after this incident, the troop pushed up on to the Jebal to take over positions at a place known as The White City, a bald feature in the heart of the mountains accessible only by foot, helicopter or light aircraft. It consisted of a barbed-wire perimeter fence which ran for about half a mile, inside which was a light-coloured corrugated metal building, erected by our CAT teams, that served as a school-cum-hospital-cum general-store-cum-local-meeting-point. It was from here that food, medical supplies and Psy-ops material was distributed to the Jebali and information on Adoo movement gleaned. Acting on this information, patrols would be sent out to investigate, and if they proved feasible, operations mounted in order to close with the enemy. When we were not out taking the fight to the Adoo, he would be using the light metal sheets on the storehouse for target practice and bringing it to us. It became almost a game. They would send a couple of Katyuska rockets over to us and we would bat back a hundred or so mortar bombs. It was not really a fair 'game', but then again, that is one of the disadvantages of being one of the 'bad guys.'

Because of these interruptions by the Adoo, we were, out of necessity, living in holes in the ground. As time went on, so some of these holes began to improve, some becoming quite palatial. A sight I shall always remember was that of two of the Regiment's Irish contingent digging away relentlessly to get their home just right. There was not much to choose between the two of them when it came to prowess with a pick and shovel. Both were large in stature and much larger than life in character. One, who looked like Desperate Dan, we called Grizzly, the other, a ruddy-faced man with an easy smile, was Paddy-the-Ditch. He had acquired the name in Malaya after driving his vehicle off the road into one of the monsoon ditches running along either side. On being pulled out by another truck, he promptly reversed straight into the ditch on the opposite side of the road. It was something he was never going to be allowed to live down. These two wanted their dug-out to be the best *basha* on the hill and spent most of one week digging it out and shoring up the sides with bits of corrugated sheeting. They crowned their effort with a professional-looking roof of wood, tin and sandbags. It was perfect – except for one lump of rock that protruded out of the floor, right on the spot where Grizzly intended to lay out his sleeping bag. Try as he might, there was no way a pick and shovel was going to budge this rock a single inch. Grizzly grew frustrated. He was a demolitions man, and finally he stormed off to get a brew and some 'fixins', saying to the

Ditch, 'Now, don't you worry about it at all. Oi'll sort it out when I get back.'

Twenty minutes later, from the general direction of their palace I heard Grizzly cry out, 'Fire in the Hole!' This was the recognised call whenever something was about to go bang. It was a big bang, too, and in the next instant the roof of their house went sailing across the Jebal. Kit and equipment were strewn everywhere and bodies quickly dived for cover as the bits of debris rained down. A huge plume of grey and black smoke hung sullenly over what used to be their home, but in place of which there now appeared a crater large enough to garage a tank inside. The Ditch crawled out from behind a rock and confronted his building partner. They were both covered in dust from head to toe.

'Oi think you put a bit too much explosive in,' he ventured, whereupon we all fell about laughing, and none more than they. Like most 'good hands' in the Regiment, these two had learned how to laugh at themselves when the occasion demanded.

Once in a while, when we received information from the Jebalis, telling us what the Adoo were up to, we would send out patrols to ambush or close with them in battle. It was during one of these patrols that our Troop Rupert almost came to grief. We had been out for a week and were due for our daily resupply of water by helicopter. The Rupert had been on the radio to our base in Salalah and had informed people there that we would require eight jerrycans of water that day. In turn, he had been asked to send out any empty cans we held. Making a tour of our positions during a quiet time, he discovered that we only held two empty cans; the other six were full. The helicopter would be with us in an hour.

'Empty the water out of those cans so that we can send them down to base,' he instructed one of the blokes near him.

'Tell them we only need two full ones,' came the logical reply.

'No,' Rupert insisted. 'Eight come up and eight go down. Empty the cans!' (This was addressed to me.)

'I'm not emptying good water away,' I told him. 'The Firqat would never forgive me. And what happens if the helicopter doesn't make it?'

It was a golden rule within the SAS, and every other unit in the British Army, never to leave yourself without water in the desert. Realising that he was not going to get anyone to throw water away, he set about doing the job himself and this is where he made what almost proved a fatal mistake. He strode across to the Firqat position, took hold of two of their jerry cans and proceeded to empty them into the sand. A Firqat standing next to me shouted to him to stop. Not understanding what was being said, the Rupert snapped a not-too-friendly remark back and continued to pour away the precious liquid. No doubt thinking that the officer had gone mad, the Arab raised his rifle and took aim at the stooping back of the Rupert. I managed to push the rifle to one side just as he was about to fire, and quickly explained in Arabic exactly what was happening. Totally unable to come to terms with the situation, the Firqat started hiding the rest of their full cans of water. Eventually the helicopter came in and delivered our water and food. The crisis had passed. The Rupert remained supremely ignorant of how close he had come to being shot in the back, but he was destined never to gain the confidence of our Firqat. From that day on he was known to them as *Majnoon*, the Stupid One.

One day we received information of Adoo movement not far from our base Madeenat al Haqe (the White City), and it was decided to move out and intercept. There were two squadrons in the area at the time, so it was to be a large operation. Two very prominent ridges ran out in a V-shape from our base with a deep wadi between them. My squadron was to move along and hold the right-hand ridge while the other deployed along the left. We would be backed up by our own mortar teams, helicopters and the Sultan of Oman's Air Force Strikemaster jets.

When we were in position, a large band of our Firqat were to move up the wadi bottom, clearing the caves and pushing the Adoo up to us on the ridges – a simple plan, which went well for the most part. The one element that did go wrong was – not surprisingly – due to the inexperience of our Troop Rupert. Coming from a non-infantry unit, his appreciation of tactics left a lot to be desired.

Up on our ridge we had come under fire several times from an Adoo sniper and had called down for supporting fire from our mortars, which were being controlled by Bronco a couple of thousand yards behind us. This was intended to flush out the sniper. Ever impatient to make a name for himself, the Rupert started to move further over the lip of the ridge. The Troop Sergeant intervened, explaining that moving onto a forward slope would leave us exposed to the Adoo below, who would then be able to see us silhouetted against the skyline.

'But I can't see the wadi floor,' was his reply, whereupon he moved forward anyway, taking with him two of the younger members of the troop.

Before he had gone far we heard the sound of automatic machine-gun fire and saw the party attempt to take cover behind a small clump of rocks and a few sparse bushes.

One of the sergeants in the troop, who had seen plenty of this type of action during his time with the Regiment and whose appreciation of the situation we highly respected, turned to four of us who lay beside him, saying, 'Come on, then. He's committed us now. We'll have to move forward and cover them back.'

Instinctively, without another word, we followed him over the brow of the hill and into a position above the by now pinned-down group of the Rupert and his men. The Adoo were firing fast and furious and the sound of bullets whined and cracked past our ears. Starting to return the fire, the sergeant called for more mortar support and a couple of Strikemasters to strafe the area of the wadi from which the Adoo were firing. Under cover of this support the Rupert's party began to extricate itself. Once they had pulled back to our positions, we began to make a run for the top of the hill and safety, working in groups of two. I was in the last pair to leave and just before I got to the lip of the hill, there was a lapse in the fire cover and the Adoo began shooting at us once again. Little puffs of smoke and dust were being kicked up around my ankles as the Adoo bullets struck the ground. I was in a bit of a fix – I could not go back and there was no cover to dive behind in the immediate area. The Adoo had got the range perfectly and it was only a matter of time before one of their bullets hit me.

Twenty feet from the top and safety, it happened. An angry, red-hot lead bullet tore into my left knee and knocked me to the ground. It felt as though I had been struck on the side of my leg with a sledge-hammer; the force was so strong it spun me round to face the way that I had come. The whole world clicked into slow motion. Looking around, I could see the bloke that I had started the run with just going over the top of the hill. The sound and sight of bullets spitting into the earth all around me looked almost comical as a total calm descended over my world. I seemed to be observing everything from a great way off. I was the central character, yet somehow abstracted from it all. I sat up and looked at my leg. The area around my knee was dark and wet with blood.

I tried to stand and run the last few yards, but collapsed in an undignified heap as my knee gave way, incapable of bearing the weight. The pain was excruciating.

For what seemed like forever I lay on that spot, expecting at any moment to feel other bullets ripping into me. I was a sitting duck for the machine-gunner and could not understand how he was missing me. Bullets rained all around, yet it was as if I was shielded in some safe cocoon. Deciding that my luck could not hold out forever, I started to crawl towards the sanctuary of the hilltop. Still some distance short, I saw the figure of the Troop Rupert running towards me and screaming for me to jump on to his back. He would carry me up the hill. It all seemed too ironic. Here was the man who was responsible for me being shot in the first place, now offering to assist me.

'Bugger off!' I screamed back at him. 'If you had listened to reason, none of this would have happened.'

It could have been an amusing altercation in other circumstances, but not in the midst of enemy fire.

'Come on, jump on my back!' he repeated.

'No! Bugger off!'

All the same I grabbed hold of his shoulder and hobbled upwards. Within seconds we had scurried back to safety and the rest of the troop. I could hear the scream of the jets as they dived in towards the wadi floor, firing their cannons at the now silent Adoo.

Lying on the sandy ground, using a rock as cover, one of the troop medics cut away my trouser leg to expose the wound. By now it was really painful and we could see that the bullet had entered the outside of my knee and gone straight through, shattering the kneecap, to exit on the other side. While the medic put on a field dressing and bandage to immobilise the injury, I took out an ampoule of morphine from the small plastic tube that hung on a cord around my kneck and injected it into my thigh. I knew that it could be some time before I got back to the hospital in Salalah.

Half an hour later I had been half-dragged, half-carried into the lea of a hill close to our mortar positions where Bronco was busy directing fire into the valley. I was later to learn that when he overheard the radio conversation about someone being shot, Bronco had said, 'That's Brum been zapped!' It was uncanny the way that he and I were so attuned to each other that we seemed to know what was happening even when separated by miles of sand and scrub.

Several hours later I found myself being loaded on to a helicopter, strapped down on a stretcher and whisked away towards the Field Surgical Team's makeshift hospital in Salalah. After a short examination, the surgeon informed me that there was so much damage, he would have to remove my patella entirely and part of my femur. By this time I was past caring, I was in such pain, even though I was high as a kite on morphine.

'If you've got to, then do it!' I told him, resigned to the fact that sometimes these things happen in wars. But I do remember thinking, 'Why me, though?'

After a pre-med I was taken into the operating room and given a strong anaesthetic. The room started to tilt and sway, voices sounded distorted and came and went, and there was a bright light.

I saw a helicopter fly over our position with the bright light following it. Suddenly there was a flash, smoke, and the helicopter began to disintegrate and fall to the ground. It had been struck by a SAM-7 missile fired by the Adoo. Just then, a small dot separated itself from the tumbling wreckage and a parachute could be seen opening above it. We started to run down a narrow track to assist the man, forgetting that it was mined. A sharp pain seared through my leg and my mind started to clear. I sat up and let out a yell. That had been a different time. What was happening to me? Everything was merging into one. Every incident that had happened during my time in this war was flashing willy-nilly into my head. I opened my eyes and all I could see was blood. My knee had been cut open and the surgeon, dressed in green, was slicing away the bone inside my leg. My mind was hazy and I felt sick. I was sitting there watching them take out my knee cap.

'He's conscious!' said the surgeon in a voice that came from a million miles away and bounced off hundreds of echoing walls. 'Give him some more!'

I fell back into the blackness.

When I woke again I was lying in a nice clean bed with real sheets and my leg was immobilised and bandaged. The troop medic had travelled out with me and sat at the bedside drinking a can of beer.

'You were lucky there, Brum. I don't know how you got out of that one. There were bullets everywhere.'

'Born lucky, me, mate,' I said. 'Born lucky.'

During the next weeks I was shipped back to the UK via the military hospital in Cyprus. In Woolwich Hospital, London, a decision would be taken whether to discharge me from the military and pension me off, or keep me on and give me a desk job. I was not keen on either. I decided that it would be up to me to convince the powers-that-be that I was capable of overcoming my disability and soldiering on. The next three months were spent in constant pain as I underwent physiotherapy, learning to stand, walk and to bend my by now stiff knee.

At the end of this period I passed a medical examination which allowed me to continue my service within the SAS. I was overjoyed. I was not going to be thrown on the scrap heap. There were still adventures ahead!

Building up to the Big Mountains

'SO YER off to Nuptse, are yer?' I said to Bronco. 'Who's doing the picking?'

'It's an Army Mountaineering Association climb, led by Jon Fleming,' he told me. 'There is a build-up in the Alps this spring.' Then, smiling, he added, 'Why don't you join the Association and try and get in on the trip?'

Well I've never been much of a joiner, not an association man at all. I don't like being organised and I enjoy my own company. But this was an opportunity not to be missed. Bronc showed me the list of climbers already on the trip and told me what they had all done. There did not seem too many 'tigers' among them. Encouraged, I asked him to give me an introduction to the leader of the Alps trip.

A week later we both stood in the office of Colonel John Peacock, a man of about my own height, with a tanned face that was creased all over with laughter lines. His eyes shone as Bronco introduced us. I knew I was going to get on with this bloke; he looked you in the eye when he spoke.

I launched straight in, 'I would like to become a member of the Nuptse team,' I said.

'Most of the team have already been chosen,' he answered. 'The final training meet and selection will be done in the Alps this year.'

Before he had time to go on, I jumped in with both feet. 'I am better than some of the ones you have already,' I stated, and proceeded to tell him why.

'I can't promise anything,' was his cautious reply, 'but why don't you meet us in the Alps and we can have a look at you?'

That suited me down to the ground. Bronco and I left. We both knew that whoever was picked for the Nuptse climb stood a good chance of going on the Everest expedition too, which was to take place in 1976.

When the time came, the Lad and I took off for the Alps two weeks ahead of everyone else in order to shake loose and acclimatise before they got there. We shook loose rather more than we had expected. There were going to be two parties meeting in the Saas Fee area for the AMA build-up climb; Bronc was to go with one and I the other, so it seemed logical for us to do our limber-up climb in the same vicinity. We chose the Matterhorn.

Arriving at the campsite in Zermatt late in the afternoon, we set about sorting ourselves out. It was great to be back among the hills. I looked up at the mountain and remembered tackling it from Cervinia in Italy with the Mountain Troop and 'Our Henry' the last time we were in the Alps. I chuckled to myself. What babes in the wood we had been then!

There looked to be a lot of snow about for the time of year, a fact confirmed to us by Fred, an old Polish climber who wintered at the Zermatt campsite every year. He was a real character and insisted that winter was staying later this year.

We wandered up into the town for a beer and to plan the next move. A day spent strolling up the valley to do the Point de Zinal should do nicely, overnighting in a hut, and then on to rub noses with the Big Fella.

Dropping our kit off at the Schöbühl Hut, we spent the rest of the day scrambling along the ridges up to the Point de Zinal. When we arrived back in the late afternoon, we were horrified to see great lines of people making their slow way up the well-worn path towards us. It was only then that we realised it was Friday afternoon: the weekenders were coming up to spend two nights in the huts. There would be singing, shouting and boozing late into the evening, something Bronco and I had always tended to steer clear of on the hill. We exchanged glances and, of a single mind, stuffed the gear back into our sacks and made a beeline for the valley.

Fred was surprised to see us down so soon, but understood our feelings. 'That's why I winter here,' he confided. 'No people in winter, just me and the mountains.'

The tent was re-erected rather swiftly and after a brew and quick meal we crashed out. It had been a long day.

Next morning we woke to find the campsite had become quite crowded. A group of Americans had arrived, one of whom turned out to be a good climber and we spent some time discussing various routes with him. Later on, while Bronco and I lounged in the sunshine outside our tent brewing up, two young American lads began throwing frisbies to one another between the tents, trying hard to impress a couple of girls sitting nearby. Inevitably, before long, the little plastic dish ended up too close for comfort to our billy, which was bubbling merrily over the little Bluet stove that Bronco was tending. Picking up the offending missile, he tossed it back to the young Americans, inviting them to take their game away from the tents. Not two minutes later the thing spun in a perfect arc and hit him squarely on the back of the head. I suppressed a grin: I could see what was likely to happen next. Bronco, normally a quiet person, was about to throw a wobbler! Snatching up the frisby, he stormed over to the lad who had thrown it and who, it must be said, was by now looking a bit sheepish, and told him that if he did not take it away to a place of safety then he, Bronco, knew precisely where to stuff it. And was more than happy do so. Personally.

Indignant, the youngster took his plaything across to where our climbing friend was sitting and complained about Bronco's vulgar threat. 'What should I do about it?' he asked. Looking across at us and smiling, our friend said simply, 'Grease it!'

As the light of the next day crept over the village, we packed our gear, left our tent once more with Polish Fred, and meandered up the track towards the Matterhorn. It was Sunday so the tourists, as we called them, would soon be returning to the valley and work. I was glad that for the rest of the week we should have the hill almost to ourselves.

Rather than pay good money to sleep in the hut at the foot of the Hornli Ridge, we took enough gear to bivouac outside. Once we were set up, we sat contentedly watching the last weekenders disappear down the track towards Zermatt. The sun was warm on our faces as it sank lower and lower in the afternoon sky, its slanting rays spilling out of gaps in the clouds that were rolling in towards us from the valley.

As the temperature started to fall towards evening, Bronco and I sorted out what gear we would need for the next day and then settled down for an early night. We would be moving before first light the next morning. The climb along the ridge from Zermatt is not a particularly difficult one and so we would not need a lot of gear; we expected to be up and down before midday.

Waking up at three o'clock we brewed our first 'mash' of the day, filling flasks with tea and wolfing down a hasty breakfast of porridge, bread and cheese. It was a cold, unfriendly morning.

In the circle of light thrown out by our head torches, we soon found our way to the start of the climb. The rock was cold and our breath turned to vapour in the wintry air. No stars or moon could be seen in the dark, cloud-covered sky. It was still early in the season for climbing and there were no guides pushing and shoving to get clients up first. This suited us down to the ground. It was going to be a good day.

Tying myself on to the rope, I started off up the first section of rock, which was very easy scrambling, and quickly warmed up as the blood began to circulate more vigorously. It soon became apparent that no one had been on the route for a while, as the snow that lay on the holds was completely undisturbed. It gave me quite an exhilarating feeling to think that this was to be both the last winter ascent of the mountain and the first climb of the new season. I brushed aside some more snow from a good handhold, a great jug of a thing about shoulder high, and gripping it firmly, started to move up.

'Below!' I shouted urgently to Bronco, who was standing underneath me, feeding out my rope. The whole jug-hold had come away in my hand and crashed down, narrowly missing his head. I had often heard that the ridge was notoriously loose, but now I had found it out for myself. We would have to go a bit carefully from now on. I could see why there are so many accidents here during the height of the season.

'You trying to kill me, or what?' demanded the Lad sarcastically.

'Missed you, din' it? What you beefing about?' I retorted, angry at myself for not checking the hold before putting any weight on it.

For the next hour or so, we zigzagged up the ridge, sometimes losing the route altogether under all the new snow that was lying about. The climbing was pleasant and made the more enjoyable by the fact that there was still nobody else about. After about three hours we found ourselves just short of the Solvay Hut and the morning well on the way to becoming light. We sat and watched the darkness slowly ebb away as the mountains dissolved from dark grey into gradually lighter and lighter tones. But the sunshine we had been anticipating to warm our cold bones did not materialise. Instead, huge snow-laden clouds, dark and heavy, covered the sky, threatening to deposit their burden all about us before too long.

'Not looking too good, is it mate?' said Bronc as we moved off in the direction of the hut.

I kicked the snow from my boots and stepped into the small cabin-like structure, perched precariously on the ridge. Bronc took in the rope and coiled it neatly, leaving it beside the door. There was time for another brew before setting off again. I closed the door on the light breeze that had started to whip up a little spindrift. The guidebook told us that we were now at 4,003 metres.

Looking back down the mountainside as we sat and sipped our tea, we could see that bad weather was starting to edge its way up the hill. Dark cloud completely obliterated the village of Zermatt far below, and was so dense that we both knew it must be snowing in the valleys. There is something special about being isolated high on a mountain like this and looking down over a fluffy sea of cloud. It is almost as though you could step out and walk across the billowing carpet to the other peaks poking their heads through it in the far distance.

Thirty minutes later the Lad and I rounded the back of the hut and made our way up a small rampway that led on up the mountain. We planned to keep going as quickly as we could in the hope that we could be up and down in time to beat the worst of the bad weather that was rolling in fast. Most of our heavier gear we left in the hut so that we could move more speedily. By the time we were on to the stanchions and fixed ropes, it had started to snow fairly heavily and it was obvious to both of us that we would be best advised to turn back to the hut while we still could. The sky had turned almost white and it was hard to distinguish objects only a few feet away. We had both been in white-outs before and had no desire to be caught out in one up here. Slipping the rope through one of the stanchions, Bronco looked at me for confirmation. I nodded. The only safe way was down. By now a wind was getting up and the snow that was falling was being blown almost sideways into our faces. Slowly we descended to the safety of the hut.

'Too bad to move down today,' Bronc replied. 'We'll have to spend the night up here, youth, along with the yetis.' He laughed.

The cabin was quite small and sparse; it was going to be a cold night, but at least we could joke and make the most of it. After all, we had wanted the mountain to ourselves, hadn't we? Well we had it, just for a bit longer than we reckoned, that was all.

The 'bit longer' turned out to be a lot longer, because the next morning it was still snowing and everywhere was white. We were going to have to hang on until it was safe to descend. The night had passed incredibly slowly as we sat huddled in the corner, chatting into the small hours, and nibbling what little food we still had, while trying to eke out the brews. The teabags were having to be used over and over again now. We could not afford to waste anything.

By late afternoon we were right out of food and our gaz stove had run out of fuel. On a shelf in the hut, in a box marked 'Emergency only', was a small packet of cheese that we had both been eyeing all day. Several times I had picked it up and examined it. It looked and smelled as if it had been there since Whymper passed this way last century.

'Seeing as I am the medic,' I announced at length, 'you have a little taste and I will watch for any reactions.' The only reaction I got was when Bronc punctured the polythene wrapper and let out the long-contained stench: both of us immediately began to retch. Quickly, Bronco opened the door and let fly with the mouse-food, out into the whiteness that engulfed us.

'That's the best place for that,' he said. We had probably saved some poor unsuspecting 'Emergency only' climber from a bad case of food-poisoning. But from now on, we were going to have to tighten the belts; that was the last of the food and the brews, and without fuel, the only way we could get water would be to compress it from snow in the relative warmth of the hut.

On the morning of the third day it was still snowing hard, but we were forced to make the decision to descend, weather or no weather. The effects of hunger and slight dehydration were already making themselves felt. Packing the gear did not take long and the anticipation of movement took a little of the cold away from our bodies. Soon we were both roped up and stepping out into the white chill of morning.

Anchoring the rope safely we started to descend. The new snow lay deep and it became difficult to find the holds – or the correct route – in the still near white-out conditions. Both of us knew that so long as we kept close to the nose of the ridge, we could not go far wrong and that the chances were we might move into better weather as we got lower. After half an hour of struggling, at times

Above: 'Born under the shadow of Everest' — home village of Hamstead with pit mound — similar in outline to the Northeast Ridge of Everest. *Hamstead Library*

Below left: The young adventurer, 1949

Below right: Dad — Enoch Stokes — all spruced up for his brother's wedding

Left: 'Soldiers of the Queen' — Coronation 1953

Right: Young soldier Brummie — 3rd Battalion of The Royal Green Jackets Rifle Brigade

Above: Best Recruit — Green Jackets, 1963, broken leg out of picture

Right: Brummie flooring opponent, Hong Kong

Below: Keeping peace on The Green Line, Cyprus

Above left: Returning from a wash in the river below 'Gunong Gajah' (Elephant Hill) Camp, Borneo

Above right: 'Gunong Gajah' – protected by Pangee pits and barbed wire with sentry posts and minefields below Pangees

Below: Moving out of a firm base, Salalah, Oman

Top: Soldiers taking part in selection training to join the SAS Regiment

Centre: SAS 'Pink Panther' desert patrol returns from exercise — North Africa 1967

Below left: Firqat forces — Dhofar

Below right: Close Quarter Battle — shooting practice at Hereford

Right: Training foreign troops in the art of storming buildings similar to the Iranian Embassy Siege, London

Centre: Teaching 'tracking', Malayan jungle camp, Brummie in black top

Below: Brummie weaving an 'Atap' roof for his leaking 'home' during jungle tracking course in Malaya 1980

Left: Bronco after the avalanche at top camp, 27,500 feet. He had only been outside clearing the snow from the collapsed tent for a few moments and came back freezing

Centre: 'Our Sherpas', Everest 1976

Bottom: Bronco, left, Brummie, right, Everest 1976

Brummie traversing the heavily corniced connecting ridge between the South summit and the Hillary Step

through knee-deep snow, we heard a great rolling rumble as tons of the wet, white stuff trundled down the mountainside in an avalanche somewhere off to our left and slightly above us. My heart missed a beat at the sound, and I scrambled frantically looking for a place to shelter. I could envisage the whole lot pouring down and carrying us off to Kingdom Come. Bronc was half-way down the rope, hanging on for dear life as a small powder avalanche hit us. I just managed to grab hold of the rope in time, but my sunglasses were knocked from my face by the cold, wet river of white. Heart beating as fast as a train, I looked down to see them rolling away into the void. I knew I should have secured them more firmly, but it was no use worrying about it now. The noise of the avalanche died away and the powder stopped raining on us.

'Glad we weren't in the middle of that lot,' said Bronc. 'Better press on, eh?' We both realised the need to be off the hill as quickly as possible.

As we descended, so the snow stopped and we could see more clearly. We had come quite a way off route and had to make a long traverse on soft unstable snow that gave way and started little mini-avalanches as we disturbed it. The whole lot was ready to go. The sooner we were clear of it, the better. With the loss of my glasses and the light becoming stronger, I was having to screw up my eyes and squint against the glare. My spare pair had been left with a cache of food, fags and goodies at the Hornli Hut, still some way below us. I knew that I was going to have sore eyes tomorrow. And it was my own fault, I knew that too.

Several hours later we dragged ourselves into the hut at the bottom of the route. It was deserted, but welcome. We were a tired, battered-looking pair. During the last hour the sun had been shining through the clouds, causing high reflection from the snow and my eyes were puffing up and feeling as if someone had thrown a handful of grit into them. I recognised it for the onset of snow blindness and informed Bronco that he would have to keep an eye on me for the rest of the way down into Zermatt.

For three days after we got back I sat in our little tent treating my eyes with Chlorampenicol to ease the pain, while our new-found friend, Fred the Pole, worked hard at keeping me amused with his inexhaustible fund of colourful stories.

No sooner had I recovered than it was time for Bronco and me to move off and join our respective groups for the training climbs.

My party was to meet in Saas Fee and Bronco's in the next valley. He was with those already selected for the Nuptse team; my lot comprised the hopefuls.

Arriving at the campsite in Saas Fee a day ahead of the rest, I made myself responsible for marking out and claiming an area for everyone and divided my time between scurrying around the shops buying in essential supplies and chasing off would-be intruders from my commandeered corner of the field. By late afternoon I was well organised, my tiny tent strategically placed not too far from the water-point and with enough food and brew-kit stacked up to enable me to have a meal ready for the others when they arrived the next morning.

Colonel John Peacock was the first to put in an appearance, smiling broadly as he saw my set-up. With him were three Gurkha soldiers who looked quite surprised to have a steaming hot flask of tea thrust at them before we had even shaken hands. I have worked with Gurkhas in Malaya and Borneo and was well aware that it is usually they who are expected to produce tea and food for the white faces, not the other way around. Soon we were a group of eight huddled around my cooking pot, tucking in hungrily while the Colonel effected the introductions.

Besides himself, there were three captains, the three Gurkhas and me. As soon as we began chatting it became apparent that the standard of climbing within the group was pretty varied. The two Gurkha sergeants, Kagendra Bahader Limbu and Narbu Sherpa, had not done an awful lot, and I was asked if I minded teaming up with them. It would be a pleasure, I replied, returning their grins.

'Ramro! Good!' I attempted to recall the few words of Gurkhali I had picked up in the Far East. They laughed at my clumsy pronunciation, and after only a short while demonstrated that their English was impeccable. If anything, the spoke it better than I did! While they finished off their meal, I set about erecting the remainder of the tents.

After downing a few beers together, John Peacock outlined plans for the next fortnight. We were to climb in two groups: in and around Saas Fee for the first week, and then move to somewhere else for the last seven days if the weather had not improved.

The climbing went well during the first few days. Kagendra, Narbu and I got to know each other better as time wore on and gradually became friends. They were totally different from one another in their attitude towards the hills. Kagendra, if anything, was a bit gung-ho! He would have a go at anything, whereas Narbu took things more cautiously. In the evenings, or sitting quietly on a mountainside eating lunch, I would ask them questions about Nepal. I wanted to know all about the Himalayas, about Everest of course, but also the way they lived back home. More than anything, I wanted to visit their country, the mecca of mountaineers that I had read so much about.

They made their homeland appear a gentle, soft land of plenty when they related family stories to me, but I knew from my books that it could also be very harsh, a place where making ends meet was a fulltime job.

Kagendra came for East Nepal, from a small village in the hills a few day's walk from the main Gurkha training camp in Dharan. 'The village is in Barimorong,' he told me, 'I will take you there when we climb Nuptse.' He smiled.

I thanked him, but thought to myself, 'How am I ever going to convince the Peacock that I should be included on this trip when we are in separate groups? He is never going to get a look at me climbing.'

The answer came the next day after we returned to camp. When we had all tucked into an evening meal the Gurkhas had prepared, the Colonel suddenly spoke out.

'There is a small traverse over in the next valley that I have always wanted to do,' he said. 'It's not too difficult and with an early start we should be able to complete it in a long day. I suggest we all go together.'

'At last!' I thought. 'Here is my chance. I'll climb them off their feet!'

Finishing my brew, I slipped away to prepare my kit and get in an early night, studying the map hard before dropping off to sleep. It did not look much of a climb, but even so, my sleep was fitful.

I awoke at 1.30, made a communal brew and took each member of the party a mug into his tent. Grumbles and groans could be heard from inside each as I woke them up and informed them it was time to go.

'What the hell time is it?' someone wanted to know.

'It's still bloody dark,' bemoaned another.

'Come on! We don't want to be all day, do we?' I chided.

John Peacock smiled at me as I sat on my sac next to the vehicle waiting to go. 'Nice morning!'

I nodded, looking at the clear sky. 'Nice early morning!'

He grinned.

We both laughed as sleepy-eyed bodies dragged their kit into the vehicle and we sped away towards our climb. To this day, I cannot remember what route it was, but I do remember leaving the truck and wandering up through meadows towards a rocky ridge that led to the top of the hill, about 3,000 feet above us. We scrambled up this and had lunch on the summit at about eleven o'clock. The climbing had been easy and did not get any harder as we traversed along the tops and started to descend the long screes on the other side. Feeling rather dejected that I had not been given a better opportunity to show what I was capable of, I chatted quietly with John Peacock towards the rear of the group.

My ears pricked up at the sound of falling rock behind and above us.

'Look out below!' I shouted, as stones the size of a man's fist rained past us. Almost immediately there came a scream from beneath me and I saw someone rolling down the scree, clutching at his head. Before he had come to a standstill, I was racing down towards him, taking care to keep to one side so as not to push more rocks on top of him.

As I ground to a halt beside him I could see he was still conscious, though very dazed and glassy-eyed. Once I had managed to prise his blood-stained hands from the wound, I examined his head. His face was splattered with blood, which was running into his eyes.

'I can't see! I can't see!' There was an edge of hysteria in his voice.

The stone had either hit him directly on the back of the head, or had knocked him over and he had hit himself on something else as he fell headlong down the slope. Whatever the cause, there was a deep gash on the back of his scalp, about five inches long and bleeding profusely.

I pulled off my sac and ripped open the top pocket where I carried a small medical pack. Opening a shell dressing, I applied it with quite a lot of pressure directly on to the cut and bandaged it tightly. By this time John Peacock arrived at my side as I was reassuring my patient, one of the young captains.

'How bad is it?' asked the Colonel, and taking him to one side, I told him that the blood had been stopped, but that he was in quite a bad way. Before he could say anything, I had pulled a map out of my sac and was telling him that he and one other should get down the hill as fast as they could, hitch a lift back to our vehicle and meet us at a grid reference which I pointed out on the map. The rest of us would start to escort the injured man down towards the spot as soon as he was able.

I had completely taken over the situation with no reference to the leader of our small party, but to me there had seemed no time for all that: the situation demanded action. With all the good grace that I was later to learn so characterises John Peacock, he left us most of his water and food, and set off with his partner in the direction of the road.

Hours later, we saw the lights of the vehicle as we moved towards our rendezvous. The others had prepared a hot drink for our arrival. I would allow my patient only the merest sips of liquid and was given some sharp looks from the others as we sped on towards Saas Fee. By now, he was quite perky.

Knowing of my SAS training and subsequent hospital attachment, I was asked if I could suture the wound in order to save a heavy hospital bill. I had all my medical equipment with me and indeed had stitched much worse cases than this in the past, but when I cleaned the captain up in the toilets on the campsite, I was not happy that I could clean the wound well enough to ensure that there were no small fragments of stone still lodged inside. Refusing, I insisted that he go to the hospital and have it X-rayed first.

'Oh well, that's blown it!' I thought. I was sure they were all thinking, 'What's the use of having a paramedic with you if he won't do the job when you want him to?' My chances of showing John Peacock what I was capable of seemed to have just flown out of the window; there was no way I would be visiting Kagendra's home next year now.

Arriving back from the hospital with his head all neatly bandaged, the captain thanked me for what I had done on the mountain and added that it was a good job I hadn't stitched him up. The X-ray had shown a large piece of rock stuck in his skull and a slight crack.

I smiled as I walked away. I had made the right decision after all, even down to not letting him drink too much liquid.

'You reacted pretty promptly back there today, Brum. Thanks,' said the Colonel, before disappearing into his tent for the night.

For our second week, we moved to the Dauphine and traversed

La Meije before returning home to the UK. I said goodbye to Kagendra and Narbu, thinking that I might never see them again, and made my solitary way back to Hereford. On the train I thought over the events of the last month. Whatever happened, I had enjoyed those four weeks in the Alps, even if Bronco and I had clocked up another epic. But it was time now to get back to work.

Nuptse

S EVERAL WEEKS passed and I heard nothing more about the Nuptse trip. Then, one morning a letter arrived from John Peacock telling me there was to be a last day of selection interviews. Would I be able to make it? He felt it important I state my case in person. Would I? It would have taken an all-out war to stop me! I intended to go on this trip, come hell or high water. Excitedly, I ran to tell Bronco the news.

'Don't be surprised,' he said, 'if they ask you some pretty daft questions. They won't all know what they're doing.'

The interviews were to be held in the old War Office buildings in London, and when the day came, I caught an early train down to the smoke, dressed in my only respectable jacket and trousers. As the carriage swayed from side to side, I tried to work out what they might ask me, rehearsing my answers. In the preceding weeks I had given quite a lot of thought to food and equipment, logistics, team make-up and a plan of campaign on the mountain, and felt pretty confident I could put up a good show.

My appointment was for 11.30, but in true SAS style, I arrived with time to spare and to eye up the opposition. Sitting in the waiting-room were three other candidates, all officer-types. We introduced ourselves and I formed the distinct impression that, as a mere corporal, they did not rate my chances very highly. 'After all,' as one of them so eloquently put it, 'the Army Mountaineering Association is, in the main, a gentlemens' club.'

With my usual steam-roller diplomacy, I invited him to 'Bugger off'!' and was not really surprised that they talked among themselves after that. My feathers ruffled, I was now ready to take on the whole selection committee. If they were anything like this lot, I told myself, then they could stuff their Nuptse trip.

The door opened to let out the last of the three before me and I was called forward. The room was large, wood-panelled and stuffy-looking; there was a long table at one end, at which sat the six members of the selection board, and a lone interrogation seat for me to occupy in the centre of an empty floor. As I took my place, I noticed one face at least that I knew, John Peacock was smiling broadly at me across the table. That did a lot to put me at my ease, but looking along the rest of the line, I could not help remarking that a couple of them appeared rather young to be choosing expeditioners.

'How do you think you would cope with being away from the UK for so long?' asked one of them.

What a funny question: that must have been what Bronc was on about. We were only going to be away for three months, for goodness' sake, and I took great delight in informing the young man that life in the SAS was one great expedition. We spent all our time working in small groups in adverse conditions: jungle, arctic, desert. We were often in mountainous country for far longer periods of time than this – and with a live enemy thrown in!

He fell silent. There followed a series of predictable enquiries, which I answered easily, and then came the big one.

'Why do you think we should include you on this team?'

This, from Colonel Peacock, was just the question I had been hoping for – which was probably the reason he asked it. Now at last, I was in a position to sell myself. For the next few minutes I elaborated on my climbing skills, my motivation, team spirit and anything else I thought might help them make up their minds in my favour. I concluded with the words, ' . . . and because I am a lot better and more reliable than some of the people you have on the team already!'

Well, that's that, I thought. Either I've sold them on the idea or blown it altogether, and I was rather surprised to hear one last question. This time it came from the other young-looking officer.

'If you walked on to a dangerous snow slope which was avalanching, what would you do?' he asked.

'Here we go again, Bronc,' I said to myself. Out loud I told him I would never walk on to a slope that was avalanching. If, however, I happened to find myself in the middle of an avalanche, then there would not be an awful lot I could do, except 'swim'. The rest would be in the lap of the Gods. At this, the young man hesitated before remarking, 'Oh, jolly good!'

As I left, John Peacock came out with me, winked, and said that he would be in touch soon. It sounded promising, but coming back on the train I tried not to let myself get too excited. Most of the others had often climbed together over the last couple of years. They had been to the Kulu Himalaya in India where they scaled a mountain called Menthosa (21,140 feet); some of them had been on the North Face route of Annapurna (26,525 feet), while others had climbed in Greenland. My own altitude record of 15,000 feet seemed rather insignificant by comparison, but having now met most of them, I felt confident I could do as well, if not better than they. At any rate I would do my best.

The team was to consist of seventeen British climbers, ten Gurkhas, three members of the Royal Nepalese Army and a Nepalese liasion officer. The leader of the expedition would be Jon Fleming, a major in the Parachute Regiment. I had met him on the Alpine meet earlier that year and got along with him quite well. By far the strongest of the climbers, as far as I could gather, were Gerry Owens and Richard Summerton. These two had climbed together for some time and always as a team. Bronco had often spoken of them and it was obvious he felt them to be very reliable. His word was good enough for me. Apart from Bronco and me, the rest were all officers: perhaps the chap in the waiting-room had been right after all – perhaps it was an officers-only club. I would soon know.

Nuptse, I knew, was the lowest peak of the Everest triangle. It rose to 25,850 feet; its neighbours were Lhotse at 27,890 feet and the Big Fella himself – Everest, or Segamartha as the Nepalese call it – towering above them at 29,028 feet. Sitting silently in the train, I pressed my face against the window and looked up at the billowing clouds. They looked miles high. Several had collided together to form a mountain shape far up in the sky, and as I gazed at it, it dawned on me that Nuptse and the rest of the peaks in the Himalaya were higher even than these cumulus formations. In fact, they would begin where the clouds finished. The magnitude of what I was getting into started to sink in.

The idea was to climb the mountain by the central ridge on its South Face. There had only been one successful ascent of Nuptse before, and that was led by Joe Walmsley, a Lancashire climber very active in the early Sixties. One of his team members had been a little-known youth named Chris Bonington. I had read their account of the climb and knew that most of the difficulties were on the lower reaches of the mountain, along a twisting, narrow ridge which consisted mainly of huge, rotten ice seracs, very prone to collapse. They had done the route in 1961 and mentioned a rock band which barred the way for about 1,000 feet at an altitude of 23,000 feet. The whole venture sounded daunting and a little dangerous; it made me tingle with excitement. Coming back down to earth as the train pulled into Hereford, I had to remind myself that first of all I needed to know I had been selected. I was not absolutely sure I had left the board with the best impression of myself. Only time would tell.

But I need not have worried; within three days I received my letter of acceptance on to the team. I was overjoyed. Roll on February! I could hardly wait to get going. Yet the next months seemed to drag by even though there was so much to do and prepare – getting gear together and going on trips to the hills with Bronco to keep ourselves in trim.

I was fortunate in being able to get time off from the SAS early, and joined Tim King, a captain from the Army Apprentices College in Chepstow, as part of an advance party in Hong Kong. Our job was to co-ordinate movement of all the expedition stores on their way to Nepal, and we were accommodated in the Sergeants' Mess of the Ordnance Depot at Kai Tak Airport. (I borrowed the stripes from our Troop Sergeant in Hereford!) Most of the days would be spent meeting military aircraft in-bound from the UK with expedition freight aboard, retrieving it, relabelling, then storing it in a large hangar until we could get space for it on one of the aircraft taking Gurkha soldiers home on leave to Nepal. On days when I finished work early, I would put a flask and a bit of food in my small rucksack and head on up to Lion Rock, which stands on one of the small mountains overlooking Hong Kong. There I would sit in the peace and quiet of the hills, away from the noise and bustle of the millions of Chinese in the city. Kowloon, with its cramped and stifling streets of stacked-box tenements lay sprawled below me. My thoughts would sometimes drift back to when I was a young soldier here so long ago, but more often they would be racing ahead, wondering what it was going to be like when I finally got to Nepal and on to the mountain.

I found this whole episode quite frustrating and was impatient to be up and moving. It was made worse when on 19 February the first party of five, led by John Peacock, passed through Hong Kong in a Comet aircraft (which was also carrying HRH The

Prince of Wales to Nepal for the coronation of HM King Birendra). They had the job of making contact with staff of the British Embassy in Nepal and arranging our accommodation, transport, porters, sherpas, and generally taking care of the thousand and one other jobs needing attention before a large expedition like ours could get on the road. I was very envious.

Eventually, by early March, we had managed to get all the equipment into Nepal and were able to board an aircraft ourselves. With mounting excitement I fastened my seatbelt and prepared to meet Kipling's green-eyed yellow monster to the north of Kathmandu. The descriptions of Nepal given me by Kagendra and Narbu when we were all in the Alps now came flooding back; perhaps, after all, I would be visiting Barimorong, Kagendra's home village, but my chief thought as I began to doze off with the vibration of the plane was of this mountain we had come to climb. Would Nuptse prove my friend or foe?

Descending slowly, ears popping as the aircraft began to decompress, I could see the ragged outline of white, snow-capped mountains away to the north, far bigger than anything I had imagined, and then, through the misty haze in the valley below, emerged a small town with dirt roads running away from it in all directions. The houses lay in no apparent order, but seemed to centre on what looked like a huge pagoda with eyes painted on its tallest spire. Minutes later, seat belts again fastened and with landing gear lowered, we made a near perfect touch-down on the small airstrip. Here at last, Kathmandu! The mysterious capital of Nepal. I could not wait to get off the aircraft.

Once through the Customs Hall, which was an epic in itself with everyone milling around shouting at each other and not an awful lot being achieved as far as I could see, we met up with one of the advance party who escorted us to our hotel. It offered cheap but perfectly adequate accommodation with no frills and was tucked away in a back street rather aptly named The Nook. During the next few days the rest of the team started to arrive and settle into Kathmandu, our home for the next week. When Bronco came, he and I set off together to meet up with the Gurkhas and the three Nepalese Army climbers who were going to be with us on the expedition. They were all living at a Gurkha transit camp on the outskirts of town, where our kit and equipment was also stored. It was here that besides Kagendra Bahadur Limbu and one or two of the other Gurkhas, I met Pasang Tamang, a rifleman with the 7 Gurkha Rifles. Friendships soon started to flourish as over the next few days we helped load kit on to a light aircraft which was to fly the bulk of our essential climbing gear and food to Lukla, a small landing strip some days' walk from Everest, where it would be stored for our arrival.

When we were not working, the Gurkhas took great delight and pride in showing us around their capital city, interspersing these sightseeing trips with stops for some of the best curries and tandooris I have ever tasted. In those days, Kathmandu still had the flavour of old-world India, a city of contrasts. There were open sewage drains running along the sides of the streets and all the relevant smells to accompany them, but there were also exotic temples everywhere, for both the Hindu and the Buddhist faiths, and inside these very impressive monuments, statues of Buddha and other holy figures, ornate with gold leaf and precious and semi-precious jewels. Everywhere you looked, people were praying or paying homage to images daubed in red dye. There were markets where you could buy anything from an old cooking pot to a large opal.

Walking down a narrow side-street one afternoon, with the sun shining brightly on my back, I discovered that the age of miracles still lingered here in Kathmandu. Outside a rather dubious-looking doctor's surgery hung a sign proclaiming 'Miracle cure of Piles'. Peering into the gloomy, dusty hallway I could make out a tray full of rusty old scissors, scapels and other ancient surgical instruments. I hurried along, hoping I would never have the misfortune to require this man's services; it would take a miracle to escape blood poisoning, let alone anything else.

Being with our Gurkha friends, we were privileged to see more of the local way of life than perhaps we might otherwise have done, and travelling through one of the outlying villages not long after our arrival in Kathmandu, we stopped beside the muddy waters of the river and watched a funeral taking place. The reality and harshness of life – and death – in Nepal is borne home very strongly when you witness the lighting of a funeral pyre under a human body. The wood stacked underneath this corpse was insufficient to cremate it completely, and I watched aghast as the remnants were afterwards swept into the river, to the loud wailing of relatives. Our friends explained that this was not unusual in poor families where there was not enough money to buy the necessary amount of wood. Only moments later, people were in the river, bathing and collecting water for daily use.

By the time 15 March came around, we were all fretting to get started. Everything was assembled at the Gurkha transit camp and we started to load the vehicles, which were to carry us along the Chinese-built Friendship Highway to a roadhead at Lamasangu. This journey was going to take about three hours of bumping along a dusty road. We sat in the backs of the trucks watching the scenery pass by. At Lamasangu, we met up with Narbu Sherpa (the other Gurkha I had been with in the Alps) and the Corporal Nandaraj Gurung, a stocky man with a delightful personality. Nandaraj would act as our guide to Lukla. He and Narbu had been sent ahead to recruit porters from Nandaraj's village in the Solu region, to carry our camping kit, food, cooking pots and fuel during the walk-in. We were in almost party mood as the twenty-five or so porters and their wives and children helped noisily to off-load the gear. It did not take long before we were settled in for the night.

As it grew dark, so fires were lit and the porters and their families began to sing and dance to music played on an old sitar-type of instrument. It was tremendous to be among real hill people at last, away from the town and the haggling of the bazaar. They had so little, but their friendship was outstanding; they were more than willing to share what they did have with us. I immediately warmed to these unspoilt people.

The route was now going to take us in an easterly direction, cross-graining the mountains. We would be crossing ridges of up to 15,000 feet, stopping each night close to rivers and villages to enable us to buy eggs and local food wherever possible. The total distance to Nuptse base camp was some 160 miles and Nandaraj warned me that walking this would take us about fourteen days. Kathmandu lies in a valley at 4,500 feet, but we had driven downhill to Lamasangu, at 2,350 feet, which meant we now had over 23,000 feet to climb if we were to reach the summit of Nuptse.

We were expecting to cover some ten or fifteen miles a day, which represented about six to eight hours of steady walking. I would roll out of my sleeping bag at around five each morning and give the cook-boy a hand getting the first brew of the day going. Cups of steaming tea – *chiya* would then be taken around to the rest of the team in their tents, and while they were getting up, Narbu, Bronco, the cook-boy and I would set off up the dusty track just as it began to grow light. About two hours down the road, we would start looking for a spot by water so that we could start preparing breakfast. This for me was the best time of the day. We were walking through some of the harshest countryside imaginable, yet every last inch was under cultivation. Tier upon tier of levelled terraces rose up the hillsides and whole families – men, women and children – would be out in the cool of the morning, driving their animals before them as they ploughed and planted. They were growing rice, maize and potatoes, which form the staples of their diet. The land was parched and rocky, but every village that we passed through had the same friendly greeting for us. The children would stand at the side of the track to watch us, clasping their hands together in front of them, bowing their heads in traditional style and crying out 'Namaste!' or 'Welcome!'

Inevitably we would be invited into their ramshackle wood and mud-built houses to share a glass of chiya, a pale and sickly-sweet liquid with a layer of grease always floating on the top that I later learned came from the yak milk. Nevertheless, it was always very welcome on the dusty trail. In return, we would share our sweets, biscuits, chewing gum and anything else we had to spare, a practice I was later to question when passing through one of the smaller villages. Two young ragamuffins with the most appealing smiles I had ever seen offered a slight variation to the customary greeting: 'Namaste! One rupee. Chocolate. Please.' It saddened me to think that expeditions such as ours, passing through with their seeming wealth of food, were ultimately responsible for teaching these proud people to beg.

As we prepared breakfast beside the road, the rest of the team would arrive and eat with us. It was a lazy time sitting and chatting over tea, sausages and beans from our compo rations – good old Army grub. During this time I gradually got to know more of the team members. One of the climbers I knew from stories Bronco had told was Nigel Gifford, a captain in the Army Catering Corps. As a dietician, he was responsible for all the expedition's food, a job he took very seriously. At every opportunity, he would seek our opinion on the rations supplied. Being me, I could not resist winding him up and would inform him in no uncertain terms that I thought it was all donkey's crap, whereupon his face would drop a mile. Having had the job of providing food for patrols within the SAS, I knew only too well how difficult a task it is to satisfy everyone's tastes, and had quickly learned that it was a wise man who just produced it and asked no questions. In fact, Nigel's food was terrific, but I was not about to tell him that, was I?

Once breakfasted, we would fill up a flask of tea or coffee, pack a lunch of cheese, biscuits and chocolate and set off for the next leg of our journey. Inevitably there would be rickety old bridges to cross, that appeared to be suspended from nothing and always swayed alarmingly from side to side. Looking down through our feet, we would see the frothing river beneath, ready to receive the unwary. Some villages would have a schoolhouse or a simple hospital building. These and most of the airstrips we passed, I later learned from Kagendra, were built by Sir Edmund Hillary. After his successful climb to the top of Everest with Sherpa Tenzing on Sir John Hunt's 1953 expedition, he decided that the Khumbu region had given him so much, he wanted to plough something back into it. His way of doing this was to send in teams of people from New Zealand, equipped and funded to undertake building projects. It was an unselfish gesture which I very much applauded.

By late afternoon we would arrive at whatever spot we were to camp at for the night. Almost always we would be afforded a magnificent view of the Himalaya, and once the tents were up, we could relax, sort out any blisters, and enjoy the evening meal. The tents, however, with the rest of the heavier camping gear and food, would arrive anything up to three hours after us, carried as they were on the heads and backs of our porters, many of whom were women. It never ceased to amaze me how these sherpanis could stride along the track with apparent ease, carrying between seventy to ninety pounds on their backs. For a full day's work they would receive the princely sum of twenty-five rupees, about £1 sterling.

At the lower altitudes during this first week's walk, Bronc and I would not bother to sleep inside a tent. Instead we preferred to roll out our sleeping bags on a karrimat and drift off into pleasant slumber beneath the stars. One of the most spectacular sights in Nepal is the setting of the sun: as it dips behind the distant snow-capped mountains, so shadows lengthen and the clear sky burns a brilliant orange, which gradually pales through various shades of yellow until in one final defiant sparkle, the last shaft of light descends beyond the hills for the night. I never once tired of this display and would sometimes slip off early to be alone with my thoughts at this special time, getting even closer to nature.

Seven days of tramping up hill and down dale, crossing rivers, passing through villages and rhododendron forests, brought us to the Lamiura Pass, 11,000 feet high, which separates lowland Nepal from Sherpa-land proper. Once over this, we could feel we were at last getting higher; we were travelling through lush, high pasturelands and the temperature would drop sharply at night. Even the people seemed noticeably different: they were still very, very friendly, but appeared shyer and quieter. Family bonds were evidently strong: little children would care for even smaller brothers and sisters, bigger children worked the fields with their parents, young teenaged girls were protectively flanked by their grown-ups and brothers.

It was not long after crossing the pass that we rounded a corner of the dusty track to be rewarded with our first view of Nuptse. It stood like a barrier, defiantly guarding the approaches to its near neighbour, Everest, which was recognisable, as always, by the long plume of snow and cloud trailing from its summit. To the right of our mountain I could see Lhotse, the third peak that makes up the Everest triangle. They all looked frighteningly high, but carried a lot less snow than I had imagined. That morning we took longer than normal over our cheese and biscuits, lying back in the warm sunshine to contemplate these Himalayan giants, each of us lost in his own thoughts.

Namche stands at 11,500 feet and is the Sherpa capital; it is a village of white-painted adobe houses, stacked on terraces up the hillside. It also serves as a police post and checkpoint for anyone moving in the area, and is the end of the road for tourists. Beyond Namche, a climbing permit was needed. Selfishly, I thought, 'Good! At last we can get away from it all and be alone in the hills again.' No man has the right to own mountains, as the words of a song have it, a sentiment with which I am in complete agreement, but it *is* nice to be able to borrow them for a while!

One day's walk past Namche brings you to what is probably the most famous of all the monasteries in Nepal. Tengboche stands alone, in the lea of a mountain which shelters it from the worst of the savage winter storms. All around are quiet pine forests. At 12,715 feet it is regarded as the gateway to Everest – Sagamartha – Goddess Mother of the World. Huge summits capped with ice and snow stand like sentinels on its left and right and echo back the sounds of the gongs and long-stemmed horns which summon the Tengboche monks to prayer. We camped in the grounds of this holy place, with a spectacular view of Everest, Nuptse and Lhotse as our 'picture window'. Though still some miles from Nuptse, the clarity of the thin air made it possible to pick out the route we planned to follow along its central ridge. It looked long and hard.

The next leg took us over small rickety bridges and close under Ama Dablam, which is thought by many to be the most perfect mountain in the world, to Dingboche, where we were to have our acclimatisation camp. I could not get over the fact that we were now over 14,000 feet, which was as high as I had ever been, and we were still not having to climb. It was still only a trek. I felt really dwarfed by the sheer scale of these mountains, yet perfectly at home at the same time.

It was snowing by the time we arrived at Dingboche. Our advance party was already there and had made all the necessary preparations. Now I met some of them for the first time: Mike Kefford, who lives in Nepal and has served with the Gurkha regiments; the expedition doctor, Noel Dilly; our Sirdar (head Sherpa) Sonam Girme and two Sherpas I was to get to know very well later, Tensing and Pasang Tensing. Introductions were followed by the inevitable cup of *chiya*, then Bronco and I set about putting up our tent. Later, as he and I crawled into our sleeping bags, I whispered, 'Massive, innit!'

'Bit big,' he agreed.

There was plenty to do as we acclimatised, sorting out stores, issuing sherpas and climbers with their high altitude equipment, and paying off the porters who had carried us in. It all passed in a frenzy of activity. Geordie Armstrong, the only member of the RAF on the expedition, and Kubirjang, another of the Gurkhas, joined Bronco and me in assisting the Base Camp Manager with his huge task of organising all the gear into manageable loads for transport up the mountain. Whenever we could squeeze a few hours off, Bronc and I would scramble up nearby peaks in order to get a better look at the hill.

Sitting on a mountainside after a hard climb, relaxing with a cigarette, made me realise just how insignificant man is when set against Nature in the raw like this. I was an ant on a molehill. One gust of wind and away I could go, lost forever in the vastness of it all. Philosophy has never been a strong point of mine, and all I was going to do if I followed this train of thought any further would be to start intimidating myself – best push it all from my mind and just enjoy the environment and the climb. From our vantage point up here, we had a good view of Island Peak, further up the next valley. John Peacock, Gerry Owens and David Brister, who had been on the advance party and were therefore already acclimatised, could be seen at 20,300 feet, making a successful ascent of the mountain. I wished I were with them.

While we were at Dingboche we were involved with the rescue of the doctor of the Italian Lhotse Expedition, led by Riccardo Cassin. He had apparently moved up too high, too quickly and was now suffering from pulmonary oedema. He would certainly have died without Noel Dilly's intervention. It was the first time that I had seen anyone with this condition, when lungs fill with water and the victim literally starts to drown in his own juices. I vowed not to let it happen to me if I could help it. Our doctor was also called in the early hours of the morning to the base camp of a Japanese womens' expedition to Everest. There had been a fight of some sort between two of the Sherpas and one of them had ended up with an ice-axe embedded in his chest. We never did find out what the two had been squabbling about!

By the end of March, our base camp had been set up next to a frozen lake at about 16,500 feet and loads ferried up to it. This walk used to take about two hours up and one down, which made it possible to do two carries in a day. There was no real necessity for this as we had yaks to do most of the heavy work, but it helped bring bodies to a mountain fitness. While we were humping up loads, Jon Fleming, the expedition leader, and Geordie Armstrong occupied the tents there with Khagendra and Kubijang. Their first problem was clearly to find a route up the rocky moraine, crossing some nasty boulder fields to the glacier where Camp I was to be established underneath the ridge.

Bronco and I watched Jon and Geordie put in this camp at 18,000 ft and through binoculars could see that the route then lay up a steep snow slope immediately above, which would bring them on to the central ridge proper. The ridge, now that we were closer, looked long, exposed and almost as it if it were made up of boulders of rotten sugar, piled one on top of the other, running away from us towards the belly of the mountain. Once off the ridge, we would need to force a route through the rock band which looked to be over a thousand feet thick. The report I had read of the 1961 expedition had indicated a long snow traverse, leading to the bottom of a steep couloir, which in turn could be climbed to a col on the skyline and from there it was straight on to the summit. From Base Camp, where we sat, it was over 8,000 feet to the top, and was clearly not going to be a doddle.

The next three days were all spent ferrying loads up the moraine to stock Camp I. Bamboo marker poles with fluorescent bits of material flapping from them were planted every few hundred yards or so to assist us with the route finding on days when it was snowing. On the way down Bronco and I would sit in private and work out a plan of campaign that we hoped would enable us to get a crack at the top. By now, the rest of the team had more or less separated into climbing pairs and were, no doubt, all individually plotting tactics, just as we were. Gerry Owens had teamed up with Richard Summerton and the two were probably the most experienced of all the climbers. It began to be accepted by everyone that they were the two most likely candidates for a summit push.

Returning from a carry, Jon Fleming announced that Bronc and I were to move up to Camp I the next day and start pushing the route up the hill. Geordie Armstrong and David Brister would go with us. I was overjoyed that we were going to get out in front and lead. We retired early after packing most of our personal gear in preparation for a dawn start the next morning.

Arriving at Camp I, we set about putting up more tents and studying the route, and I prepared the evening meal. For all four of us the excitement was almost electric that first day and we had to fight hard to contain our enthusiasm. We were so enjoying our freedom and happy to be the highest people on the expedition. It was agreed that Bronco and I would lead out the next morning, the others following closely behind, supplying us with extra ropes and karabiners and further securing the fixed ropes. By installing these ropes, everyone coming up with loads later on would be able to attach himself to them by means of jumar clamps (safety devices that run freely up a rope, but bite in and hold fast if the wearer falls), and thus be able to move more quickly and safely. That evening as we lazed about after dinner, the valley below reverberated to the strains of Geordie's sea shanties.

Bronco was awake before it was light and set about making the brew at the entrance to our small two-man tent. Huddled up like a dormouse at the back of the tent, I could tell it was cold outside from the way Bronc kept stuffing his hands down inside his sleeping bag which was dangling from his waist as he knelt over the stove. Soon I was sipping hot sweet tea and forcing down milky porridge. It was funny how my taste in food had changed. As we went higher, the blander the flavour, the more I liked it and I was constantly aware of the necessity to drink plenty of liquid to offset dehydration. Bronco and I had long since worked out a domestic routine. He would prepare breakfast in the morning, fill the day's flask and pack lunch, and I would attend to the main meal in the evening.

Just as it was getting half-light, we stepped away from our tent and moved across the hard, frosty snow on crampons that crackled and crunched as they bit into the icy crust of the glacier.

Before we had gone too far we came upon the first of our obstacles, a large and deep crevasse. Fixing one end of the rope to a metal stake, Bronco edged out over a snow bridge with me belaying him and the rope snaking out between us. Once across to the other side, he hammered in another of our stakes and lashed the rope to it. Clipping my jumar – which was attached to my harness by a short length of tape – on to the rope, I set off after him.

Krmmph! The whole bridge slumped and resettled. My heart leapt into my mouth and the hairs on the back of my neck stood rigidly to attention as snow to the left and right of me crumbled away and disappeared into the darkness of the chasm. I expected at any minute to be left suspended in air. Luckily, there was no further movement and I crossed safely.

'Hope there aren't any more like that,' I muttered, as I drew level with Bronco. He chuckled and shouted down the slope to Geordie, who was by now standing outside his tent, advising him to find a better bridge than that one.

'Not the best way to start a day,' he agreed as he once more set off up the snow. By now the angle was steepening and we were beginning to enjoy it, taking turns to lead out the lengths of rope. Pushing up for about 800 feet on good snow and ice, we at last found ourselves on the crest of the ridge with panoramic views all around. I felt I was on top of the world and said. as much to Bronco.

'If we are, then we're on the wrong *bukit*,' he said, pointing. 'The roof of the world is around that corner.' We both laughed.

Turning left, we headed along the easily-inclined ridge until the way was barred by a huge rock gendarme.

'My lead,' I said, and rounded it awkwardly to the left. By now

I was panting with exertion and finding it hard to draw sufficient breath. Fixing a piton into the rock I tied off the end, shouted to The Lad to come on up, and collapsed back against a boulder to rest. When he plumped down beside me I noticed that Bronc too was blowing rather hard and I told him of the difficulty I was having breathing. He pulled out the altimeter and informed us we were at 19,200 feet. The distance was just about right for a day's load-carry and as if to confirm our judgement, a few feet further on we came across the outlines of rock platforms that had been used by Joe Walmsley's party. Dumping our gear, we claimed the site for Camp II and awaited the arrival of Geordie and David. When they came, we took out a map and started to put names to some of the larger peaks that we could see off into the distance: Ama Dablam behind us, Island Peak to the right (we were almost as high as that), Lhotse, Baruntse, and a long way back, poking its head between the two of them, we could see Makalu (27,790 feet.) The campsite would be just big enough for three tents, but we must be careful not to get them too close to the 2,000-or-so-foot drop on either side of us. The big gendarme looked like the pope's hat, so Geordie named it 'the Mitre'.

We quickly descended to Camp I and spent the next three days bringing up enough gear and food to allow us to live at Camp II and push on even further.

The day we finally moved to Camp II a bag of mail arrived in Base Camp. It was the first to reach the expedition, and David volunteered to stay behind until it came up to I, so that he could bring ours with him. There turned out to be two letters for Bronco, but one was obviously a bill. The other, he could see, was from his wife and he weighted it down carefully with a small rock while he prepared a mug of tea so that he could settle down and enjoy it properly. Lying back in the sunshine, he lit a fag and reached for the letter. His hand knocked the stone by accident and a gust of wind lifted the precious paper tantalisingly beyond his grasp. He watched in forlorn amazement as it floated gently down to the West Lhotse Glacier, two thousand feet below. All I could do was howl with laughter beside him. 'Still got your bill, though, mate,' I said consolingly, and moved off quickly, out of his reach, still giggling.

The route between II and III was on very steep snow and ice, except for one short, sharp rock pitch that had been graded VI by the 1961 party. I found out why when I started to lead it. At ground level a grade VI climb can be enjoyable, but at 19,600 feet, with bags of exposure and the rock covered with verglas, it is a very different matter. The pitch was only about fifty feet, but it proved very steep and overhanging at the top. By the time I reached the last move I was puffing and panting like an old steam engine ready for the breaker's yard, and was relieved to spot an old peg with a bit of rope embedded in the ice a few feet above me. Grabbing hold of it, I told Bronco to stand by for a nonsense and pulled down on it, hard. The whole lot came away in my hand: rope, peg and half the mountain went trundling down towards the glacier. I clung on with only one hand and one foot on the rock, thinking if I don't do something quickly, I'll be on the way down too. I made a desperate lunge for a handhold high above me, beyond the overhang. My fingers wrapped around a big jug-hold and with one last heave, I pulled myself over on to easier ground and banged in a peg. That was the nearest I had ever come to a big fall and clipping myself to the piton, I rested long enough to ease the pounding in my chest. Fifteen minutes later, with the rope secured, Bronco had jumared up to join me.

'Nice lead, youth,' he said. He would probably never know just how much nervous energy it had drained from me. He took over the lead and I was not sorry to sit for a while and rest as I paid out his rope. We were now back on steep ice.

The last few pitches up to Camp III were led by Geordie Armstrong and rounded two huge rock blocks up a narrow ice gully on the left. This was a very impressive lead. The campsite was hacked out of the side of a large ice tower at 19,800 feet. The platform we made was both airy and unnerving to sleep on and as an added safety precaution we secured the tents to the mountain with several ice screws and ropes. It was never a pleasant spot to stay, especially in a bit of wind.

I was not sorry when Bronco and I were relieved at the front and went back to Base Camp for a couple of days' rest. Descending through the lower camps I could feel myself breathing more easily. We chatted with other team members who were by now occupying these rapidly growing, tented villages and stockpiling equipment for upward movement.

During the few days that we were lazing about down at Base, David Brister and Geordie Armstrong, backed up by John Peacock, Tim King, Nigel Gifford, Charles Walshaw and Crispin Agnew had forced a route which zigzagged along the rotten ice ridge, through towering unstable seracs of ice, as far as a small notch about three-quarters of the way along the ridge. This was to be the site of Camp III (20,400 feet). Once a tunnel tent was in position, Jon Fleming, Crispin, Bronco and myself started to push on further, up towards Camp IV. This section was short and very steep and gave good practice at front-pointing on blunt crampons. Very hard work! The route was exposed and quite exhilarating to be on; it finished by ascending a vertical 400-foot snow and ice face, which brought us to a large col where the ridge was fused to the main body of the mountain.

Four days later we had enough equipment at IV to allow it to be occupied. Load-carrying from III to IV was always hairy as part of the route traversed along the side of the ridge and was constantly avalanching with powder snow. Even on the fixed ropes I never felt completely comfortable and the glacier below was a long way off! On one of these carries, Nigel lost his footing and his load of a tent and foodstuff went crashing 3,000 feet down the hill to be lost for ever. He was lucky not to have gone with it.

The plan now was to get everyone stocking up the camps all along the route so that we could occupy the top camp at 21,000 feet.

During this phase of the climb, Gerry Owens and Richard Summerton, who had been ferrying kit between the lower camps, started to move up the mountain. By now, it was getting on towards the end of April and we were experiencing snow storms that were so bad that climbing was out of the question for days on end. During these 'festering' periods we would lock ourselves in our tents and rest. It provided a good opportunity to bring the diary up to date, write the odd letter home, or cook up a special meal. The food we were eating was a mixture of Army composite rations, dehydrated meats and soups. Nigel had worked out exactly how many calories we should take in each day, but in order to maintain this level, we would need to have eaten everything that was put in the day's ration-pack, including the toilet paper.

As our palates adjusted to the food, so we learned to concoct different dishes. Bronco used to knock up a decent rice pudding and mix it with dehydrated apple flakes, and my culinary speciality was potato cakes made from mashed potato powder with chunks of tinned fish tossed in and served up with peas and a bit of curry. It tasted delicious – well, at least I thought so.

By 27 April, Camp IV was occupied by Tim King, Nigel, Pasang

and Krishna Bahadur Karlo, one of the climbers from the Royal
Nepalese Army. It had taken us the best part of four weeks to
climb the ridge and we now had to complete the whole expedition
in less time than that. Moving out from IV was a cold affair
because as the camp was in the shade of the hill, the sun never got
to the tents until late in the day. Still with 5,000 feet to climb, we
could not hang about; the lead team set off to find a site for Camp
V. The climbing was easy to begin with: there were some
'cramponable' snow slopes, the odd patch of blue ice and one or
two small crevasses. Then it was necessary to traverse left on to the
face of Nuptse proper and climb steeply for about a thousand feet
over mixed ground until a large open crevasse was reached at the
foot of the rock band. This crevasse provided an ideal spot to place
the camp at 22,350 feet and easily accommodated three tunnel
tents. Directly above the camp was what we believed would be the
last major obstacle on the face, the rock band. I was quite worried
about this 1000-foot section, because on the way up I had been
watching how the rock and ice tumbled down it. Luckily the camp
in the crevasse was well protected from the danger. Not so, poor
old Tim. He used his knee to stop one of the falling rocks and had
to be assisted down. Nigel and Crispin were now joined by Gerry
and Richard, who had moved up through the camps in order to
occupy Camp V and force the route on through the rock band.

Meanwhile, Bronco and I, teaming up again with Geordie and
David, moved into IV and started to bring up supplies to support
them. The rock band proved easier than expected as Crispin
discovered a narrow ice gully cutting through the worst of it. This
very impressive lead brought us on to a small snow ledge on which
we sited Camp VI. Over the next three days, a platform was cut
out of the ledge and two tents erected on it. On the nightly radio
call to Base Camp, Gerry informed them that the camp was now
operational at a height of 23,350 feet, and that due to frostbite in
his fingers, Nigel would have to descend the next day and would
require assistance.

On 6 May, Gerry, Richard, Geordie, and David occupied VI
and started to push out the route towards the final camp. This was
quite a long job as the way now led along a traverse of over half a
mile of fairly steeply-angled snow. Taking along everything
required to establish the camp, they had a long day and decided,
because it was so late, that they would put up the tents and remain
there. Our general strategy was always to come down the

mountain to sleep after gaining new height, but the difference in altitude on this day was not that great, only some 300 feet. They were hardly likely to suffer any major effects from altitude sickness, even though Gerry and Richard had moved up quite fast during the past few days. The tents were placed at the side of a snow couloir which led to the col on the summit ridge. Our top camp now stood at 23,800 feet.

The next day, Geordie and David descended leaving Gerry and Richard to rest in preparation for a summit bid the following day. Crispin and Krishna, who were to form the second summit team, moved across to join them, carrying another tent. I felt envious as I ferried a load up to V and wished that it was Bronc and I over there getting ready to go for the top. I knew that our chances of becoming a summit team were now very slim and that by the time these two pairs had been through, the expedition would be running out of steam. We were all tired, as it was. That night we slept at the crevasse camp below the rock band. We were all excited by the fact that at the same time tomorrow we could be celebrating a summit success.

It was not to be.

Leaving the top camp at 7.15 a.m. on 9 May, Gerry and Richard headed up the snow couloir towards the col, from where it was only 400 feet along the ridge to Nuptse summit. Everyone on the mountain who was in a position to see the final couloir remained glued to telescopes or binoculars, willing the pair onwards and upwards. Keeping to the right-hand edge of the couloir, they made good progress and by ten o'clock that morning were over half-way up.

Then tragedy struck. Either they were hit by a rockfall or one of them slipped; whichever it was, the pair fell headlong down the couloir in a mini-avalanche, past Camp VII where Krishna was watching horrified, and all the way down to the Nuptse glacier far below.

A hush fell over the mountain for the rest of that day and the following night. We waited in agonised torment, hoping there could have been some mistake. Perhaps it had only been a rucksack or some gear that had fallen out of the couloir and not Gerry and Richard after all? But confirmation soon started coming in over the radio from various climbers along the ridge and from Base Camp where the accident had also been witnessed. The next day Nigel and John Peacock tramped up the glacier and identified the bodies of the two men. It was not a pleasant task, and we all felt for them.

It fell now to the leader of the expedition, Jon Fleming, to take stock of the situation and decide whether or not to abandon the climb. I did not envy him his position. He chose to continue, which was a popular decision with the rest of the team. But first, there were several problems to sort out. Krishna at Camp VII had been struck on the head by a stone and had lost a crampon during the rockfall caused by the falling pair. We had somehow to get another crampon up to him and escort him down. Geordie Armstrong, too, had got a frostbitten hand by this time and had to pull off the mountain. We planned one more summit bid, but this time as a foursome. David Brister and Pasang Tamang, who were up at Camp VI, were to take a spare set of spikes across to Krishna and Crispin at VII to enable them to descend, and then wait for Bronco and I, so that we could all make a final push for the top together. To add to our worries, the weather began to deteriorate.

The morning of 12 May started cold and grey as Bronco and I moved off along the terrace that led to the start of the half-mile traverse to Camp VII. It had snowed in the night and the fifty-degree ice traverse was covered with a new layer of wet snow. No ropes had been fixed beyond Camp VI, so Bronco and I were forced to move slowly, kicking steps along the route; we were linked together by a 150-foot climbing rope. Our packs were quite heavy as we were lifting all our own gear, extra food and fuel for the others and a radio. Looking down was a bit of an eye-opener. The slope ran away from us for about 300 feet and then fell 3,000 feet to the glacier below. I was conscious that the new snow we were on was not as stable as I would have liked. After about two hours of steady plodding along the traverse, belaying each other as we took turns to lead, I saw the tent of Camp VII about a hundred feet above and to my left at the mouth of the final couloir. Pointing this out to Bronco, I headed on up towards it. I was sixty feet above him when the snow under my feet collapsed and I started to slide downwards. Within seconds I was out of control, on my back with my sack pushing me over on to my side, and gathering speed. The world started to slow down: I was on the outside looking in. Sitting up, I saw a look of horror on Bronco's face as I slid past him.

'Stop yourself! Stop yourself!' he screamed. 'I'm not on very good.'

'Hold me, hold me!' I shouted back, as I sped towards the big drop.

My mind was alive, adrenalin flowing in rivers, and I was acutely aware of everything that was going on. Strangely enough, there was no panic. I knew that unless I arrested myself, or Bronco stopped me, we were both going to go freefalling over the cliff. I remember thinking, 'Is this how it was for Gerry and Richard?'

Jamming my axe in the soft snow I pulled myself over on to my belly and tried to brake the fall. After what seemed like minutes, but must only have been fractions of seconds, I started to slow down. Bronco was still screaming at me as the rope between us tightened and began to tug gently at my harness. I came to a halt and frantically started to kick a safe platform on which to rest and pull myself together. I was shaken and slightly unnerved as I gazed in amazement at the spot below me where we would have parted company with the mountain and taken to the air.

'You all right, Brum?' Bronco's voice came from another world. Looking up, I could see from his face that he, too, must have had visions of this being our last climb.

Twenty minutes later we had climbed up to the camp and were sitting in the snow, sipping hot tea from our flasks. David Brister and Pasang were inside their tent which had rather a lot of snow on top of it. By now the cloud and mist was all around us and it had started to snow heavily. In all the excitement I had not noticed the weather turn so bad. After digging out a platform and putting up another tent, Bronco and I crawled inside and sorted out stuff for a meal. I was still shaken from the fall.

He said, 'I thought we were gonners then, youth!' But I chose not to discuss it and lit us both a cigarette instead.

'Don't look too good for the top tomorrow,' I said, making some comment about the snow that was already building up on our tent. From here, at 23,800 feet, there was less than another two thousand to the top. It did not seem an awful lot and certainly there was no technical climbing involved. It would all depend on the weather next day. A plan was discussed between the four of us and, satisfied that all was in order, we jumped into our sleeping bags for an early night.

There was no let-up in the snow during the night and it started to build up on top of our tents. The weight of it was so heavy that the side nearest the hill started to sag inwards and had to be propped up with our rucksacks. Later on, I heard a rustling on top of the tent and realised that avalanches were flowing down on us. This happened with increasing frequency as the night wore on and we feared that we might be swept away completely. Luckily for us, we had dug the platform in such a way that the snow started to bury us and slide over us, rather than push us off. Most of the night was spent pushing snow off the top of the tent from the inside, to leave us room to move. The space inside was rapidly being reduced by the weight of the snow pouring down. Things were not looking too good at all.

By the time morning arrived, it was impossible for us to get out of the tents, let alone go for the top. All we could do was stay put and wait until the snow and the avalanches stopped. We were rapidly getting into a survival situation. Over the radio we were informed that no movement was possible anywhere on the mountain and that there was a peculiar magenta glow in the sky which heralded more snow on the way. We arranged to talk with the expedition leader over the radio every four hours for updates.

No movement was possible outside the tent that day at all. In fact, it was taking us all our time to keep a liveable space cleared in which to brew tea and warm up our food. Another of our problems was that the cooking was done on a primus stove and the fumes, when it was in use, were making us feel nauseous due to the lack of air circulating. We were trapped, entombed in an igloo of snow, with the tent acting as an inner skin and stopping the fresh air getting to us. Sometime around mid-morning we cringed as we heard the roar of a monster avalanche crashing down not far away. It missed us but several inches of powder snow settled on us in its wake. We later learned that it had wiped out a tent at Camp V. Fortunately there was no one inside at the time.

Our worry was that the monsoon had arrived early and it might not now stop snowing for a week or more. Not knowing how long we would be here for, we started to ration our food and drink supplies. Receiving a weather report from Base Camp, which told us of more snow, Jon Fleming made the decision to evacuate the mountain. He ordered us to return to Base Camp. That, however, was easier said than done. We could not move anywhere in this.

The rest of that day and night passed by, the seconds ticking away like hours. It was a struggle to maintain a sense of humour and we must have told each other every funny story we knew three times over. Always in the back of our minds was the thought of what had happened to Gerry and Richard, of my fall, and the fact that we were going to have to descend in even worse conditions than those on the way up.

Waking from a fitful doze on the morning of the third day, I could almost hear the silence – it was so deafening. It took several minutes before my brain registered the fact that we were no longer being avalanched upon. I looked over to where Bronco lay in his by now wet sleeping bag, his head poking out of the top. He looked tired and drawn; his eyes were puffy and red from the effects of the fumes from the stove. I knew my own must look the same.

'It's stopped,' he said flatly, without feeling, and started to stretch his cold bones. There was no need for idle chatter, now. We both knew what had to be done. As he prepared a last brew and a quick breakfast, I set about packing our gear in the cramped space. Shouting across to David and Pasang, we learned that they were awake and in about the same shape as ourselves; we would all leave in about an hour's time. I reached across to grab the welcome brew that was being offered me by Bronco. I was cold and feeling claustrophobic, trapped in the confines of our buried tent. I knew that we must be a fair bit underground by now, because during the night I had pushed my arm out of the vent at the end of the tent to allow some air to circulate, and had been unable to clear the snow even at arm's length.

When we were both dressed, Bronco tried to clear a way out, but found that there was just too much snow to be able to get out that way. Taking my Swiss army knife, I ripped a gash down the outward side of the tent and with the loose snow pouring in, pushed up into the new day. My lungs drank down the clear, fresh air, thin as it was. I was glad to be out; we had been cooped up in there for three days and I was so stiff. The sky was still dark and heavy with snow as I kicked a space clear between the two tents. By this time, Pasang had cleared away the snow from the front of the other tent and was kneeling outside, looking dishevelled and weary. Because of the amount of snow that had avalanched upon us, a lot of our stores had been swept down the mountainside and we could only find one rope between us. Putting the trusty Swiss knife to good use again, I sliced the rope in two, giving half to David and Pasang. I asked them if they wanted to descend first or to follow after us. David chose the latter, saying that it would be easier if we kicked the steps and made the route through the fresh snow as we were the more experienced.

They told us they would have a brew and something to eat, then follow on. Informing Jon Fleming of our plans over the radio at 10.30, Bronco and I tied ourselves together on the short rope and set off down. The snow lay deep and was so unstable that every footstep triggered minor avalanches below us. Progress was agonisingly slow as we kept having to knock away the snow that was balling up under our crampons. Taking it in turns to lead the break trail, we both wished that there had been fixed rope along this section. After an hour, looking back the way we had come, we could see David and Pasang setting off from the high camp.

Towards mid-day we had reached a spot where we had to cross an obvious avalanche runnel. The snow here was much deeper and at times we were wading through four feet of it, up to our waists. It had also started to snow again and we could only see about twenty feet in front of us and soon lost sight of the following pair.

By 4.30 in the afternoon the clouds started to lift a little and we could see the other two were not far behind us. Bronco was just starting to traverse around a particularly tricky rock pitch which ended up at the terrace that led to Camp VI and safety. I shouted up to the others to ask how they were going and was told by David that they were OK. When I had crossed the rock pitch I could see that there was only one tent standing at the camp site. After a quick confab, Bronc and I decided that we should leave the tent for the other two to sleep in, and that we would try to get down to the lower camp. Shouting back our plans in the by now foul weather, we set off down the fixed ropes, glad to be once again anchored to the lifeline.

The descent to Camp V took a lot longer than we had imagined and it had been dark for a long time when we stumbled into the crevasse camp by the light of our headtorches, to be welcomed, fed and given hot drinks by Tim King and Charles Walshaw. Throughout the day we had been fighting through small avalanches and hearing many more of varying sizes all over the mountain. It had been a long, hard slog and for the first time in days, I slept properly.

The next morning, 15 May, Bronco and I moved slowly down the mountain, looking back towards Camp VI for signs of David and Pasang leaving their camp. There was no movement around the camp all day. Over the radio at Camp IV we heard the voice of

Geordie Armstrong, who was at Base Camp, explaining to Jon Fleming that he had noticed a 'new black dot' on the face under a crevasse. The spot he indicated was directly under the place we had last seen David and Pasang. Bronco mirrored my thoughts when he said, 'Hope it's a rock.' We both secretly feared the worst.

Tim and Charles, who were still up at Camp V, climbed back up to VI to see if the pair were still in the tent, but when they arrived, the camp was deserted. There had been no one there since Bronco and I had passed through. The 'black dot' was in such a position on the steepest and most dangerous section of the cliff that it was impossible for Tim and Charles to investigate. That night John Peacock at Base Camp radioed for a helicopter to search for the bodies. In an *Alouette* belonging to the Royal Nepalese Army, John flew close to the black dot the next morning and confirmed that it was in fact the body of David Brister. There was a rope leading up from his body into the crevasse. On the end of this rope, we knew, would be Pasang Tamang, our Gurkha friend. The mountain was evacuated under a cloud of gloom and sorrow.

When we arrived at Base Camp, Bronco noticed that he had got frostbite in his toes and had to be flown by helicopter to Kathmandu. I hitched a lift as well in order to look after him in the hospital. The last thing we saw as we left Base Camp was the large metal cross that had been erected on a stone cairn to commemorate our four lost friends.

The flight out to Kathmandu lasted less than an hour. It had taken us two weeks to walk in. Things seemed somehow out of all proportion.

Bronco's frostbite was only minor and when the rest of the team arrived in Kathmandu, having flown out from Lukla, he was allowed out of the hospital for rest. The British Ambassador and the Defence Attaché, Mr Jimmy Lys, who had assisted us throughout our expedition, very kindly looked after him. They also arranged a memorial service in the British Embassy Chapel for the four who had died.

Being told that we had two weeks to wait before we could fly back to the UK, I accepted Kagendra Bahadur Limbu's offer of a visit to his home in Barimorong, to the east of Nepal. The time we spent away from the rest of the team enabled my friendship with Kagendra to grow, and allowed me time to 'wind down' and reflect on the last few months. I now knew what Himalayan climbing was about; I had learned a lot about big mountains, friendships, tragedy; I had learned to love this beautiful country and the people who live in it. I was looking forward to coming back to Everest next year.

To the Top of Everest

I T DID not take the others on our Joint British and Royal
Nepalese Army Expedition long to realise that this young
sergeant and corporal from the SAS were going to need some
watching. We were competing right from the moment we
arrived in Lamasangu, the little village on the Friendship
Highway which links Nepal with Tibet, from where the walk-in to
Everest starts. First off the wagons, we picked the best spot by the
side of the road where straight away I began to lay out the sleeping
mats and bed rolls while Bronco put on a brew. That done, we got
stuck into helping the porters unload the rest of the gear.

'Let them do it themselves. That's what they get paid for,' said
one of the Army Ruperts with us.

We looked at each other, and Bronc let his breath out slowly. I
knew him well enough by now to be able to read his thoughts from
the merest twitch of an eye. He was as good as saying, 'Selfish
bastard! Hope we don't have to rely on him later.'

Tents were being put up for everyone – everyone else, that is,
except the porters and ourselves. Being at relatively low altitude it
was still quite warm and the sky was clear; we had already decided
we'd do better to sleep out now and start acclimatising right away.

A few minutes later, I nudged Bronc. 'Cop a load of this,' I
whispered.

Out of one of the tents had stepped an apparition, tall and aristocratic, a figure dressed in paisley pyjamas and carpet slippers. He was holding out a personal mug, hopefully.

'I say,' (the voice was Scottish), 'is there any tea?'

It was like something out of the Raj. Bronco and I rolled around, helpless with laughter. We couldn't believe our eyes.

By six o'clock the next morning, The Lad and I stood looking down on the first signs of stirring in the campsite from high up on the side of a hill. We had been up and away two hours before, and not a soul had seen us go. The psychological war had started. The rest of this team was going to have to get used to our backs; that was all we intended letting them see. We led out first every morning and it became normal for the others to catch us up at the Breakfast Stop further along the trail, where we would already have hot water bubbling over fires and breakfast cooked. As they sat down to eat, we would finish off, pack a flask and a day's food and be gone again.

It was good to be out in the morning air with the sun warm on our backs. There was no rush; from time to time we would just stop and stare at the hills and the snow-capped peaks all around. Passing through villages, we started to meet people we had made friends with the year before on our Nuptse trip. Such a shame that had all ended in tragedy.

After ten days we reached the Dudh Kosi river, where we turned north. The walking was easy and pleasant, and all the time we were slowly acclimatising. We arrived at Lukla Airstrip, a tiny ribbon of grass and rubble stuck out on a peninsula of land high above the early morning cloud at ten thousand feet. This was the spot to which the bulk of our ten tons of stores had been flown by small aircraft. The pilots were uncanny. Loaded with people and equipment, they crabbed up the valley, parallel with the strip and heading directly into the belly of the mountain, then at the very last moment, they would quickly swing the planes round a full 180 degrees, cut engines, and float gently down on to the strip. All the time, cross winds and downdraughts would be buffeting them from every direction. Once the wheels touched down, they had to throttle back hard and stop within seconds or they would collide with a sheer 2,000-foot rockface. Dotted all along the side of the runway were the rusting remains of all those that hadn't quite made it. Talk about flying by the seat of your pants!

Fortunately for us, all our kit had got in safely, but I was glad we had walked and not flown in by air. Besides, it would have been a pity to have missed the last week and a half's worth of local culture and exquisite views.

At the famous sherpa village of Namche Bazar we picked up our Sirdar, Sonam Girme, and continued on up the track to the Tengboche Monastery. This is where you get your first real glimpse of 'the hill' as it pokes its nose over the long ridge of Nuptse. Seeing Nuptse again brought on a rush of feeling. I could vividly remember the joy last year of being on my very first trip to a big bukit and the exhilaration of climbing to high altitude. Equally, however, there was a wash of sadness as I remembered the death of Gerry Owens and Richard Summerton, and then Pasang and David Brister.

That night, sitting round a campfire, we had a good old singsong and a lot of Gurkha rum, in between swopping war stories and old climbing lies. An American trekking party, bound for Base Camp, was also camping at the monastery and its members tried vainly to out-sing us. Just after two in the morning, the normally patient monks came across complaining about the raucous din, and our adversaries slunk off to their sleeping bags, defeated.

Before pushing on the next day, the monks held a *puja* for us, a ceremony during which they offered up prayers for our safety, wished us every success, and presented each of us with a holy scarf for our protection. For the rupee equivalent of a pound a head, it seemed cheap at the price.

Two days later we were firmly established in our acclimatisation camp above Pheriche at 15,000 feet. The time had come to pay off all the porters and sherpanis who had carried our equipment this far. It was a good day. Lots of laughing, joking and back-slapping as everyone wished us luck, before disappearing back to Namche Bazar – some of our gear, as we afterwards learned, disappearing with them. We were to spend a whole week, here, sorting out and issuing the climbing kit to both sherpas and climbers, and making sure that we had indeed got sufficient quantities of food and climbing hardware to complete the climb.

When we were not helping out, Bronco and I would take off for the day and climb one of the small peaks in the neighbourhood, gaining one or two thousand feet in order to get ourselves into trim. The general rule for Himalayan mountaineering is to work high and sleep low, pushing the body a little higher each day but always bringing it down to a lower level to rest at night. This way, gradually, the body's metabolism makes some slight adjustment that gives it a higher degree of altitude tolerance.

After a week, Tony Streather, the expedition's leader, made the decision to send off what later came to be called 'the Heavy Gang' to locate a site for Base Camp at the foot of the infamous Khumbu Icefall. Eight of us moved up the valley with a couple of yaks to reconnoitre. I still sometimes wonder what the rest of the team made of our sick sense of humour when they followed up a few days later. We'd added a flourish of toilet paper to every pile of yak dung to indicate how house-trained our yaks were!

On arriving at Base Camp, Bronco and I just stood gaping at the icefall. We had not been prepared for such a huge river of ice cascading down the mountainside, right to the point where we were standing.

'Bit vicious-looking, innit?' muttered Bronco.

'It'll go,' I replied airily, and staggered over to find a basha spot. 'Fancy a brew?'

I have to admit my stomach was turning over a bit as I started to light the stove and get out 'the fixins'. The base camp was situated right on the bend of the icefall at 18,000 feet, two hundred feet from a wall of rock, snow and ice that rises sheer for five thousand feet to the Lho La, the notch on the border ridge between Tibet and Nepal, which runs right through the summit of Everest. Privately, I thought, 'He's right, you know. It's bloody vicious.'

The icefall is formed from the collected rivers of ice sweeping down off the flanks of Everest, Nuptse and Lhotse, which then all get squeezed through the Western Cwm before tumbling off the side of the hill in a great white and blue frozen waterfall, 2,000 feet high. It is estimated to be moving at a rate of three feet per day, and is made up of hundreds of thousands of huge ice towers and blocks that crumble and sift against each other like lumps of granulated sugar. The surface is criss-crossed with open-mouthed crevasses, some up to 300 feet deep and forty feet across. It is always precarious.

'Could give us a bit of bother, this buggar,' I mused.

That afternoon, after the others had joined us and all the tents were erected, we sat around studying the fall through binoculars, trying to spot a safe-ish route up through it.

Bronco and I had both made out the obvious way through the fall. Straight up the centre, no messing, and so keeping away from the avalanche dangers off the sides of Nuptse and Everest. Not only that, you had to be blind not to have seen the line of red marker flags, crushed and dotted about in a rough line up the middle. Suck it and see!

'Early birds off to bed again, eh? Must get their beauty sleep!' joked someone. Bet he got a bit of shock when he woke up in the morning to find that Brummie and Bronco, yet again, had been gone for hours, and even now could be seen well into the icefall, ferreting out the best route.

There was method in all this early start business. Not only was the snow at its most stable then, before the sun got to it – and therefore at its safest – it also meant we would be finished for the day by about one o'clock, back at base, brewing, feeding and sunning ourselves. By the time the others rolled in sometime in the late afternoon, tired from having to plough through all that soft snow, we were fresh, rested and packed up for the next day, our plans made and talking sense. By now, the mould was set.

Route-finding through the icefall was desperate. True, the odd red marker flags pointed out the general line taken by previous expeditions, but none the less we still had to negotiate under and around some horrific, teetering ice towers. We felt sure they were about to collapse on our heads everytime we went near them; the sounds of the ice cracking and creaking in the early morning cold played havoc with our nerves.

Many people, we knew, had died coming through here. Thinking you had found some nice easy section to crampon your way up, would invariably prove false, and reliable looking snow-bridges had a nasty habit of slumping suddenly into hidden depths, leaving you quaking on the brink of a giant chasm. You became increasingly breathless from the effects of altitude and from so many narrow squeaks.

For safety's sake, we had decided we must install fixed ropes the full length of the icefall, to allow climbers and sherpas to pass through as safely as possible. This would be done by lead climbers running out 300-foot lengths of 9mm rope and tying them off to 'dead men' belay points. (A 'dead man' is a kind of snow anchor, resembling a normal spade-blade in size and shape but with a wire loop-fixture in the centre; if rammed well into snow, the harder the strain put upon it, the deeper it would work itself in. Or, sometimes it might be fixed to a three-foot metal stake driven into hard-packed snow.) A back-up team of two then followed on behind, anchoring the ropes at intervals and making the route safer. Reading reports of previous expeditions made it clear that ladder sections would be needed to span some of the wider crevasses, and our team engineered some pretty fancy bridge-work, but struggling like Himalayan window-cleaners through the ice towers with these six-foot ladders was no easy task.

Daily now, we would wake while it was still dark, breakfast on milky porridge that Bronco had made the night before, fill our flasks for the day and struggle out of our warm sleeping bags into our windproofs and harnesses. Then, lifting the day's load on to stiff backs we would crampon off for the high point of the day before, to push the route a bit further. There was no room for complacency. Sometimes we would find the whole scene had changed overnight because a serac had crashed down barring the way or a ladder had dropped into the gaping mouth of one of the crevasses as it widened with the movement of the icefall. One morning Geordie Armstrong was jumaring a stretch of fixed rope when a tower started to lean, tightening the rope that linked it to the next ice pinnacle. Inevitably the rope snapped under the strain and poor Georgie was catapulted into the air, like an arrow from a bow, to be left suspended on his jumar clip half-way up the ice tower on one end of the broken rope. He was so badly shaken, he decided to come back down and collect his wits before he could do anything more. We plied him with hot tea and made a joke about it, but were all secretly glad it hadn't happened to us.

After two weeks we had set up Camp I at 19,300 feet and started to equip it for occupation, but it was never a popular place. Perched as it was on top of a huge ice serac that groaned as the ice contracted every time the temperature plummeted in the late afternoon, we could never feel sure that it would still be there the next morning. It always was, and in fact was sited in an excellent position, as it had a great wide crevasse above it which acted as a collection point for all the avalanche debris that was constantly falling from the face of Nuptse and the shoulder of Everest's West Ridge. Once this camp was in place and the rest of the team had moved up to base camp, 'the heavy gang' retreated down the hill for a rest, where Tony Streather, the expedition leader, had now taken up his director's position. Tony had celebrated his fiftieth birthday the day we set up base camp; it was an emotional moment for him as it was also the twenty-first anniversary, to the day, of setting up base camp on Kangchenjunga for the successful first ascent of that mountain when he had been one of the four to reach the summit. On his very first climbing expedition, Tony had been to the top of a major peak (Tirich Mir, unclimbed at the time), and in 1956 had showed great courage in leading the survivors of a student expedition to safety after an epic of Haramosh in the Karakoram. But he had not been to the Himalaya for seventeen years at the time he was invited to lead our expedition. All the same, he was a popular and, as it proved, an ideal choice. In accepting, he became one of the first men to have been on expeditions to all three of the world's highest mountains, Everest, K2 and Kangchenjunga.

With Camp I occupied, it was now the job of the lead climbers to force the route over the lip of the icefall and into the Western Cwm, where they were faced with a different problem, that of overcoming some of the bigger crevasses, and running the gauntlet of avalanches from the West Ridge as the route ran close under the shoulder of Everest for three hundred yards. We now had a third member of the SAS climbing with us, Steve Johnson, a powerful, tall man who had just joined the expedition after completing his Mountain Guides course in Germany. As well as being instrumental in leading this section of the climb, Steve also took on the job of filming, earning himself the nickname Cecil B. De Mille. It wasn't long before Camp II, which was to be our Advanced Base Camp (ABC), was sited at 21,000 feet, way up in the Western Cwm.

The first sight that greeted climbers as they reached the spot was intimidating: hundreds of tons of snow avalanching with a deafening roar off Everest, Lhotse and Nuptse. Bronco and I, by this time back up at Camp I, were feeling very fearful for the safety of those out in front, but we need not have worried. If anything, this tremendous fall of snow had shown them the best place to site the new camp, well out of harm's way in an avalanche-free area in the centre of the Cwm.

The next week was spent stocking Camp I and ABC, so that the next team, led by Terry Thompson, could take over the lead and allow the party that Steve was in to drop back down for a well earned rest. Before this happened though, a comic and rather stupid event took place. One of the young captains who was in the lead party, Henry Day from the Royal Electrical and Mechanical Engineers Regiment, decided, instead of thawing out his small Bluet gas cartridge by leaving it overnight in his sleeping bag, as we all did, to speed things up by holding it over a candle. It was quick all right. Containing a 40/60 mixture of butane and propane, the resulting bang and flash that echoed around the Western Cwm reminded us of one of the mortar attacks in Marbat. Henry, who had the candle between his legs, stopped some of the splinters of metal, but the injuries, luckily, were only slight – more to his pride than anything else, though he did have to retire to Base Camp for a while.

Once the camps were well stocked and occupied, the new lead climbers set out early one morning, searching for a place at the foot of the Lhotse Face for Camp III at 23,000 feet. After a long, hard slog, Captain Terry Thompson and Geordie Armstrong found just the spot we had been looking for, and dumping off their gear returned to the safety of ABC. They arrived back late in the day, absolutely shattered from their efforts, and crept straight into their tent for the evening meal and sleep. It was then that tragedy struck.

During the night Terry must have got out of his tent to answer a call of nature, and in the darkness stumbled into a crevasse. Alarmed that he did not return to the tent, Geordie alerted the rest of the team and a search was organised. Soon Terry was located at the bottom of a crevasse, but despite attempts to save him, his injuries were so bad that he died before he could be brought to the surface.

We tried to bring in a helicopter to transport Terry's body back to Kathmandu, so that he could be buried in accordance with his family's wishes, but this proved impossible due to high winds. The helicopter was blown off course and only narrowly escaped crashing itself. Aborting the mission, we decided to bury Terry there on the mountain. His body was lowered gently into a crevasse and a short simple ceremony held at the spot as the storm blew in around us. It was a bleak moment.

Not surprisingly, morale was badly affected, and not helped by the fact that the storm raged on for the next few days, keeping everyone pinned inside their tents with nothing to do but dwell on the events that had just taken place. All of us felt that Terry would have wanted us to carry on, and in the end it was unanimously decided this was the right thing to do. Once the winds died down and the sun came out again, things began to look a little better and we resumed stocking up Camp III.

Some members had decided by this time that their ceiling had been reached, that this was as high as they could go. The constant nausea and headaches of climbing at high altitude were beginning to take their toll and theirs now would be the job of daily going out into the icefall, the most dangerous section of the whole climb, to keep the fixed ropes and bridges in a state of good repair. I did not envy them the task.

Camp III was on a platform cut into the foot of the Lhotse Face, big enough to accommodate two tents. Bronco and I moved into one of these to back up Phil Neame and Steve Johnson, who were now leading the steep ice face. The climbing here became more exciting as the angle increased, and soon we were cramponing our way across glistening hard blue and green ice, catching the occasional glimpse of the plume blown off the summit ridge, which indicated high winds of anything up to 130 knots up there. The fixed ropes, anchored to the face by ice screws and pitons, meant that we could move quite quickly up the slope. There was the opportunity for some marvellous photography as the sun came over the top of Lhotse and burst into flame directly behind the silhouette of the climber in front, jumaring up the ropes with spindrift blowing around his ankles.

Heading up the steep snow and ice, we kept in touch with Tony Streather by walkie-talkie. He was now up at ABC overseeing progress, watching us through his spyglass. His well-intentioned advice of 'It looks better off to the right' or 'Try a little further to the left' received some choice remarks from those in the lead.

It was at this Camp III that some of my high-cost medical training was put into practice. I discovered one of our Gurkhas sitting on his side in obvious agony after carrying a load up from ABC.

'What's the matter, mate?' I asked him.

Embarrassed, he finally admitted to suffering from a bad case of piles. They were so bad that he was unable to return to ABC that day. I persuaded him that I would need to take a peek in order to see how best I could treat him, and managed to get him to lower his trousers. The sight that confronted me was horrendous, like a bunch of grapes hanging from a vine. It was easy to see that the poor man had a severe case of strangulated haemorrhoids – no wonder he was crippled. Over the radio I described the porter's conditon to our doctor, Philip Horniblow, urging him to come up the next day with his bag of tricks. By the time he arrived, the poor chap was in even worse agony, lying face down in the tiny tent.

'With your medical training,' said Philip, 'you can assist me on what will probably get into the Guinness Book of Records as the highest-ever operation.' With our patient kneeling, his nether regions pointing skywards, our high altitude surgeon took aim with his scalpel and struck three times at the ballooning append-age. Effluent spat everywhere, covering the three of us and the tent. Letting out a scream, the brave Gurkha collapsed in a heap, relieved that it was all over. Turning to Philip, I asked, knowing the answer, 'And just what job did you have in mind for me?'

Smiling, he said simply, 'You get to clean up and bandage the patient!'

Meanwhile the lead pair had found a spot at 25,000 feet for Camp IV. This was situated on an avalanche-prone slope half-way up the Lhotse Face. This, like our Camp I, was never a popular place to be, with its continual snow slides, but it did offer spectacular views back down the valley as the sun went down and the afternoon cloud rolled in, spreading itself like a carpet at our feet.

Shortly after this camp was stocked and the route was being pushed on through the Yellow Band towards the South Col, Bronco and I were informed by Tony Streather that we were to be the first summit pair.

Descending to ABC, we started to prepare our kit. The small summit tent was erected to make sure that all the bits were intact, and rations, oxygen, radios and stoves were made up into manpack loads and ferried up to the South Col by our high altitude sherpas. One of them, Yonge Tenzing, made the climb from Camp IV to the col three times in consecutive days without the use of oxygen. We were impressed. Once Bronco and I started to move up above 25,000 feet, we started to use our oxygen systems. We were working on a diluter demand system, which only allowed the warmth of the oxygen to flow into our lungs when we inhaled, thus cutting down on the oxygen wastage normally experienced with constant flow circuits.

The move up was a long, slow plod, interspersed by the best wishes of all the team members we met descending the fixed ropes from the col. The path had been opened up and the camp on the South Col prepared for us and our back-up party, all ready for the final push.

Gaining the col, we stared in disbelief at the mass of rubbish that had accumulated there from previous expeditions: old oxygen cylinders and fuel containers lay scattered everywhere, fused into the ice by countless storms and high, jetstream winds. At 26,200 feet this was a bleak and windswept place for a camp. All the same, it felt good to be up this high, knowing that tomorrow we would be starting on the final bit of the climb.

The plan was for Bronco and I to follow our back-up party up the right-hand couloir to gain the final ridge, and get as high up it as we could before placing the last camp. The others would then disappear back to the South Col, leaving us to sleep in the new camp that night, ready to go for the top the following morning. While we were away, the second pair would then come back up to take over occupation of the tent, so as to be in position for a second attempt the day afterwards if conditions held. Bronc and I were to return all the way to the South Col after our summit climb. A simple plan, but alas, not one that was to run smoothly.

Excitedly, we set about preparing our evening meal and summit kit. Tomorrow would be our big day. It definitely warranted an early night for Bronco and me.

On the 14 May 1976, 'the Lad' and I left the South Col trailed by a support party of four. Towards late afternoon we had arrived at the spot of Camp VI at 27,500 feet and, in worsening weather, began cutting out a platform for it. After dropping off the tent and some food and oxygen, the others wished us well and descended towards the safety of the South Col as fast as they could. By now, it had really started to snow badly.

During the night we suffered one of the worst storms either of us had ever encountered. About six feet of fresh snow fell on us and we were avalanched in our tent and fortunate not to be swept clean away. It meant that the next morning, instead of going for the summit, we were digging ourselves out and re-erecting the tent. We radioed down to the South Col and, through the climbers there, were able to 'speak' to Tony Streather. We managed to convince him that we had enough food, oxygen and fuel to stay another night and go for the top the next day. Initially, he refused but soon cottoned on to the idea that we were only prepared to go in one direction – and it certainly was not down!

The morning of the sixteenth dawned fine, but in the distance we could see the monsoon rolling in from India. As a result of all the activity the day before, we did not get away until six, late by our standards. Shortly after leaving our lone tent, we each cached half a bottle of oxygen and continued with one cylinder apiece.

By the time we had struggled up to the South Summit, we were counting each hard-earned step. It seemed we were going back two for every three forward. Even breathing was a chore. Already, it was past midday, and we had made a pact before we started that if we were not at the top by then, we would turn back. But safety plans were readily forgotten when we looked ahead to the heavily-corniced ridge connecting us with the Hillary Step and the summit beyond. Selfish ambition and the thought of all the hard work and back-up given us by the rest of the team made up our minds for us. A quick Chinese Parliament and we went on!

I started to lead out the rope, just below the cornice, and remember thinking, 'Somewhere round here must be the snow-hole where Dougal Haston and Doug Scott spent the night.' We both knew that the body of Mick Burke, who was last seen going for the summit on that 1975 Southwest Face Bonington Expedition, was likely to be in it. I didn't relish finding it, but need not have worried: with all this fresh snow about, there was no chance of finding anything.

'*Krrrmp!!*'

My heart leapt into my mouth as the whole precarious slope shifted under my feet. Adrenalin surged into my system like a dam giving way, and my head began to pound violently. I went rigid, holding my breath and not daring to move. My whole body was aching and I remember wondering if Bronco felt the same.

Then, gingerly, I edged on, to the foot of the Hillary step, where I sank gratefully into the snow. I lit two fags for when Bronco joined me.

'Hear that?' I asked him.

'Hear what?'

'The whole lot moved, for chrissake.'

'Didn't go through, though, did it,' he grinned, plumping himself down next to me and taking his cigarette. After five minutes he led off again, up the Step, half on the rock and half in the snow, waist deep, pushing on up.

'Best lead he's ever done,' I thought. I'm not sure I could have done as well after the scare on the cornice.

We seemed to be wading through snow for an eternity before finally landing on the top, where we both collapsed in a heap. It was nearly a quarter past three. We were grinning like crazy, but I could see a tear in Bronc's eye and knew my eyes were streaming, too. We shook hands and hugged each other tightly. No need for words. From relief, from elation, I don't know what, we cried like schoolkids. We had done it!

The moment was all too short-lived. We spent a few minutes scrabbling about looking for the Chinese survey tripod which must have been buried somewhere under all the fresh snow, but the weather was getting worse all the time. It had already robbed us of our summit-view, if not of the summit-feeling. We each took some photos, then started back down.

Leaving an abseil rope on the Hillary Step, we retraced our steps over the South Summit in almost white-out conditions. I took off my glasses to try and see the way. Most of the track was already covered by the new, falling snow. After a while, my eyes felt gritty. I guessed the worst: I was in for another dose of snow-blindness. How easily it's done! Just below the South Summit, at around 28,000 feet, Bronco spotted our spare oxygen cylinders, but there was no way we could go any further. In the even whiteness, everything looked the same. We would either fall off into Tibet, or slip down the Nepalese side into the Western Cwm. There was nothing for it: we were going to have to spend the night out.

Gone now was any euphoria. Survival was the only issue at stake. We were carrying no bivouac equipment because we had wanted to move quickly, and the only food we could muster between us were a few sweets and a sticky old piece of Kendal mint cake that had glued itself to the bottom of one of my pockets. All our liquid had been drunk hours ago.

After digging a small open snowhole for shelter, Sod's Law decreed that the wind changed direction and started to blow straight into it.

Bronc and I sat facing each other, our feet tucked into our climbing sacks, knowing that we would have to see this night out. We dared not go to sleep or we would never have woken up again. As soon as one of us dozed off, the other would attack him to wake him up. We pummelled and massaged each other throughout the night to keep the circulation functioning, but both knew by now there was little we could do to stop the frostbite that was already starting to numb our toes and feet.

When our oxygen began to run out and we were down to the last half cylinder, even by taking off one set of gloves, try as I might, I wasn't able to change over the metal coupling that secures the masking system to the bottle. Without the precious warmth that comes from breathing oxygen, we knew we would die. Bronco did not hesitate. He took off both sets of gloves to give himself added dexterity and quickly made the change. It was the frozen metal to skin contact even for that very short time that resulted in his fingers becoming so badly frostbitten.

While we were sharing this last cylinder of oxygen, passing the mask from one to the other, I was surpised to see Bronc take a few lungfuls and then pass the mask to his left.

'What are you doing?' I asked, for I was sitting to the right of him.

'He needs some as well,' he said.

Throughout the rest of the night, we both felt the warm presence of a third person sharing with us. People have often said to me since, that it's not unusual to hallucinate at altitude without oxygen. Well, we were at altitude, certainly, but we weren't without oxygen – and neither of us believe we were hallucinating. We were being looked after!

Unknown to us, perched as we were above the worst of the weather, the rest of the team were all battened down in their tents undergoing a really bad snowstorm and wondering what had happened to us. Over the radio, Tony had been advised that we had not returned to the top camp, which by now was occupied by John Scott at Pat Gunson, the second summit pair. He told them they should set off for the top the next morning if the weather was OK, keeping a lookout for signs of our bodies, or try to see where we might have fallen off. A feeling of doom had descended over the expedition.

As the light started to turn grey, then brighter as the sun came up early the next morning, so our spirits rose also. Dishevelled, frostbitten, battered by winds and exhausted, we started to descend, both profoundly moved by the night's experience. Someone up there likes us, we both felt sure of it.

Shortly afterwards, we could see the outline of two people struggling up to meet us. When John and Pat spotted us, they immediately abandoned their own chances of getting to the top and assisted us down. By this time, I was totally snowblind and we were both suffering heavy frostbite. On hearing our story, they were the first to congratulate us. I was so overcome, mostly with relief at having met up with other human beings (I don't mind saying there were times during that night I doubted if we ever should), that tears again started to flow down my cheeks.

Down at the top camp they gave us more oxygen and, more importantly, drinks. It had been over twenty-six hours since we had last had any liquid. Over the radio the rest of the team, spread out between all the lower camps, were informed of our success. You could feel the atmosphere of joy and relief even over the airwaves, and no one was more delighted than Tony Streather.

The decision was then taken to withdraw from the mountain, in the light of the fact that Bronco and I were almost casualties and that the monsoon was now upon us. Coming down the Lhotse Face, quite unable to see, gave me a great respect for blind people who take up climbing. Abseiling down the ropes was terrifying. I was put on to a stretcher when we reached the Western Cwm, but quickly abandoned it after hearing all the oops and whoa's from those assisting it over the crevasses.

It took three days to get down to Base Camp, from where we were flown by helicopter to the hospital in Kathmandu. I asked the Doctor how he intended treating us.

He replied, 'Rest only. Until we have to amputate, maybe in two month's time.'

Amputate! I rang for a taxi and discharged us both. We retreated to the Yellow Pagoda Bar. I dare say we looked a right mess, but we did not care. We had climbed our mountain. We were alive, and almost well. That was the good news. The bad news was that we had frostbite on all our toes, frostbitten noses and ears, and Bronco's fingers on his right hand were also all affected. To add to that, I was snowblind and we were both totally exhausted.

I had left England as a healthy eleven-stoner; I was going back a flyweight of eight stone two, but was happy. Ours had been a successful expedition, not only because we had been to the top, but for other reasons too. It had been a happy trip and this I felt was due to three reasons: not least the leadership of Tony Streather. I don't say this just because he chose Bronco and me to be the summit pair, but because he was a very astute man and an accomplished climber; it was his capable hands that had steered a well-managed ship. It helped too that we had no prima donnas in the party. None of us were 'professionals', and therefore had none of the pressures of having to get to the summit and write books about it afterwards. Instead, we could just enjoy the mountain for it own sake. The third thing was the team spirit. Everyone was prepared to work for the common good; there were several self-sacrificing moments I knew I would remember for ever. I thought particularly of the crew in the icefall, who played 'Russian roulette' day after day to keep the route safe for all of us, of the Sherpas who uncomplainingly carried our loads high, of Big John Scott and Pat Gunson, who when they found us at 28,000 feet, took one look at our condition and gave up all hopes of a summit climb themselves, although they were so close, choosing instead to assist us down. Most of all, I remembered Bronco in the snowhole taking off his gloves in order to change the oxygen cylinder, an act that without doubt saved both our lives, but one too for which he would pay for the rest of his days in lost fingers. This was self-sacrifice and friendship of the highest order.

Paying the Price

MOUNTING THE steps of the aircraft in Kathmandu was a harder job than climbing the mountain had been, even with the help of the beautiful Thai Airways hostess. By now my feet had turned really black and any exertion left me breathless and in pain. I was led gently to my seat, presented with an orchid, a copy of that day's *Times* (which carried a report of our expedition), and a glass of chilled champagne. Unused to champagne, I sent it back and ordered beer instead. The doctor had given Bronco and me a supply of morphine-based pills which we were to take every four hours or so to help combat the discomfort of the journey. Coupled with the alcohol, these pills saw to it that both of us were in the air long before the aircraft left the runway. We had said goodbye to our Gurkha friends, old and new, and were soon winging our way home, back to our families in the UK.

I had mixed feelings over the sort of reception that might await me when I arrived home. Somewhere along the years, I had married a Hereford lass, whom I adored, but who was now beginning to change her mind about spending the rest of her life with me. I was her second husband. She already had a small son when we married, and the boy and I had grown very close over the past few years. I looked upon him as my own, and thought ruefully that he at least would be pleased to see me. I was anxious to be home and, looking out of the window, willed the miles away. Perhaps things would be better now; perhaps we could still make a go of it; we would have to see.

The stopover in Bangkok remains a blur in my mind. The rest of the team quickly disappeared into town to celebrate, but whoozy from the effects of all the drugs we had taken, Bronco and I were barely able to stagger on throbbing feet to the nearest restaurant for a meal and a beer, before crashing out for the night. We both thought that as soon as we touched down in the UK, because of the security under which the Regiment normally operates, we would be met by a car and whisked quietly away to Hereford, leaving the others to face all the fuss of cameras and pressmen without us. How wrong we were!

Two wheelchairs were waiting at the foot of the steps of the aircraft to save us the long walk down corridors to the customs hall, but once through there, we found ourselves pushed into a brightly-lit, crowded room. Flash bulbs popped and for forty-five minutes we were the centre of attraction, subject to a barrage of stupid questions. What did our wives think about the climb? Did we see any yetis on top? Not amused, we felt somewhat let down at being submitted to all this exposure at a time when we really were not up to it. But unknown to us, the Regiment had been having a bad press during our absence: an unpleasant border incident in Northern Ireland had hit the headlines, and our climb of Everest, it seemed, had come at just the right time to take off some of the pressure and portray the SAS in more favourable light. It was publicity Bronco and I could well have done without. It meant we became known as members of the SAS and would have to be extra careful in future when working in certain areas of the world.

When eventually we did get back to Hereford, we were given a grand reception by the Regiment and the people of the town. We were treated almost like heroes and carried along at roller-coaster speed, invited to functions all over the country – charity balls, wedding receptions, cocktail parties in our honour – every day something different. It seemed that everyone wanted to know us. I thought it was great, and the only sad thing was that my wife would not come to any of the events with me. She had definitely decided that living with someone like me was too much for her and she had to leave. I could not understand what had gone wrong: I loved her so much, and only now do I wonder if perhaps that was at the root of the matter, maybe she felt stifled by all my love.

I did not know how I was going to live without her; I was devastated, but at the same time, determined not to show it. I made a point of going to every party in town, pretending I couldn't care less. I also started to drink heavily and to drift in and out of relationships, but they brought nothing but disappointment and tears. I was looking for some meaning in life, but it eluded me.

Luckily, I still had a lot of friends, many of whom knew the depth of my hurt and did their best to help me, but in the end I realised that I was the only one who could sort myself out: I had to see things for what they were and adjust accordingly. Life had to go on.

Meanwhile, there was still the frostbite to sort out. The doctors had been able to have a good look at our toes and Bronco's fingers by now, and it was clear they were eventually going to have to amputate. It only remained to decide how much should come off, and when. The answer came from Dr Michael Ward, one of the country's leading authorities on frostbite injury, who kindly agreed to come to Hereford to see us. His advice was that everything should be left alone for two months, because by that time it would be apparent which tissue was going to die off and which could be saved. That seemed fair enough to me. It just meant that we were in for a bit of an uncomfortable couple of months.

The summer of 1976 was a particularly hot one, and pretty soon, as the toes started to get blacker and to separate from the good flesh, they also began to smell terribly. They were, after all, just lumps of rotting flesh attached to the ends of our feet. After the first month, I noticed that tiny maggots were eating at the dead tissue in between the frostbite that had gone hard and the healthy flesh on my foot. A gap was appearing between the two that began to expose the bones of my by-now dead toes. I was naturally quite revolted by this and at first tried to remove them, but eventually came to realise that they were helping to get rid of all the decaying flesh and, however disturbing, ought to be left to get on with their grisly job.

Every other day the regimental medic would pop around to my quarters and take photos of my rapidly decaying feet. He wanted to ensure there would be a pictorial record of the various stages for teaching purposes in future; no opportunity is ever wasted in the SAS!

While I sat around doing very little besides waiting for the operation, I decided to learn another language to fill in some of the daylight hours. Arabic was my main foreign tongue, but as I had picked up a smattering of German on my trips to the Alps, that was what I would attempt to master next. The Education Officer from the Regiment very kindly supplied me with a series of books and tapes, from which to learn the basics. It helped take away a little of the boredom, but being still affected by the break-up of my marriage, I found myself looking forward to the evenings when friends would pop round and take me into town for a drink or a party. One of these parties was to prove a rather amusing and somewhat painful experience.

There were about twenty people in one of the flats in town which was renowned for its wild parties. This night, however, we were all sitting quietly on the floor in a circle, chatting and drinking and telling each other lies. Several of the girls were nurses from the local hospital, whom I had got to know over the years. They were a jolly crowd and good fun to be with, but nurses do have a tendency to be inquisitive and very down-to-earth, and as I was squatting on the floor with my feet stretched out in front of me, swathed in light gauze dressings to hide the discoloured toes, one of them turned to me and asked if she could have a look. She had, she said, never seen a case of frostbite before. I warned her it was not very pretty, but she didn't seem to mind, so eager to oblige and numbed by the effects of alcohol, I began carefully to discard the dressings. As the fresh air got to my feet, I noticed she reeled slightly at the smell. The other people were all looking pretty disgusted by this time, but full credit to her, my nurse hardly batted an eyelid as she knelt to study my gangrenous toes.

'For crying out loud, cover those things up!' someone shouted, as a trolley was wheeled in bearing a meal of curry.

It smelt delicious and I was hungry, but instead of helping me replace the dressings, the girl began asking about the maggots and wondered if she might be allowed to actually touch my toes so that she could know what they felt like. By now the toes were all hard and wrinkled and completely dead.

'Some women are never satisfied,' I muttered to myself, as she gently touched the dead tissue.

'Would it hurt if I squeezed them?' she enquired, and being pumped full of painkillers and booze, I told her to help herself.

The next thing I knew, a sharp pain was shooting up through my ankle and I looked down to see her fainting at my feet. She had tweaked my big toe hard and it had crumbled away in her fingers. Now it was lying, forlornly, on the carpet – although not for long. The dog saw to that. Two more girls fainted and several people were sick. It was all very embarrassing and the only good thing to come out of it was that there were not many customers for the curry. I had two helpings before falling soundly asleep on the floor.

Bronco and I had deliberately not gone to a military hospital for our treatment. We knew if we did that we were likely to be pensioned off as disabled once we'd had our operations, deemed unfit for further service. So, to avoid this, we had arranged through friends of Dick Hardie, the expedition's doctor, to have the deed done by a local surgeon at the hospital in Hereford. Frostbite was not something that is dealt with an awful lot in small market towns, especially not in the middle of summer. Because Bronco would need to have the fingers of his right hand amputated as well as all his toes, it was decided between us that it was only fair I should act as the guinea pig and have my operation first. No one was clear how much of the toes and forefeet would need to be removed in order to allow sufficient good tissue to be left at the end of the foot to effect a healthy suture line. That was something the surgeon, a Scot, could only find out with practice and he would have to practise on me.

The night before the operation, my friends threw a grand party for me to say farewell to my defunct digits. Hungover the next morning, I steered my wheelchair into the ward and presented myself to sister. She was a charming lady who informed me that they were all expecting me, showed me to my bed and jokingly warned me against the dangers of her nurses taking off the rest of my toes before I got into theatre. She had obviously heard of the escapade at the party.

The rest of that first day was spent getting to know the other patients and staff; they all seemed very cheerful and I knew that even under the circumstances, I was in for a pleasant stay. About twenty people turned up to see me at visiting time, all carrying six-packs. The theory is that alcohol is one of the best treatments for frostbite, as it dilates the blood vessels and promotes circulation through damaged tissues. It was the first time I have actually been encouraged to drink beer for my health. Ward sister was a good soul and only began to remonstrate when one of my visitors pulled out a guitar and started to play folksongs. Then, in the interest of the other patients, as she put it, she had me transferred to a private side ward, one which even had a fridge to keep the beer cool.

The next morning I was given a pre-med injection to calm me down in preparation for the operation, then wheeled into theatre by one of the nurses I knew from my party nights. I held out my arm to the anaesthetist, who inserted a needle which made the world go away. My head seemed to be swaying from side to side; there was a ringing in my ears and I fancied I saw myself hobbling along a dusty lane on crutches, dragging my useless feet behind me. Coming towards me was the surgeon, walking his dog, and he stopped and chatted for a while.

'I don't know how much of your feet I am going to have to cut away,' he told me, 'until we get you into the theatre. I will obviously only take what I have to, but you must prepare yourself for the eventuality that you may have to spend the rest of your life on crutches or in a wheelchair.'

My voice was full of venom as I yelled at him, 'No, no, I won't! I don't care what you say, I won't use sticks.'

'What's the matter, Mr Stokes? Come on now, wake up. Wake up for me.'

The voice of the kind ward-sister wafted into my ears from a long way off. It washed over me as I blinked open my eyes and looked into her smiling face. I realised that once again I was back in the tiny side ward and my bed. I moved my head and looked around, then putting my elbows underneath me, lifted myself up. There was a sudden searing pain all the way from my feet to my knees. The last time I felt anything as remotely painful as that was when I had been shot through the knee in Dhofar, and I was not even sure that had hurt as much as my feet hurt now.

I wanted to know how much had been taken away – or more importantly, how much I had got left. The sister explained that I still had half my feet and that the doctor was pleased with the way things had gone. I fell back against the pillow as the effect of the drug chased away the burning pain. I felt better now that it was done. I was clean again, now that the maggot-infested, black, horrible mass of gangerous flesh had been removed; and letting out a sigh, I fell back into an exhausted sleep.

It was over, though poor Bronc still had it to come. When I next awoke it was visiting time and among my visitors were my Mum and Dad, and my brothers and sister, who had travelled down from Birmingham. I could see the strain in my Mum's face and tried to put her mind at rest by telling her that everything would be all right and that before she knew it, I would be back climbing again. She attacked me verbally, as only mothers can, and told me that I must on no account climb again, that I should take up a more sedate hobby.

Bronco had his amputations the next morning. His feelings of relief at being free from the affected parts mirrored my own, but of course he was going to suffer pain not only from his feet but from his hand, too. His fingers had been removed at the end-joints, but more of his feet had been saved owing to the new-found experience of the surgeon. I was glad that I had been the guinea pig. Poor Bronc was going to have a harder time coping with things than me, and even a few centimetres could make a big difference. I tried to cheer him up, as he lay groggily recovering from the effects of the anaesthetic.

'Never mind, lad,' I joked, 'look on the bright side! I will be able to get a job as a male model, modelling shoes for Mothercare, and you can always be a shorthand typist in a small arms factory!'

During the next few days I became more and more determined to walk. The morning when Bronco had gone down for his amputations I had tried to stand up by the side of my bed and as the blood rushed to my feet, was given a sharp warning that it was going to be a long, hard, painful business.

I made gradual progress over the following weeks and was eventually getting about on my own with the aid of crutches. It became a race now between Bronc and me to see who could make it the furthest without having to rest our throbbing feet. When the time came for us to leave the hospital, it was obvious I was not yet ready to manage on my own in my own house, and it was lucky that two friends of mine, Norman and Jenny, were prepared to take me in.

Living in their house meant that I could get to see the little boy whom I had looked upon as my son, and he was frequently allowed to come up and visit me. Losing him was going to be the hardest part of my marriage break-up, but I knew that in order to be fair to my ex-wife, I was going the have to distance myself from him eventually. He still saw and loved his natural father and I realised that if she ever married again, it was going to be an impossibly confusing situation for a six-year-old to accept. I cried often during the ensuing years as this became the case.

Those years were full of pain for me as I slowly learned to walk without crutches and finally to throw away my stick and walk into town unaided. I felt ten feet tall as I shuffled about the streets, attempting to walk naturally. I had been warned that my balance would be affected by having no toes, and I must expect to fall over fairly frequently; stories were constantly being related to me about some great cricketer who having lost his big toe, was unable to bowl again; but shrugging off all these old wives' tales, I remembered reading of Douglas Bader, the wartime pilot, who had lost both his legs and yet still walked and flew aircraft. All I had lost were toes and a kneecap. I had coped with the loss of the kneecap sufficiently to manage to climb Everest, so I was damned sure that ten tiny toes (nine of which now sat in a jar in a medical museum in London) were not going to stop me. Determined to walk properly and do again all the things I had been able to do before, I set about a daily physiotherapy programme.

The day would begin with a swim which helped to soften the hard scar tissue that had formed along the front of my foot. This was followed by three or four hours down at the hospital, learning to walk in a natural way, and two hours touching the end of my sensitive feet in an attempt to harden them up. Gradually, I started to win. My walk was slow, but not too far removed from that of a normal person with toes. There was a tendency for me to stand on my heels, which resulted in bad back pains, until I pushed through the pain barrier and forced myself to put more and more weight on to the tender bits on the front of my feet.

Six months after having the toes removed, I attempted my first run. I launched myself forward, as I would normally do, and let out a scream as my foot hit the floor and a sharp pain shot through it. Telling myself not to be such a moaner, I moved forward a few more steps. Each one was agonising. 'Just two more,' I thought. Then, two more after that, then one more, and so it went on. I stopped, sweating and in pain, and looked back towards my starting point. I had covered less than twenty feet, but was very pleased with myself. I may not have looked very stylish, but then again, I never had been.

In fact, as I increased my distance over the next months, the style, if anything, got worse. The important thing was that I was on my feet and running. That was progress.

During these early months, Bronco and I were presented with our British Empire Medals at a small 'do' at the SAS camp in Hereford. A few days after this we received a letter from an organisation called RADAR in London, informing us that we had been made 'Men of the Year' and could we make it to the Savoy Hotel for a dinner to mark the occasion?

In some ways, looking back and reflecting on the events of this period of my life, I possibly was affected by city influences. I was out partying every night and had grown very 'hard' emotionally. Life consisted of booze, good times (that weren't really good times), and dozens of different girlfriends. I was, I think, trying to prove to myself, after a broken marriage (my one and only failure in life, so far), that I was still attractive and was not going to have to go through the rest of my days being rejected by people. Half of my problem was that I had lost touch with nature. I was no longer off out into the hills where I could sit on my own, watching some sunrise or sunset to put life's problems into perspective. Instead, I was too wrapped up in feeling sorry for myself. Things, I knew, would have to change.

Unknown to me, it was going to take some five years before I would be able to get out and climb again to anything like the standard that was acceptable to me. During those years I was to do many different tasks. The first, and biggest one though, was to convince myself and other members of the Regiment that I was still capable of carrying my weight and able to put something back into the SAS. To dispel any fears as to my staying power, I latched on to the Selection Course and did some of the marches over the Brecon Beacons with the new recruits, culminating in the endurance march of eighty-five miles. No one could now point a finger at me and say that I was not up to it. But even more important, I had proved to myself that I was still capable of doing it. My timings had been slow, but that apart, I had convinced myself that I still deserved to be a member of the Regiment. I had always been a hard disciplinarian and the first to denounce someone if they weren't up to their job. I was big enough to realise that the same set of rules also applied to me.

Having been in on the setting-up of the first anti-hijacking team, I was given the job of training teams of the younger members of the Regiment in the skills required to carry out such tasks. My days would now be full of instructional classes teaching Close Quarter Battle (CQB), hostage and prisoner handling, how to enter buildings from above and below, the art of abseiling down the side of high-rise flats and forcing entry through windows without harming yourself, as well as a thousand and one other things. I prided myself on my ability and agility, which enabled me to enter a room full of people with a loaded pistol, shooting at targets of terrorists as I went, and extract those taking the part of hostages unharmed. Most of all, though, it was very rewarding for me to see the enthusiasm with which some of these younger SAS soldiers learned their lessons and even more rewarding to watch, some years later, that training put into practice as some of them stormed the Iranian Embassy in London.

It was picture-book stuff, straight from the training manual. The equipment that they were now working with was a far cry from what we had used in response to the first ever hijacking of an aeroplane in the UK. The vehicles in which we then raced to Heathrow were underpowered and overloaded with our cumbersome ladders and armament of gas masks, hand grenades (designed temporarily to blind and deafen), and other associated equipment. Screeching to a halt on the apron of the main runway at Heathrow, we were led by the police to a hangar for briefing and to prepare ourselves for assault. A Ugandan Asian, we learned, had boarded a British aircraft abroad and pulling out a pistol, informed the cabin staff and pilot that he also had a bomb in his travelling bag, which he fully intended to detonate unless he was flown to the UK. The aircraft had arrived and so had we. The policy of the Government was, quite rightly, that Britain would not treat with terrorists holding people and property hostage, and that if negotiations of a peaceful nature failed to defuse the situation, then the leash should be slipped from our necks and we would be allowed to go in to rectify the situation – permanently. We had reached that stage, and four of us now stood at the rear of the aircraft, one behind the other, gas masks on, pistols in hand, listening intently to a running commentary of what was happening inside over our tiny radio earpieces. Opening an emergency door at the rear of the airplane, one by one we crept aboard, hearts beating fast and fearful of making any noise that would spook the Asian, who now stood only feet away from us on the other side of a loo door in the main cabin. One false move and we knew he would start shooting the hostages, and might even detonate the bomb and blow us all to hell! I had already made a plan in my own mind that if I heard anything that indicated his intention to start shooting, I was going to push open the door, step inside, move to the left of the door and put two bullets into his chest.

In situations like this, events change so rapidly that the final word to move in is given by a controller who is positioned where he has access to all the relevant up-to-the-minute information and a hotline to Government. Crackling over the radio earpieces, came the words that we had all been waiting for, 'Stand by! Stand by!'

We were poised in anticipation for the 'Go!' but the word that would have sent us hurtling into the fuselage of the aircraft to take the terrorist didn't come. Instead, the Controller was screaming, 'Stop! Stop! Stop! and telling us that things on the aircraft had taken a turn for the better, and that we should get off as soon as we could without being discovered. Making our secret exit, we returned to the hangar to be told that they had negotiated the release of the hostages in exchange for an onward flight to the continent. We were all still in a state of wound-up aggression and very frustrated, until we learned the next stage of the plan. The aircraft would be allowed to take off, but instead of flying to the continent, it would gently make a slow circle of the UK and land at Stansted Airport, where we would again be lying in wait. Boarding another aircraft with all our equipment, we jetted across to Stansted.

The whole area had been cordoned off by Police, so that we could contain the situation. When, eventually, the aircraft drew to a halt on a section of the airstrip, away from the main terminal, the illusion of this being an airfield somewhere on the continent was shattered by a uniformed policeman who walked past the stairs that had been positioned at the doorway of the aircraft. Totally devastated by this turn of events, the Asian called to the policeman and gave himself up, handing over the box of electrical wires that had been his bomb and a wooden replica pistol. It had all been a bluff to get into the UK. All the man wanted was to become a British citizen. He would probably never know how close he had come to owning his own six-foot plot in Britain.

Having done 'team jobs' all over the world, trained bodyguards and actually done some bodyguard duties, one of my next jobs was to instruct on the Bodyguarding Courses (BGs). One course I ran was for members of the Royal Bodyguard, all big strapping lads from the Police Force. The courses were particularly interesting as the students were so varied – some were American soldiers who arrived full of big ideas and with even bigger pistols. It was not long before the inevitable happened and one of our American students was picked up by the local police in Hereford as he was sitting in a pub, packing his Colt 45. Because we tried to make our training exercises as realistic as possible by practising armed VIP escort in local hotels, restaurants and pubs, this character had assumed that we all went round carrying guns all the time. It was quite embarrassing having to collect him from the local jail and explain to the Duty Sergeant, whom I knew personally, that Wyatt Earp here was temporarily attached to the SAS, and that I would see that this sort of thing did not happen again.

One of the things we always stressed to our students was the importance of keeping weapons concealed. Carrying out an exercise in one of the local hotels – the object being simply to move in a public place without drawing attention to yourself – this lesson of keeping weapons hidden away was perfectly illustrated. Having followed his 'VIP' into the bar of the hotel, one of our young BGs ordered a drink from the girl serving cocktails. As he reached into his inside jacket pocket for his wallet, the girl saw his pistol tucked nicely away in his shoulder holster. Thinking this must be some sort of hold-up, she snatched up a soda siphon, hit the fire alarm and while showering him with water started to scream for help. Falling about with laughter, we managed to rescue our six-foot charge from the wrath of this quick-thinking young woman and calm her down sufficiently to explain the situation.

As the scar tissue on my feet grew harder, so I was able to do more and more varied jobs. For a year I travelled around the world advising on security matters in embassies and British consulates. One of the countries I visited was Argentina, where I learned of the claim made on the Falkland Islands. I was not to know that years later, this insight was going to stand me in good stead during a small war. I found the Argentinians to be very hospitable, if a little excitable at times. On a subsequent trip I trained a group of police bodyguards and got an inside peek at the problems faced by the people of that country.

I had heard of people disappearing in the middle of the night, never to be seen again, but did not really believe the stories until I was running the course along the banks of the River Plate one morning and stopped to watch as two bodies were recovered from the water. Both had gunshot wounds in the back of their heads. The police politely ushered me on, saying that it was the work of gangsters.

I might have believed this, had I not been the subject of a beating by a police crew myself a few nights earlier. I had been out for a meal and a beer in the White Fly, a very popular, cheap restaurant in downtown Buenos Aires, and was returning to my hotel when I was stopped by two policemen, who informed me that they were special police. They hit me on the back with a long night stick and forced me to spread-eagle against a wall. I was generally roughed up until they had satisfied themselves that I was a British subject, as I claimed, and not some 'hoodlum' or 'fascist pig'. Holding myself back from punching one of them, I was informed in no uncertain manner that if I did throw a punch, I just might find myself in the river with a bullet in my head. It made me glad to be a Brit, and not living under oppressive military law.

Around this time I also went to Northern Ireland, where I worked as a liaison officer for the Army and the Police Force. It was a sad time for me as my picture of Ireland was one of green hills, folksongs and friendly people. That was the way I remembered it from my Green Jacket years as a young soldier. Now, when I returned, all I could see was hatred and mistrust, a nation divided against itself.

Testing myself to the limit in different 'theatres' of the world to see how my feet stood up, I moved from a job training the anti-hijack team of a friendly Sheikh-dom in the Gulf to one of Tracking Instruction in the jungles of Malaya and Brunei. Gradually, I had proved to myself that I was as good at most things without toes as I had been with them – well, almost.

I found that when it came to climbing hard rock I was still prone to a lot of pain from my feet. I had begun making short visits to the Yat whenever I was home, to attempt some of the easier climbs I had done years ago, and I was wearing the same old climbing boots as I had then. It hurt, but the will to climb was just too strong. Pain or no pain, I was going to get back into the climbing game. My pride was injured more than my body as I constantly fell off easy rock pitches when the toes of my boots folded upwards as I put my full weight on them. People had been right when they told me that it would be very difficult to climb hard again without toes. Modern technology saved the day for me with the introduction of rigid-soled plastic double-boots. I found that so long as I put soft insoles inside them, I could stand the discomfort, and that the boots compensated for my lack of foot-length. I was back on the right road to the big hills.

It was during this period, too, in 1978, that I met a girl with whom I fell madly in love. I had promised myself that I would never again trust another woman, but as soon as I saw this one, I knew that she was for me. Her name was Lynn, and she worked part-time in a pub that I used to frequent. She was a lot younger than I was, had blonde hair which reached half-way down her back, beautiful big hazel eyes and a ready smile that lit up the whole place. She so captivated me, I just had to take her out, and invited her to dinner one night. I had little trouble finding girlfriends in those days, and was quite unprepared for her reaction to my invitation. She turned me down flat. Not being one to take no for an answer, I persisted for months, but whether I asked her to lunch, dinner, a party, the movies or for a drive in the country, the reply was always the same. 'No, thank you. I'm sorry.'

I began to think that there must be something wrong with me after all. Daily, I would send her roses and gifts – all to no avail. I bribed the owner of the pub not to order her a taxi to take her home after work, so that I could drive her myself. That, too, failed. It gradually began to sink into my thick skull that she really did not want anything to do with me and I was making a fool of myself. I forced myself to stop asking her out. For the life of me, I will never understand the logic of human relationships, but blow me if two nights later, on her first night off, she didn't come over to me and ask me to take her for a drink!

I was overjoyed and it must have shown in my face, because it drew the remark, 'You can take that smirk off your face, too! I'm only doing it 'cos I feel sorry for you.' But from that night on, friendship grew to love on her part too, and the happy ending was that we eventually married and had two wonderful boys.

Sam and Ben are as different in character as can be: Sam is a wiry, agile thinker, no one steals a march on him; while Ben, our youngest, walks through walls and breaks his Tonka toys. Lynn has helped, too, with my rehabilitation. Being a runner herself, she accompanied and encouraged me on many training runs. She drew the line at climbing after an epic walk along the Snowdon Pyg Track one winter's day, but recognising my need to get out into the hills, she has always helped with the organisation of my many climbing expeditions, and cheerfully 'holds the fort' while I am away. For that, and so much more, I love her more than I can say.

During this period when I was teaching and training others and based in Hereford, I was called out from home one evening and asked to help with a rescue in the Brecon Beacons. One of our selection courses had run into trouble when the lads were caught out in a rather bad snowstorm over the tops of the Pen y Fan area. Most of them managed to make it down to the roadhead safely and sought shelter in surrounding farms, but there were a few people still unaccounted for. Our job was to scour the route taken by the course in the hope that we could locate them.

Putting together a team of ten well-equipped men, I led them to a starting point where the missing people were last seen. As I plodded up the side of the hill with the wind and snow blowing hard in my face, I tried to recollect when I was last out in the hills in weather as bad as this. Not for a long time, certainly. Dark clouds hung full of snow in the chilly night sky. We had been informed by two of the Selection Course members who had made it to a telephone box that one of the officers accompanying the group had been taken ill and had collasped on the top of the ridge somewhere. I did not hold out much hope of finding him this night.

Slowly, following footprints in the snow, we wound our way up the track that led to the top. Once there, the prints showed signs of confusion, with footmarks disappearing in all directions. This was obviously the point at which the weather had got so bad that the decision was taken to descend rapidly into the valleys. In a bomb-burst of snowprints, people had split up into smaller groups and scurried off the hill. There was one set of footprints that appeared to be following an erratic path, running parallel to a set that were quite steady. I decided to follow these, and not long after, came upon a discarded brick and bits of ballast that had been thrown out of a rucksack to lighten the load. Several yards further on was the impression in the snow where someone had stumbled and fallen to the ground. I started to fear the worse. Looking ahead along the ridge, starlight reflecting off the snow revealed the shape of a small snow igloo, about half a mile away. Following the tracks, which by now told me that one of the people was being half-carried, half-dragged, we neared the snow-covered mound.

Not wanting to shock the occupants with our sudden arrival, I started to hail them, 'Hello, the snowhole – hello, the snowhole!'

Concerned at not receiving any response, I moved in closer, calling out as I went. Then, kneeling outside, I could see the construction was a circle of snow blocks covered over by an old poncho shelter.

'Anybody at home?' I queried.

'I'm all right, I'm all right,' came a feeble reply from within.

Relieved, I asked how many were inside. 'Two of us,' said the voice, 'but *he* hasn't moved for quite some time.' There was just an edge of hysteria in his tone.

I was anxious not to let the wind into the hastily-built shelter and opened up a gap at the top, just big enough to pass in a cup of hot tea from my flask and to enable me to feel the still form of the person next to our survivor.

'Drink this!' I said gently, as I withdrew my hand. The other man had felt quite lifeless and cold. I would have to get inside and examine him further to see if anything could be done to save him.

Telling the others to erect the two tents we had brought with us, I crawled into the shelter, where a thorough examination confirmed my worst fears. The officer was dead, and had been for some time. This fact was confirmed for me by the attitude of the other occupant, who was lying inside his sleeping bag with his back to the lifeless figure. I have seen situations like this several times over the years and recognised that the man had switched himself off from the reality of things that were happening around him. He had probably been like it for some hours. The best thing that I could do was to get him out of the shelter and into one of the tents with the rest of the blokes as soon as possible.

Shuffling out of his sleeping bag, he slid out of the tiny confinement of the snowhole, still with his back to the body of the dead officer, and taking a breath of fresh air once he was outside, was escorted into a tent. He was put into some warm, dry clothing and given more hot, sweet tea to sip. Soon he began to relax, openly relieved to find himself once again in the company of people.

With the situation contained and no one else in immediate danger, we radioed to the base from where the search was being co-ordinated, requesting a helicopter pick us up at first light the next morning. It had been a tragic end, made all the worse by the realisation that they had done all the right things by building a shelter to get out of the wind, and getting into their sleeping bags to keep warm. None the less, it served us all a sharp reminder not to take the hills for granted. When the weather gets harsh on the mountains, the only thing you can do is get off them with all speed.

Shortly after this incident, I was informed that I was to be posted to a training school in Bavaria for two years in order to set up a winter warfare course. Before I left, I managed to wangle a trip to Canada where I really would be able to test my feet, both climbing and skiing.

Working from a base hut at a place called Mosquito Creek, we climbed some of the easier peaks in the area and then set off on skis for a tour of the high peaks. I had read somewhere of a ski-mountaineering trek which traversed these hills from the Bow Valley to the Yo Ho Valley, and took the opportunity to follow the same route. Loaded up with climbing ropes, food, fuel and maps, I arranged for a vehicle to pick us up at a pre-arranged rendezvous on the other side of the mountains.

With skins fixed firmly to the bottom of our skis, we moved off in single file over the ice and snow covering Bow Lake. The weather was perfect, with clear air, crisp white untrodden snows, and the sun hanging in the pale blue yonder warmed our backs. Navigating our way up through the Bow Valley, we started to zigzag up the ever-steepening mountainside until we emerged high on a wide plateau which overlooked the lowlands spread out at our feet. Lush pine forests gave way to open riverlines snaking their way down into the valleys below. On our way up, we had disturbed deer that had skittered quickly away from us, and crossed the tracks of two bears and numerous small animals out foraging for scraps of food. Now, as we sat on our packs basking in the sunshine, watching an eagle as it lazily sailed above us searching out easy prey for its dinner, I marvelled at the beauty of nature, as I always do, and thanked God that I was now fit and fortunate enough to be here in this place.

For three days we traversed these mountains, skiing effortlessly down slopes that had not been skied on for months, then climbing back up to the rock bands on our skins. We scaled peaks by day, spending the nights in huts dotted along the route. We were completely alone in the mountains. It had the feel of pioneering to it. In reality, of course, the route had been skied many times before, but to us it did not matter. Today it was ours and life was definitely worth living.

The nights in the huts would be spent chatting and watching the sun go down over the peaks as they changed colour from brilliant orange through to grey, and then the night air would turn bitterly cold as it became dark. Our meals were composed mostly of spaghetti or other pasta, as this tended to be the lightest to carry. The problem was, of course, that this type of food has a tendency to fill you up straightaway, but half an hour later you are starving again. This was certainly the case with Archie, Big Mac and Ginge, who were all big lads and took a lot of feeding.

On the last day we descended a steep-sided cliff and crossed a frozen waterfall which proved to be the highlight of the trip for all of us. We fetched up in an untidy heap at the bottom of the hill!

We had really enjoyed ourselves and had only to complete the long, easy run down along the valley bottom to link up with our vehicle, which would be waiting at the rendezvous. Following the track which cut through the pine trees lining the river, we were rounding a sharp bend when we all pulled up sharply, one behind the other, confronted by a fully-grown bear. On reflection, it must have been the sight of all of us bumping into one another and falling over at his feet, that caused the bear to turn into the trees and amble away, shaking his big head as if in bewilderment. Perhaps he had a sense of humour.

Days later, as we packed up in preparation for our journey home, I reflected happily on our adventures. It had been an exciting few weeks. I had coped all right and the thought that I couldn't keep out of my mind now was, 'I wonder if I could still hack it on a *really* big hill? Everest again, maybe?'

After two short weeks in Hereford, Lynn and I started packing to move to my new post in Germany at the Long Range Reconnaissance Patrol School. It did not take long for me to settle into the job after we had driven across France and Germany to get there. To be situated not too far from the Bodensee (Lake Constance), Europe's largest inland lake, was for me an ideal spot. The Bavarian mountains were less than an hour's drive away and the borders with France and Switzerland about the same distance. Lynn had to put up with quite a lot during this period as much of the time I was away, running courses up in the hills, or working all hours day and night.

The officer in charge of the school had a bee in his bonnet about getting as many students through the course as possible.

It doubtless looked good on his annual report, but resulted in some rather embarrassing moments for me. Being an international school, it was our job to train the special forces from all the NATO countries. One winter I had thirty soldiers, who had travelled from as far afield as Greece and America, standing outside my office waiting to participate in a winter warfare course. This course would involve skiing, snow-holing and cross-country tactical movement on skis, as well as a host of other skills needed to work and fight in snow conditions. I had prepared all the equipment needed weeks before: food, transport, accommodation, tentage, everything was ready. We had all we needed – except the snow.

I had been insisting for weeks that the course be cancelled

because of the absence of any white stuff, but no, the Rupert knew better.

'It will snow by tomorrow,' he said, sending me off into the beautiful green hills to await his prediction. Needless to say, after three days of this, I threw a wobbler and sent them all home with my apologies for the stupidity of the school's commander, who, to my eternal shame, was an SAS colonel.

Before leaving the UK, I had completed a German-language course which stood me in good stead as the German sergeant-major who was working alongside me spoke little English. I got on well with Hans, who helped me with my German and introduced me to many local climbers and leaders of other mountain training centres in the area. He was a qualified mountain guide himself and many an hour was spent recalling incidents that had taken place during the times spent learning our skills. Hans had trained with the German Army Mountain Guides' School and I had started at the Ecole de Haute Montagne, the French guides' school in Chamonix, where I had completed both climbing and skiing phases.

Hans had laughed at my stories when I related them in our little office in the LRRP School, and had his own tales to tell. It was then that I confided in him of the plan Bronco and I had to go back and climb Everest once again. It was now five years since we had reached the top, and my feet had stood up well to the bashing I had been giving them over the last few years. It had been painful, but the urge and need to climb again was proving too strong to concede to the pain. I was going to have to get on to the big hill once again. Hans expressed his concern and asked whether I was sure I was ready yet?

The truth was that I wasn't sure, but the only way to find out would be by trying. We would see.

North to Alaska

THE MAIN regret Bronco and I felt after our ascent of Everest in 1976 was that the adventure had not been shared by the rest of our mates. We had been the only members of the SAS on the team. Obviously it was our climbing ability that ensured we were selected – although I have to say sheer bloody cheek played a part in it, too – but all the time, through the preparation period and during the trip itself, we couldn't help thinking that a unique training opportunity such a climb would be for the Regiment. How marvellous it would be if we could find enough skills within the unit to be able to mount a totally self-contained SAS Everest Expedition.

This was our dream. We voiced it first one sunny afternoon in the Annapurna Tea House, Kathmandu, just before we flew home from Everest, but it took seven years before we were in a position to make the dream come true. All that time, through the long years of rehabilitation after our frostbite amputations, it remained a source of inspiration in the backs of our minds.

In 1978 Bronco was flying back from Germany and happened to find himself sitting next to a senior officer in the Canadian Army. The conversation turned very quickly to climbing. Why didn't the SAS come to Canada for their high altitude practice, the officer asked, the Rockies would afford an ideal training ground.

Bronco wasted no time in following up the idea, and before long an exercise had been set up to enable four Mountain Troops to train in the Rocky Mountains, with Bronco and I going along as supervisors.

This proved a huge success, as well as being a real morale booster for the pair of us, showing we were fit enough once more for high altitude climbing in harsh conditions. But what was especially exciting was the fact it had demonstrated that there really was sufficient talent and enthusiasm within the Regiment for an expedition to be put together which stood a good chance of reaching the top of the world's highest peak.

All the while Bronco and I had been laying our plans for a Himalayan expedition, in traditional SAS style we had not taken any of the officers into our confidence; yet we would need official sanction if we wanted to pursue the idea further. This was finally secured at the end of a period of jungle training when our CO, Colonel Mike, a good sort, came out to visit the squadron. Bronco and I went out with him for a Chinese meal; we saw to it that he was well plied with the local grog before Bronco broached the subject of the expedition. His reply was enthusiastic: 'What are you waiting for?' he asked. 'Get on with it and let us see something down on paper.'

Never one to rush for a pen, this was the moment to tell Bronco he could be leader of the expedition. I was happy to be his deputy, I assured him, but it was the leader's job to organise the paperwork.

Outline plans were drafted: we still wanted to keep Everest as our objective, although we were not too particular about route. We needed permission from various levels of the military hierarchy, and deliberately kept the budget low so as not to raise any resistance on that score. We also needed, of course, a permit to climb the mountain. Signals were sent to both Nepal and China to see when we might be allowed to go. Nepal's reply arrived back first and it was not promising: the first available date was for a spring climb in 1986. That might be fine for the Regiment, but it looked hopeless as far as Bronco and I were concerned. We could well have left the SAS by then, pensioned off as old men. However, within days, an answer came from Peking, too. The Chinese Mountaineering Association were keen to help, and (for a price) a booking could be made for the spring or autumn of 1984. We cabled back accepting the spring option and from that moment on it was all systems go to get the team and equipment organised in time.

Bronco and I were invited to go to Peking to sort out the details with the CMA about getting the equipment into China, along with paying a deposit on the booking. This trip clashed badly with an unforeseen happening: the Falklands War. However, a week was set aside which did not interfere with the task in hand, and the two of us set off for Peking as planned. There seemed to be two options for getting the outfit to base camp: either we could drive in from

Nepal and then march up the final miles to the foot of the mountain, or we could have everything flown into Lhasa and trucked to Everest from there. The negotiations continued throughout the week, interspersed with trips to the Great Wall and various other monuments, until on the final day, all the relevant documents were signed and a celebratory dinner was given us by the five officials of the CMA.

Returning to England through Hong Kong, we went to the army HQ there to let them know we were passing through and to check if any messages had come for us. When the Duty Training Officer was confronted by two SAS soldiers casually mentioning that they were en route from Peking, his face went ashen and we were whisked off at once to the intelligence section. The situation was quickly clarified, but there were a few raised eyebrows.

With approval for the expedition from the Ministry of Defence, and the Chinese anxious to assist, Bronco and I now had to finalise the thousand and one finer details to ensure the best chance of success. But first, we had a small war to attend to – the Falklands War.

Not the least of our problems as far as Everest was concerned was how the heck were we going to scrape together the £130,000 we needed for the expedition. I tried a bit of optimistic realism.

'Right,' I said. 'Each of us puts in a month's wages. We get a grant from the Army Mountaineering Association – they should be good for five hundred or so. We talk nicely to the bloke who holds the bread in the Mount Everest Foundation – he's bound to slip us a thousand. Then we make a big list of 'Potential Sponsors' and get our Ruperts to approach them personally. Come on, Bronc, we're almost there!'

Well, that proved a trifle naïve. We had a long, long way to go even after donations from various trust funds and well-wishers began to trickle in. The name of the Regiment was always good for a few bob, but we would not have had such an easy ride if it were not for George Williams turning up like the knight in shining armour depicted on his Anglian Windows glazing-firm's logo.

'How much do you require? A hundred thousand? OK, you've got it!' With not so much as a blink of the eyelash!

We could not believe our luck. George had started his business life in the Worcester area and felt an affinity for the Hereford-based team. The first time I met him, I knew this was a man I could get on with, and that was not just because he was the man behind the cash. He was a self-made business man, spoke straight and dealt straight; there was never any beating about the bush with George.

That was the first hurdle overcome. Next, we needed a patron. Although it was never publicly announced, His Royal Highness Prince Charles agreed to support our expedition. Bronco and I had both had the pleasure of meeting his Highness on a number of occasions in the past, and found him extremely knowledgeable about Himalayan mountaineering and indeed about climbing in general. Someone else we approached for patronage was Colonel David Stirling, the founder of the SAS. I had seen him several times on his visits to Hereford, but never met him personally; I was, therefore, a little apprehensive when Bronco and I were shown into his office in London to lay our proposal before him. I need not have worried. With a ready smile, he said he was honoured that we should have asked him, and promised to do all he could to assist the expedition. From the wistful look in his eye, we even got the impression he would have liked to come with us.

Bronco and I were over the moon. Ever since I had read the book *The Phantom Major*, telling how David Stirling first started the SAS during the Second World War and equipped it to fight and destroy convoys and aircraft behind enemy lines, I had had enormous respect for this man. To be sitting now in his office, listening to him retell some of the old stories, egged on by Bronc and I like two children eager for more, was a situation I could scarcely believe. Over the next five years, however, I got to know him a lot better, and he was to help and guide me through many aspects of business protocol in my dealings with sponsors and film people. I learned, too, that before the war he had been quite a climber himself, and had once even planned an attempt on Everest, which was still unclimbed at the time.

'What happened? Why on earth didn't you go?' I wanted to know.

He smiled. 'A man called Mr Hitler started up a spot of bother, and I had to go and set up the SAS instead.'

Now I knew why he had showed so much enthusiasm for our enterprise, and wondered what it would have been like to climb alongside such a dynamo of a man all those years ago. Bronco and I will always be grateful for the support he gave us during our Everest years.

A basic kit list was put together, broken down under such

headings as: Rations, Climber's Personal Kit, Stoves, Tentage, Hardwear (for the hill), Walk-in Kit and Chinese-element Clothing.

It was decided at the outset that we were not going to be a rag-tag and bobtail outfit, dressed in half-civilian, half-military gear. We had done that so many times in the past when we were just forming the Regiment's Mountain Troops. But to obtain top-class climbing kit meant that someone would need to be given this task as a fulltime job, as it would obviously be too much for Bronco or me, along with everything else we still had to do. Andy Baxter and Tony Swierzy agreed to take it on and immediately began rushing around asking people which side they dressed and what their inside leg measurements were! They took great delight whenever they persuaded some company or other to give us something for nothing. The fruit of their enthusiasm was the fact that we must have been the best-dressed, best-equipped team to have visited the mountain for a long time.

Locating likely team members was relatively simple. Every member of the Regiment's Mountain Troops had been knocking on the door for weeks, asking Bronco or me if they could be put on the ever-growing list of climbers for consideration. It soon became a task not of who should go, but rather who should not. With such fierce competition, everyone was determined to stay fit and safe: parachuting was only undertaken reluctantly, or rugby, only with a thought to avoiding all the other players.

Most of the candidates had already had at least ten years' climbing experience. Some had been to the Himalayas, some had not. There were climbers who had completed French Alpine courses and German Alpine Guides courses, but that was not going to be enough to qualify them for a place on the team. It was decided that a training climb was an essential part of the Everest build-up. We were going to be high on the mountain for a very long time, so it would make sense to ensure that everyone could at least perform happily at 20,000 feet. With this in mind, Mount McKinley in Alaska was chosen as our proving ground.

Known to the American Athabascan Indians as Denali, the Great One, McKinley stands at a height of 20,320 feet above sea level, dominating an ancient, glaciated landscape. It is the highest peak in North America, a huge white dome rising above the green and yellow tundra. It lies fifteen degrees further north than Everest and is reputed to be the world's coldest mountain. If our lads performed well in such an environment, then the chances were good that they could also work satisfactorily on the 'Big E'.

After staging through Anchorage and sampling the hospitality of the American Army Base at Fort Richardson, we moved by train to the old mining village of Talkeetna. Set on the banks of a salmon-and otter-filled river, this is still very much a sprawling frontier town, straight out of the Wild West, and it readily absorbed the wild bunch that hit town that night. We made straight for the Talkeetna Fairview Bar to sink a few jars with our pilot, Doug Geeting, who was to fly us into the mountains the next day. I had met Doug the year before: he is a striking, red-haired tiger of a man, whose number one love is flying, closely followed by playing songs on his beautiful Ovation guitar. The night rapidly degenerated into a boozy *ceilidh*, culminating with two of the locals standing face to face in a Mexican stand-off, screaming, 'I'm going for my gun!' Bodies began flying everywhere – through the windows, over the bar – and the batwing doors were torn off their hinges as the two gunslingers were evicted. Big Rosie, the barmaid, stood her ground, defying the brawlers to re-enter.

'She's truly beautiful when she's mad,' sighed Doug, quickly taking to his heels as she made to throw a bottle at him. We followed him out. It was already after three anyway, time we got some shut-eye, and we headed off up the road. It had been a good night.

Rudely awakened again at six by the roar of an aeroplane engine in my ear, I staggered across to the window, much the worse for wear, and peered outside to see our red-haired fire-drinker starting up his little Red Baron stunt trainer.

'Just goin' up to check the weather,' he said and taxied off along the dusty, narrow landing strip that had been carved out of the forest. On his return a short while later, we both climbed aboard his Cessna, together with all my kit. After a twenty-five minute flight we caught sight of the tiny snow-covered airstrip on the south fork of the heavily-crevassed Kahiltna Glacier. I was glad to be set down on firm ground at last and watched the little Cessna disappear back down the mountain. Complete silence. I was alone in what was to be our base camp at 7,400 feet.

Doug and his partner ran a shuttle service throughout the day, ferrying in the rest of the team and their kit.

'What a stupid way to turn up on the hill,' I admonished Mel Parr when he arrived, shivering and cold. 'Look at you, you're soaked!'

'Well, thanks a packet, mate,' he retorted. 'Seeing how it was you that's responsible for my state!' Stumbling about in the dark at four o'clock that morning, I had apparently located a locker with all his gear inside in mistake for the *khazi*. Mumbling my apologies, I slunk off to get his brew fixed up. I was going to have to suffer for this for the next few weeks, I just knew it!

It had been a long hard day. I was glad to jump into my sleeping bag after we had eaten our evening meal. Mel, lying next to me, said sarcastically, 'Hope you've got your pee bottle handy tonight.' I pretended to be asleep already.

There were twenty-nine of us in the party, which was rather large for a hill of this size, but I had wanted to get as many people as possible to the top, or at least to get them as high as we could, so, that we could see who was going well. Our team for Everest would only be fourteen strong, so I anticipated a lot of competition on this trip.

The route was to be the easiest on the mountain and would entail a five-day trek up the valley to the foot of the West Buttress at 14,300 feet, a period of acclimatisation there and a week rotating people through to the summit. There is no technical climbing along this route and the only danger was likely to be from avalanches and crevasses. All the members were well versed in mountain rescue techniques, so I was not too concerned about our welfare. I was, however, acutely aware of the ever-changing weather patterns on McKinley, and of the fact that it could get extremely cold. Waking early the first morning, this cold was very noticeable and the ends of my feet where my toes used to be felt like blocks of ice as I pulled on my boots and prepared breakfast for Mel and myself. Bronco was not on this trip, which meant that I would not be getting my early morning tea in bed. Instead, it would be up to me to take over the role and do the 'earlies' for Mel. I was going to miss The Lad, if for no other reason than that.

Once we had breakfasted and prepared ourselves for the day, Mel and I set off up the glacier with a load of tentage and food for the next campsite. The idea was that for the first couple of days we would all stretch our legs and have a look at the area by doing 'carries' up to about 9,000 feet. I didn't want to rush any higher until we had all acclimatised a little. Loading up our tiny plastic sleds the night before, I deliberately did not put on too much weight. I was glad of this now, as slowly we inched our way over the snow with the crampons biting into the hard surface. The sled was fastened to my harness at both hips by five feet of thin blue line and, as we moved uphill, trailed behind me nicely with a steady downwards pull, but whenever the ground changed to a slight downhill incline, the thing would rush at me with great speed and hit me in the heels. I had also made the mistake of making my load too high so that when we began to traverse a snow slope, the sled and load would topple over on to its side. After the tenth time this happened, I found myself becoming extremely frustrated, but without rigid poles, there was not a lot I could do to rectify the situation. I just had to grin and bear it. I now knew how the poor horses must have felt, that used to pull the barges along the canals in Birmingham. Pretty soon my hips were raw with the constant rubbing of the harness. I could see that I had a lot to learn about Alaskan sled-pulling.

It was a fantastic setting to be in, though, despite the awkward load-hauling system. The campsite by the airstrip lay in the bottom of a glacial valley under the shoulders of Mount Hunter and North Peak, with the mighty Foraker Mountain poking its head proudly into the blue sky just across the valley from us. Foraker was the second highest in the area and looked very inviting. McKinley itself loomed above us, heavy with new snow, as if defying us to venture on its flanks. And to add emphasis to this appearance of disdain, rivers of billowing white powder could be seen high on the mountain's shoulder as an avalanche rumbled its way down to the glacier below. I was reminded once again of the majesty and ferociousness of big mountains.

The morning had dawned fine and clear blue skies. The air was clean with that bracing feel to it that is peculiar to the high country. It was good to be out and about and crunching our way up the glacier, threading a route between the more obvious crevasses. Crossing one of the many snow bridges, Mel remarked how privileged we were to be in a place like this, and I could only nod my agreement.

After four hours of plodding up the glacier, we arrived at a spot where some previous party had built several circles of snow-block walls as protection for their tents from the wind. Dumping off our kit, relieved at last to be rid of the weight of our sleds, we sat on our packs and basked in the sunshine. The others could be seen snaking their way up slowly towards us. We commandeered the best of the snow circles and I smiled secretly to myself at how, once again, the early bird had caught the worm. The others would have to fashion more snowblocks and build their shelters up.

Mel had long since been chosen as one of the definites for the Everest trip and as we sat waiting, we chatted over the merits of several of the hopefuls before descending back down the way we had come. Now that all the alcohol was finally out of my system, I felt a lot better and looked forward to moving up properly to the new camp next morning. In the course of the next few days we were to make our way on up, through places with such names as Kahiltna Notch, Motorcycle Hill, Windy Corner, until we finally arrived at the foot of the headwall at 14,300 feet.

The site here was a delight. A natural suntrap, it was protected from most of the wind by the mountain itself on the right, and the West Buttress on the left, the steep walls of the hill forming a semicircular amphitheatre that was big enough to accommodate two rugby fields. It reminded me of some of the plateaux you get in Nepal. The Ranger Service which administers the National Park has erected a prefabricated observatory up here which doubles as a hospital emergency post and during the height of the season, there is a doctor permanently in residence. Because it is such a popular spot and attracts many climbers, the rangers, conscious of the need to keep the place clean, have also built what can only be described as one of the best loos with a view that I have ever seen. The great wooden thunderbox bestrides a deep crevasse, and looks back down the route we had just travelled up, affording a magnificent panorama over Foraker and the surrounding peaks. Seldom have I found a place where it's possible to answer the call of nature in such comfort and at the same time view Nature in all its glory. There is something special about watching the sun go down in the late afternoon, seated on a throne like that!

Two days after we arrived at this spot, the rest of the team reached us too, closely followed by several other parties of various nationalities. There were Americans, Canadians, Brits, Germans, Italians, French, Japanese – you name it, they were there! Soon a village of tents of all colours and makes had sprung up. The atmosphere was electric; it was like being on an international climbing meet. Climbers both famous and infamous were soon rubbing shoulders and swopping stories. One of the French climbers, Jean-Pierre Troillet, who was guiding a New York taxi driver called Frank up the mountain, told me of his desire to solo the North Face of Everest, the route we were training to do. I wished him well and tucked heartily into the bacon sandwich that he had offered me half of. Frank, whose funding of this outing included the food, gave me a sideways look of disapproval as I greedily wolfed down his buttie.

The next stage of our journey proved a little more exhilarating as we clipped into some fixed ropes and jumared up the two-thousand foot headwall on to the ridge proper, continuing from there to our last camp at 17,600 feet. This place was known as the Iglooplex. It was a flat windswept area where the ridge joined the main core of the mountain; half a dozen igloos had been built there over the years and used as accommodation for the countless numbers of climbers who come up this route. Once inside one of these tiny ice caves, the bitter wind is neither heard nor felt, which was a comfort. The problem, however, was that some of the climbers who had sheltered here must have been too exhausted to drag themselves outside whenever nature called. As a result, too often the inside was a disgusting foul-smelling mess of yellow show. Archie Scutt, my partner, preferred not to risk contamination and set about building a new snow cave in which to spend the night prior to our summit bid next day.

We set off in the cold half-light next morning, carrying with us flasks of hot tea and food for the day, tucked away safely in our rucksacks. We headed for the beginning of the traverse to the col, 1,500 feet above us. Our breath froze as it left our mouths and we trudged slowly upwards in a mist of condensed vapour.

My rhythm was constantly interrupted by having to stop and gasp for air every twenty paces or so, and a headache developed, brought on probably by a mixture of altitude and the freezing cold of the morning. Even with my double boots and Gore-tex gloves, my feet and hands were cold. I began to look forward to reaching the col where we would be in the direct rays of the sun and have a chance of warming up. The last thing I needed was more frostbite: there was nothing else I could afford to lose! I began talking to myself in my mind.

'What on earth are you doing here, what are you trying to prove?' I demanded. 'Why didn't you quit when you were ahead?' Having already 'done' Everest, why was I going to so much trouble to go back there? This kind of thinking wasn't doing my resolution any good and I endeavoured to force it from my mind as I took another step upwards. I heard my crampons bite into the hard icy snow, when suddenly, unbidden, another voice inside me screamed, 'Because I want to, that's why!'

Annoyed at myself for no particular reason, I gritted my teeth hard together and forced myself to take fifty more steps before I stopped for another breather. When I looked back, I could see Archie watching me and shaking his head, no doubt thinking I had gone stark-staring mad, storming up the hill like that. Half an hour later we were sitting in sunshine on the col, although unfortunately it was also very windy. We could not afford to hang about there for long and pulling on our duvets and windproofs, we set off again slowly up a slightly steeper section.

We were following a line of bamboo marker poles left by a considerate party of long ago but felt the need to stop and catch our breath with increasing frequency; the altitude was clearly beginning to get to us. A thick cloud descended about our ears, which made us grateful for the markers showing us that we were still on the correct route. Turning left as we neared what we thought was the top, the cloud just as suddenly cleared and showed us that we still had a good way to go. The summit was several hundred feet above us, and the sickening thing was that we had to descend into a small bowl, losing a hundred feet or so, before we could reach the foot of a steepening wall, which led up to the summit ridge.

We stopped for another drink of tea from our flasks, dumped our sacks and started the final climb to the summit. The snow was rock hard, whipped solid by years of wind, and we had to kick viciously with our crampons to get them to bite into the surface. Climbing was not technically difficult, but by now my feet had frozen solid and I was growing increasingly alarmed about frostbite: the sooner we could get up and back down, the better. Putting my head down against the wind I set off upwards once more, and after what seemed liked hours of crabbing up the slope, I found myself on the ridge which led to the top. Feet throbbing and my heart pounding away, I made my way steadily along the corniced edge and on to the highest point, which was festooned with bamboo markers stuck in at all crazy angles.

I had made it. This was the highest point in all of North America. I was totally elated now, feeling tremendous to be standing on such a magic spot. The questions that had passed through my mind earlier could all now be answered. Why do it? For this, that's why. For this feeling of overcoming one's fear and doubt; for proving to myself that no toes need be no handicap; for being able to stand here like this, alone on a mountain, alone with raw elements; for enjoyment; I do it, in short, for myself. Archie came slowly up beside me and after taking a few snaps, I left him alone to savour private moments in his turn, and kept on down with the chill now gone from my bones. I had cracked it. I now knew that nothing and no one could stop me. I was fully fit. Everest, here I come!

Waiting for Archie at the spot where we left the rucksacks, I drank the last of my tea and ate a Mars bar while still congratulating myself on the climb. It was not that there had been any real climbing involved, it was more of a high altitude slog than anything else. But that didn't matter; what I felt was important was having coped with it. When Archie arrived, I congratulated him too on his first 20,000-er, and set off down towards the ice caves. Descending the traverse from the col to the Iglooplex, we were met by two people on the way up, who asked how far it was to the top. 'About two hours,' I answered, but judging from their slow speed, I seriously wondered whether it might not be nearer four or five, if they got there at all that day, that is.

That night we spent in the snow cave and descended to 14,300 feet early the next day. The rest of the team were by now rotating through the top camp and going for the summit. My job was that of a mother hen, sitting under the headwall and monitoring all our climbers as they made their attempts. During that last week, twenty-five of the team made it to the summit, and Andy Baxter and Merv Middling made a record fast ascent of Foraker as well. While waiting for them to finish, I assisted in the rescue of a climber who had gone too high too fast and was suffering from pulmonary oedema. He was brought down the headwall by Wolfgang Nairz from Innsbruck in Austria, a climber who I later learned had also led an expedition to Everest. McKinley, I decided, was definitely the place to go if you wanted to meet people.

Doug's face was a picture as I told him of our achievements on the fly-out to Talkeetna. By the time all the team were back in town, there was a great shindig taking place, and we eagerly joined in the festivities. The air seemed so thick down there that you could almost eat it. Not having had a real meat meal for a few weeks now, we almost ate the town out of all its stock of food for the winter. It had been a good trip, and I now knew who would be going to Everest and who not.

Everest, the North Face

B Y AUGUST 1983 all our kit and equipment had been procured and was packed, manifested, labelled and loaded into two twenty-foot sea cargo containers hired from a local firm, and shipped out to Hong Kong. Several weeks later I was to fly out and check that the gear had not been damaged in transit and transfer it into Chinese containers for the onward move to Tienshin. Here the Chinese Mountaineering Association would arrange for it to be moved by rail and road up to Lhasa in Tibet, to be stored for our arrival in 1984. The CMA insisted that our equipment be in their hands three months prior to our arrival. This was the only way, they informed us, that they could guarantee its being in Lhasa on time.

The team had now been finalised. Of the fourteen members, Ricky Villar, who was the Regimental Medical Officer was the only Rupert on the trip and doctors don't count as real Ruperts, so that was OK by us! This was to be a real SAS Trogs-only climb. Not that it was ever the intention to exclude officers, just that the only one that fitted the bill when we came to make our selection was Ian Crozier and he was unavailable.

Last-minute checks were now the order of the day: passports up to date? Visas all applied for? Dental examinations made? And had we had all the Gamma-globulin and other injections to protect against weird oriental diseases? Several hours were spent down at the local travel centre in Hereford, where David Mills, my favourite travel agent, was busy arranging a cheap flight for us from Hong Kong to Peking (or Beijing, as it is now known).

We were all itching to get started and wishing away the next few months so that we could be off. On 13 February 1984 Bronco and Mel left for China; theirs was the job of making sure that everything was cleared by the CMA in Peking to enable the rest of us to follow without any last minute hiccups, and for Mel (who was to be Base Camp Manager) to check through the gear in Lhasa. I was glad to see them go; it meant there were only two weeks to wait before the rest of us could leave as well.

But excited as I was, it was a difficult time for Lynn and me, and for the two boys. As the day of departure grew closer, there was a definite atmosphere about the place: it was important for me to try and spend some extra time with the boys and to spoil Lynn to show her how much I valued her support in all this. Inevitably, I asked myself whether I was being fair to them in going off and leaving them to worry about me while I enjoyed my mountains, but Lynn dismissed this with characteristic generosity and logic by saying, 'Brum, if you didn't have something to do with climbing in your life every now and then, life around here would be pretty unbearable. You go and have a good time, but just remember to come back to us in one piece, that's all.'

I must admit it does make me feel better about things hearing her say that, even though I know that every day I am away she will miss me as much as I will her and my boys. But at the heart of it, I know there is no other way for me – I will always respond to the pull of the mountains, to their beauty and the enjoyment they give me. These are forces too strong to deny.

When the day came, I said goodbye to Lynn and the boys at the airport and made my way with the other expedition members through passport control and into the departure lounge for a last pint before boarding the flight to Hong Kong. There was a buzz of excitement throughout the team as we chatted, with one eye on the departure board. We knew each other pretty well by now and had all climbed together, so expected no personality problems during our time away. People had already paired off as far as preferred climbing partners went, but there was enough unity within the team to enable any member to work with any other. Two of the strongest snow and ice climbers, Andy Baxter and Tony Swierzy, had teamed up together and were constantly teasing the others, telling us we would need to be up early to get ahead of them. The banter went on to-ing and fro-ing throughout the flight and a healthy competitive spirit was born, kept in trim by the dry humour of Phil Mallard and Merv Middling.

After spending two nights in Hong Kong, we stumbled, bleary-eyed on to the CAAC aircraft that was to take us on to Peking. I sat back and smiled at the mixed reactions of the team members as for the first time they came face to face with the 'real' China. A sombre-faced air hostess welcomed us aboard – if that is the right phrase. She was dressed, not in the trim, fashionable suit you come to expect on international airlines, but a green serge Chairman Mao uniform, unpressed and baggy, with red stars on the collar and a matching cap.

Uttering a curt 'You sit here!' she ordered us to our places and thrust a complimentary plastic mirror and comb at each of us, before marching off to deal with the next customer. Having been to Peking the year before to sign the protocol, I had quickly learned then that people in China are severely regimented and do not readily exhibit any sense of humour.

The airport in Hong Kong is one of the trickiest in the world. With limited space for take off, the pilot has to spin his wheels fast before making a headlong dash down the runway, then zigzag unnervingly from side to side to avoid huge skyscrapers. Once you are safely airborne, it is with some relief that you settle back and look forward to your in-flight refreshment. In Hong Kong we had been spoiled by all the good food: there were mountains of it and it was rich and varied and exquisitely cooked, but now we were in the People's Republic we found both the fare and the service more austere. It did not help either that there seemed to be no washing-up facilities on board and the bowls we were served all bore the greasy traces of earlier meals.

When his tray was put in front of him, Archie, a Scot, turned to me with a look of disgust and said, 'This rice is like porridge gone wrong,' an observation with which I was forced to agree, as I pushed the soggy, grey pile to one side and reached in my travelling bag for a tin of corned beef. I had learned my lesson the hard way last time; now it was their turn.

'Bon appetit!' I said and tucked into my tinned cow while they chased some unidentifiable pieces of stewed fish around with their chopsticks.

Some time later, the aircraft plummeted towards the ground in a dive that would not have disgraced a *kamikaze* pilot, straightening out at the last minute to land rather bumpily on the airstrip in Peking. We had arrived. Most of the passengers leapt immediately to their feet, grabbing their belongings and surged towards the exit, intent on getting out before the plane had finished taxi-ing. Customs was chaotic by any standards, but made slightly easier for us by a member of the British Embassy who had managed to force his way through the crowds in order to act as interpreter on our behalf. Even so, the next hour was spent sorting out documents and having long discussions with officials for the release of cameras and other attractive items that we were carrying with us. Finally we emerged on to the streets outside the airport to be met by Mr Chen Rongchang, who was to be our expedition liaison officer, and other members of the CMA.

They took us to a small hotel, the Bei Wei, our home for the next few days. Our hosts were very anxious that we should see the sights of China. We were taken to the massive square that was dedicated to Chairman Mao, and to the Forbidden City, an area of over a square mile enclosed within huge walls to keep out the peasants. Inside was the most beautiful palace, which housed treasures from all over China and Tibet. It was quite sad to realise that all this had been built for the benefit of just one man – the Emperor. He used to live here with his concubines, apart from his people, but as an absolute ruler, leaving them in no doubt of his ultimate power over their lives and deaths.

The people we met on our travels in Peking, thousands of them milling around everywhere and all dressed in either green serge military uniforms or the drab blue of civilians, reminded us still of this bygone age. China had only recently opened its gates to tourists, and being among the first, we found ourselves a constant source of interest; we were stared at wherever we went.

The Great Wall of China was a huge disappointment to me. Though it stretches all the miles to the horizon, most of it seemed to be in ruins except for the few bits accessible to visitors. I learned from our interpreter how, when the wall was built to keep out the Mongols, whole villages had been driven to work on it for years – some people, he suggested, were separated from the rest of their families for thirty years or more, and many died building it and were buried inside the wall without marker or trace. I could well believe it.

From Peking, we again had to brave the hazards of an internal flight, this time to Chengdu, the principle town of Szechuan. Chengdu is a much smaller city, with only some five million people compared to the capital's nine million, and it was here that we were fortunate enough to stay in one of the new hotels that are fast being pushed up to cater for the tourist trade. The rooms were good – each had its own bath and toilet, but alas, the food hadn't changed in appearance or taste – everything swam in soybean sauce or grease.

One evening, in desperation to get something cooked to suit our British tastes, two of us entered the kitchen to see if we could persuade the chef to fix us some scrambled eggs. Looking round, there were only two things we recognised instantly: one was the carcase of a dog that was being butchered on a big wooden bench, and the other was a pack of rats fighting for the remnants that had been thrown into the corner! I will eat, and have eaten, most things in survival situations, but then I lost my appetite completely. Roll on Lhasa, I thought, when we can break into our compo rations. I did have one last can of my emergency stock of bully beef, and slipped away to my room. I don't know whether they smelt it, but minutes later the door crashed open and in marched the rest of the team demanding fair shares: a small tin of meat does not go far between twelve hungry men.

The next day we woke early and drove in darkness the two hours from the town towards the airport. Even starting at 4.30 like this, the loudspeakers were already blaring on every street corner, accosting the crowds of people shuffling along the dark lanes to work.

'What is it saying?' one of the blokes asked our interpreter.

Mr Lin, who was a college student and had been assigned to the expedition for practical experience, replied in his halting English, 'It is telling the people that we have a new rule today: no spitting in the streets. A large dustbin has been placed at all the corners of the main streets and people must spit into them.' He could not understand why we found this so amusing, and thinking back, I recall that when I was a kid in Birmingham, we had signs something like that and there were spittoons in all the local pubs.

The take-off from Chengdu seemed very little smoother than that from Hong Kong or Peking, and I began to wonder what the odds were of ever getting to the mountain, let alone climbing it. Once it got light, we could see we were flying over vast ranges of snow-covered hills that I later learned were little explored and included peaks of over 20,000 feet.

The descent into the valley which houses the airport in Tibet was breathtaking. Mountains of up to 12,000 feet flashed by the wingtips as the pilot fought with crosswinds to keep the aircraft steady as he headed down into the valley bottom and on to the ribbon of gravel that served as an airstrip. As we skidded to a halt, the sound of people clapping drowned out the noise of the engines, and I even joined in the applause, more out of relief to be down than any appreciation of the pilot's skills. Finally, after the usual scrimmage for the door, we emerged in the burning heat of the afternoon sunshine and walked across the dirt to a waiting truck. Bronco had come out to meet us.

'Bring any grub with you?' I asked, hopefully.

'Yea, I've got some in the bus. I knew you would be wanting some after the crap you'll have had on the journey.' We gathered up our baggage and climbed aboard thankfully.

The trip into Lhasa was interrupted several times while we waited for road workers to clear away blasted rock – they appeared to be making this road only one jump ahead of us. Gangs comprising hundreds of men, women and children could be seen scrabbling to fill large baskets with broken rock and ferrying it across to stonemasons, who were busy fashioning flagstones which would eventually be used on the new road. Their tools were crude: wooden spades and rakes, and cement that was being mixed by the children with bare hands, like mud pies, and then spread (again by hand) by women on bended knee. Every so often, standing beside the road, would be a Chinese soldier with his rifle slung casually over his shoulder, almost as if overseeing the labour of the Tibetan workers. We were instructed by our Life Manager (whose job was to ensure that we did not subvert the Chinese members working with the expedition) not to take photographs of this road-building. He assured us that this was not forced labour and that the people liked doing it as it kept them busy and happy. The cameras clicked in secret.

Five hours of this bone-jolting travel brought us into Lhasa, the Forbidden City, dominated by a huge stone building with a golden roof, which stood proud and alone on a small hillside in the centre of the town, a white-painted, majestic block with hundreds of glassless windows staring out blindly over the open valley. The red-ochre edging to the doorways and windows contrasted brightly with its white walls. This was the Potala Palace, former home of the Dalai Lama, the religious leader of Tibet, who fled to India in 1959 after the Chinese occupation.

There was plainly much to see during our few days' stay in this interesting city, but first, wouldn't it be nice to get off this truck, sit down comfortably and have a real cup of tea? In a mug, with milk and sugar – and hot! We pulled into the CMA compound where we were to stay, met up with Mr Tang, the official who ran the Tibetan side of the organisation, then Bronco showed us where we were to sleep.

That evening, walking around the dusty, noisy small streets of Lhasa with their mud and stone houses painted in the same traditional style as the Potala, and listening to the sound of musical instruments coming from the temples, we felt in touch at last with true Tibetans. Women, dressed in long, black robes of cotton-drill, edged with colourful braid, and often wearing wide-brimmed hats though rarely shoes, would giggle and point at us as we passed, their red, weather-tanned faces creased in smiles. We were the only Europeans in Lhasa at the time and consequently something of a curiosity. Children in the market, and grown-ups too, were fascinated by our fair hair and pale skins. Building up confidence, as we chatted and bargained with the stallkeepers, they would creep up and touch us, plucking at the hair on the backs of our hands and arms. Body hair, it seems, is something of a novelty; they grow little or none themselves. I immediately took to the Tibetans, with their natural friendliness and good humour. Throughout the time we were in Tibet, they would invite us into their colourful little houses for yak-milk tea and rancid butter on bread. Like the Nepalese, whom they resembled in many ways, family life was obviously very important to them.

Men from nomadic tribes passing through the city, looked hard, rugged and self-sufficient – which they obviously were – as they strode proud and tall among the market stalls, their families trailing behind. Knives and old muskets hung casually from their belts. I later learned that these tribesmen, who had resisted the Chinese takeover and resented any intrusion by outsiders into Tibet, still earned a living by hunting and trapping 'snow lions' and selling their skins in the market. I would have loved to be able to speak their language and learn more of their way of life. They would not converse with me through our Chinese interpreter; as soon as he made any advances towards them, they would disdainfully wave him away and walk off in the opposite direction.

We were three days in Lhasa, which was useful acclimatising time since the town stands at 12,000 feet above sea level. We found the height slowed us down quite a lot at first. Just walking around for a few hours would leave us feeling tired and out of breath, and it would have been utter madness to have charged up the hundreds of steps to the Potala Palace for fear of bringing on mountain sickness. The Palace was a maze of stairs and rooms, housing countless figures of Buddhas, demons and gods, prayer wheels of differing sizes from small ones operated by hand to huge ones that must have weighed tons. Everywhere you looked, were statues and brilliantly-painted decorations; precious and semi-precious jewels bedecked idols of long-dead lamas, priests and shamans. They were all housed in darkened, dusty rooms, lit only by the flickering light of hundreds of butter lamps, little brass bowls of rancid oil giving off a curious, sickly smell. A constant queue of worshippers shuffled around the rooms, rotating hand-held prayer wheels and chanting in a hushed tone, *'Om mani padme hum . . . om mani padme hum . . .'* This sound was drowned every now and then by the long low blast of the horns, gongs and cymbals played by the monks who lived within the palace confines.

Of more spiritual importance to devout Tibetans than even the Potola, is the Jokhang Temple, which is situated in the old centre of Lhasa. During our time in Tibet, we were fortunate that a major religious festival was taking place, giving us the opportunity to see for ourselves one of their most ancient rituals. Pilgrims arriving in the city, many after travelling for weeks on horseback or foot, have to circumnavigate the temple three times by throwing themselves prostrate on the floor, rising and shuffling forward about two feet, then repeating the process, until after their third circuit they finally make it to the main entrance of the temple. There they remove their sandals, rotate a huge, gold-encrusted prayer wheel (taking care to pass it to the left) all the while praying, *'Om mani padme hum . . .'* Though normally open to the public, on this occasion we were not allowed to follow them into the temple.

During our stay we also witnessed a Tibetan 'sky burial'. Tibet's stony and often frozen ground makes normal interment virtually impossible, and wood is too scarce for cremation on any scale, so that sky burials have become the traditional way of dealing with dead bodies. In Lhasa, they take place on top of some flat rocks outside the city, not far from the municipal rubbish dump. Professional body breakers have the gruesome task of stripping flesh from the bones, then dissecting the corpses into small cubes for feeding to the multitude of birds of prey that gather for the occasion. Finally, the bones are crushed and burnt and the dust thrown into the wind, releasing the dead person's spirit for reincarnation. Dinner, the night after we had seen this ritual, did not sit easily on the stomach.

When we were not sightseeing, time was spent in the CMA compound, checking and loading our stores on to Russian-style, Chinese-built lorries in preparation for the onward move to the mountain. We had over six tons of equipment that had been held for us by the Chinese, and we now had to ensure that it was still in good order, for we would soon be out of touch with civilisation for a long time. There would be no chance then of replacing anything: what we didn't have with us, we would have to do without. It says a lot for Chinese organisation, however indecisive officials some-times seem and insistent on mountains of paperwork, that not a single item of our gear had been damaged in transit. On 5 March, three vehicles loaded to the gunwales with kit left the compound, closely followed by us, travelling in a battered old minibus and an ex-Chinese Army jeep that had seen better days. It was going to take three days of travelling along the Friendship Highway, the road that links Tibet with Nepal, to bring us to our Base Camp at the foot of Everest.

The first leg of the journey was rather boring, endless miles of dusty road through terrain not unlike the Gobi Desert. For hours we saw nothing except telephone wires, anchored to the top of mud-built towers lining the ungraded road. Eight hours of bump-ing about inside the minibus with surgical face-masks covering our mouths and noses to keep out the dust, brought us to our first night's stop in the town of Xigatse (Shigatse).

Aching, we climbed out of the vehicle, glad at last to be able to stretch our limbs. Here we would get our last bath of the trip in the spartan accommodation of the hotel, followed by yet another bowlful of glutinous rice, which we had all become accustomed now to throw to the dogs. The saving grace of the meals was the side salad of green cabbage, lettuce and beans. This was some-thing we could all look forward to. That is, until the next morning when squatting over the hole in the floor of a concrete ramp, which served as the toilet, I discovered what our meal was nurtured on. Down through the hole, a sideways shaft of light suddenly appeared as a trapdoor was opened and a tiny hand darted in to snatch away the tray – even before I had finished. Seconds later, looking over the wall at the back, I saw a young girl carrying two buckets on a pole balanced over her shoulders. She was off to the fields to pour fresh manure on to the young plants. Talk about getting your own back! Salad meant rather less after that, and I was glad that Ricky, our doctor, had insisted on us having so many injections.

Sitting back and opening a tin of compo cheese as the bus pulled out of Xigatse, with the sun just peeking its head over the horizon, our intepreter, Mr Lin, informed us that the route today would be more spectacular than that of the day before. That was not saying a lot, I thought, unimpressed, remembering the miles of sand and dust. But he was right: we crossed a couple of high mountain passes that day and glimpsed snow-capped peaks away in the distance that we were told had never been climbed. We passed the tented villages of nomad families, whose young, brightly-dressed children came out to wave excitedly as our convoy trundled through, alarming their horses which grazed lazily in the nearby fields. Four hours' drive from the town, we stopped on the banks of a huge, fast-flowing and muddy river, waiting for the ferry that was to carry us across. This was the mighty Brahmaputra, one of the major waterways of Asia.

Throughout the journey, the voice of Mel could be heard at the back of the bus, relating stories to our ever-attentive interpreter of Welsh bowmen and mighty battles fought by crusaders in far-off lands. The young man found it hard to believe that an army of British soldiers had once tramped its way to Lhasa over this very ground that we now travelled, in order to subdue the Tibetans. On more than one occasion, he was taken to one side by the Life Manager, who we surmised was lecturing him about not listening too much to the war stories of the Brits and to remember Mao! After crossing the choppy waters, we made our way into the town of Xegur (Shekar Dzong) for what would be our last overnight stay in a building for some time to come.

The little town was tucked under a hillside which had once been overlooked by a grand hilltop fortress, or *Dzong*. We could see the ruins of the *Dzong*, which had been destroyed by Red Guards during the Cultural Revolution. Our Life Manager was reluctant to answer questions on the subject and put it down to the actions of rebellious Tibetan youths. Xegur, we found, had been an important centre for religion in Tibet with a renowned monastery, but little now remained except one small *gompa* with a handful of resident monks. Wandering around here late one evening, Andy had been called into one of the courtyards and covered with white ash, but the significance of this we never did find out.

Inside the CMA compound we transferred our kit from the minibus on to lorries. Tomorrow we would be leaving the Friendship Highway and heading into the hills, so this was as far as the bus could go. It seemed strange to think that Kathmandu, across the border in Nepal, was only some eight hours drive from here, and that if the Chinese had allowed us to enter Tibet by this route, we would have been here a week ago. When Bronco and I were negotiating with them in Peking (years ago, it now seemed), they had categorically refused to allow us to do this, saying that we could not cross international borders. By insisting that everything travel through China and Tibet, considerable revenue was put into CMA coffers. Still, at least it had given us the privilege of seeing Lhasa and sampling Chinese cuisine! We retired into our cell-like accommodation for our last sleep on a bed.

During the day I had been talking with our liaison officer, Mr Chen Rongchang, who had a somewhat scarred nose. I learned, when I asked him how it had happened, that he had been part of the Chinese team that went to the summit of Everest in 1975, and that while walking across a glacier, his partner had fallen into a crevasse. Not knowing how to tie him off properly to effect a rescue, he had stood and held him for hours until help arrived, by which time it was too late for him to avoid frostbite. His nose was affected and his feet and fingers, so that he later had to have bits amputated. Bronco, he and I comprised the first Anglo–Chinese Everest Frostbite Amputees Club in Tibet.

In the daytime, travelling along the road with the sun beating down upon us, we had been quite warm, but now, sitting in the back of the lorries the next day as we rattled across a field to get back on to the road, even wrapped in our duvet jackets, we could feel the chill of the early Tibetan morning. Half an hour later, the convoy came to a halt as the lead vehicle burst a tyre and the drivers jumped out to assist in changing it. I was amazed to see that not only did they change the wheel quite quickly, but they also managed to repair the damaged one by the old method of vulcanising it. Impressed as I was by this show of self-sufficiency, however, I wished that it had happened later, after the sun had risen. We were soon on our way once more and passing through the Police Checkpoint at the junction of the Friendship Highway and the track that we would now take towards Everest.

Leaving the road, we wound our way up a valley, passing through a couple of small and remote farming villages, and then began twisting and turning as we snaked up the side of a mountain eventually to arrive, with engines labouring and steam blowing from overheating radiators, on the top of the Pang La pass at 17,000 feet. By now the sun had been up for quite some time and the sky was a deep, clear blue. Here, looking through a clump of fluttering prayer flags that had been placed in a shrine beside the road, we got our first sight of the mountain we had come so far to climb. Everest was still some sixty kilometers distant, but it was an incredible view from where we stood. We were looking at the roof of the world, and the initial reaction was one of stunned silence as the eye struggled to take it all in. Then excited voices began identifying the different routes.

We began picking out the other giants in the long line of peaks on the skyline: Makalu, Cho Oyu, Pumori, Lhotse, Nuptse, and way over in the distance, Kangchenjunga, alone and sombre. We stayed and had lunch at this spot, enjoying its remoteness and the complete stillness now that we had cut the lorry engines. Every so often as we chattered and made plans, our eyes would return to Everest and we would wonder if in three months' time we might have climbed its North Face. We were now at about the same altitude that our Base Camp would be, so sitting here for a while would help us acclimatise. No one seemed to be suffering any ill-effects; that was a good sign in itself. It would take us about six hours or more to get to Base Camp from here, but we were reluctant to move because we knew that as soon as we descended into the valley on the other side of our high pass, we would lose this magnificent view of the mountains.

The drive, at breakneck speed, with the drivers hauling the vehicles around tight bends down the steep hill, made me wonder if perhaps all Orientals are born with a death wish. I was glad to be on the valley bottom and rattling and bumping along the stony bed of a dried-up river bed, which had been adopted as the thoroughfare, and passing again through small farming villages with the people hard at work in the fields, tending the season's crop of barley.

Stopping on the outskirts of a village to refuel from the fifty-gallon diesel drum that we carried, we were descended upon by hoards of children, clamouring for sweets and chocolate. It would seem that even the few expeditions that had been through to Everest since travel here was permitted, have been sufficient to become identified with free handouts of food, just as they are on

213

the Nepalese side of the border. It is hard to say 'no' to kids like these when you realise that some of them only just get enough to stay alive. What did we want with all this chocolate, anyway? The load was once again lightened and we continued on our way.

After following the line of the river a little further, the point came where we finally had to ford the icy waters of the Rongbuk River, which flows down from the Everest glaciers, before turning up the valley towards the mountain.

A rough boulder-stewn track, snow-covered in places, brought us over the final lip of a rise to within sight of the Rongbuk Monastery, and there was our mountain in the background, reaching high into the sky! I was totally unprepared for a view of this magnitude. It was so unreal, almost like a cardboard cut-out that had been pasted up as a backdrop for an advert. It looked much bigger than ever it had in 1976 when we climbed it, but then from the southern side, there is nowhere that you can get a vantage point high enough to afford a view like that. At long last, after all the planning, fund-raising, administration and heartache, we had arrived at our Base Camp at 16,000 feet. The enjoyable bit of actually climbing the mountain could now begin. It was 9 March and the worst of the winter weather had gone although there was still a chill in the air as we offloaded our vehicles on to the grassy bank a hundred yards or so beyond the Rongbuk Monastery.

Setting up our accommodation tents, we were visited by some of the monks and nuns, who live in the famous monastery. Could we let them have some sugar and any spare food that we might have? I began to question the wisdom of our camping here. We had initially intended to move further up the valley towards the hill, but because of all the snow barring the track above us, we had been unable to do this. The site we were now in was that used by the pioneers of this side of the mountain in the early 1920s, and as I sat, I tried to imagine where General Bruce's tent might have been pitched.

There was a historic feel about the place for me as a climber, but also a sense of sorrow when I looked at the monastery which now lay pretty well in ruins. It had been sacked, like so many others, by the Red Guards, but even amidst the broken-down walls and piles of prayer stones, it was easy to see why the place was referred to by many as the Tibetan Shangri-La. There was a peace and tranquility here that I have found nowhere else in the world – and it was all presided over by the majestic form of Everest. I have never thought of mountains as things to be 'conquered', nor felt them unfriendly, rather their beauty, serenity and changing moods are all just part of the wonder of nature. You cannot 'conquer' big mountains like this, all you can hope is to sneak up and down, when nature is looking the other way. And no one will ever convince me that beauty such as this was ever born by chance, from a ball of gas and molten debris somewhere off in outer space. There has to have been a sublime creative plan to produce such perfection.

Over a period of ten days at base camp, acclimatising by daily scrambling up the sides of the surrounding mountains to get an even better look at our mountain, our heap of equipment was sorted out into manageable loads for the onward move uphill. The vehicles had long since gone, but we had maintained the tiny jeep as an emergency wagon, and this was used every now and then to pop back down the valley to purchase fresh potatoes, or barter for them with spare tinned goods.

Climbing up a mountainside with Mel one day we were rewarded with the sight of Cho Oyu towering above us, and which as far as I was aware, had never been climbed from this side. Studying its huge snow-covered face with massive avalanches roaring down it, I was scarcely surprised. It rose in one horrendous sweep from the mists of the valley below me, with innumerable hanging glaciers clinging to its belly like limpet mines, ready to blow. I sat and marvelled at this giant, which was so close it seemed I could reach out across the valley and touch it.

During our time on this small hill, we had been able to study the route we should take up the moraine towards the foot of the North Face of Everest and the site where we would place our Advanced Base Camp at 20,300 feet. It all looked safe enough and the only real danger appeared to be on the glacier below the camp, which was pockmarked with crevasses, large and small. I had seen enough to make me feel happier about the approach to the face; if all went well, we should be on top in less than six weeks. We descended to camp for dinner.

That night the plan was made to send off the first team to establish a route up through the moraine to the Central Rongbuk Glacier, and to find a good spot for the next camp. Once installed there, we would abandon this spot, to be looked after by our Chinese mountaineering representatives, and all move, with the help of yaks and porters, to the higher base camp. The next stage would be to push up to a camp below the North Face, from where we could begin work on the mountain proper.

Several days later I found myself picking my way up the moraine track and over the lower parts of the glacier between huge fins of blue ice, and crossing frozen rivers, closely followed by our yak train with their bells jingling and the shrill whistles and calls of the herdsman urging them on. Yaks are shy and unpredictable and can only really be managed by the one yak-man they are used to. It was going to be a good day for me, the camp had already been set up and I was carrying my personal gear so that I could move into it for good. I was pleased at long last to be going out front again where I felt I belonged. I was no good as a follower and needed to feel as though I was pioneering something. We were not on a new route, nor doing anything that had not been done before, I knew, but if we succeeded in making it to the top this way, we would be the first Brits to do so. To me, that made it a worthwhile objective. I had long ago recognised that I was a red, white and blue flag-waver and loved it when Great Britain was in the news for having done something good, rather than for being involved in disruptive strikes or fighting at football matches. It would also make me feel great if I could take George Williams back a photograph of his Anglia Windows pennant flying side by side with the Union Jack on top of the world. After all, without his backing, we would not be where we were now, enjoying ourselves in the best school of the universe, the Great Outdoors.

Putting all that to one side of my mind, I started to sing a folk song that had been buzzing around in my head for some time, only to stop abruptly as I rounded a corner and saw the tents of the camp nestling beside a small pool of meltwater. It was a great spot, protected from the wind by the row of green ice fins that projected starkly from the gravelly surface of the moraine. It was like walking into a hidden box canyon. A mug of steaming hot tea was thrust into my hand by Graham Tucker, who had been up at the camp for a day or so organising things. I smiled my thanks and sat down on my pack, slightly out of breath from the long walk. It had taken me almost five hours to get here. For me, that was slow. I would have to step it out a bit if I was to keep up with these young bucks.

That evening Bronco moved into the camp as well, and as we cut away a platform for our two-man tent, we discussed the plan of action from here on up. Over the next couple of days we would find a safe route up the remainder of the moraine and on to the glacier proper, and try to find the best place to site our Advanced Base Camp (ABC) somewhere near to the foot of the North Face. First, we would need to stock it with enough gear and food to enable me and four others to occupy the camp and then begin pushing the route up the face. Once we had got high enough on the mountain, we would see who was going strongest and decide upon summit teams.

We were now just a little over 18,000 feet with our bodies adapting well, some of the 'beef' deliberately accumulated beforehand dropping off each day. We were hardening to the task. Some of the climbers arrived late into camp with our yaks and yakherders as we finished erecting tents and preparing meals for the evening. They were tired after their slow journey up escorting the animals. Normally, the yak-men could be left to make their own way up to camps, but unfortunately we had found them rifling through our kit and stealing things, so it had become necessary to escort them everywhere for fear of losing things we could not do without. They were a hardy bunch of men, and quite colourful characters, and we didn't mind them pinching the odd tin of food. That was all part of the game, but when our high-altitude boots and bits of oxygen equipment started to disappear, it became a different ball game. After that, it was a battle of wits to see just how much they could get away with undetected.

A few days later, after winding our way through the lower part of the moraine, in and around the ice fins, climbing at a steady pace, the route opened out into a wide expanse of crevassed glacier. We were now almost opposite the Lho-la, the start of the West Ridge, which lay off to our right; the towering ice slopes of Changtse rose to our left. From this vantage point we could look directly up the North Face, and pick out the line of the climb, giving us a much better impression of the snow and ice slopes. We could see right into the Hornbein Couloir, which we intended to follow, but from which we would have to exit away to the right near the top in order to gain the summit ridge. Up till now, there had been no necessity to wear crampons or ropes as there was neither sufficient ice nor potential danger to warrant them. However, every step closer to the mountain from now on, this potential danger would increase, and so for safety's sake we roped up.

The long plume of cloud and snow streaming from the summit was a reminder of the great winds that blow high on the mountain. For the time being, we would be protected to some extent by the high wall of the West Ridge and by the North Col and Changtse. A huge granite boulder stood on its own at the point where the glacier met the moraine and this became the spot where we all left our crampons and ice-axes whenever we went down to the lower camps. It was a convenient and relatively pleasant spot at which to sit and eat lunch and drink from our flasks as we admired the view. Leaving Archie Scott and his team of three to push up the route towards ABC and find the safest path across the crevasses, Bronco and I set off for the Lho La, so that we could have a look down into Nepal and see once more our base camp of 1976. Gazing down from up there on to the Khumbu Icefall with its huge towers of ice leaning at crazy angles, threatening to fall at any minute, and the masses of open crevasses barring the way in whichever direction you looked, I was amazed that we had ever got through it without a major accident. I still remembered the Icefall as the worst part of the whole trip, and could not imagine ever going back into it again.

Looking off to our left, we picked out the route that would be taken by any team climbing the West Ridge. There was supposed to be a Polish team on this route now, and we saw some of their kit and equipment scattered about, but no signs of human activity. We came to the conclusion that the lead climbers must have just reached this point, dropped off their loads and descended back to their base camp at the foot of the Icefall in Nepal. The border between Tibet and Nepal runs down the West Ridge and across the Lho La where we were now standing, and it was funny to be able to stand there with a foot in either country. After taking a few snapshots for the family album, we moved back across the glacier, parked our crampons by the boulderstone and headed down towards base. Archie's crew had found a line which wove its way up the lefthand side of the glacier, with not too much danger from rockfall off the sides of Changtse, and were now making their way back down towards us.

We stopped to allow them to catch up and to hear their news. They said that apart from a couple of large crevasses and the odd stone rolling off Changtse, the route was safe, and that they had got to within 500 feet of the proposed site for ABC. This was good news. Things were going well, we were already a week ahead of schedule and going strong. Bronco and I decided over dinner that night to make a carry the next day, following Archie's team up to ABC. Eating my meal, I noticed that already my appetite was changing. It was the bland taste of things like mashed potato powder and porridge that my body was crying out for, and more sugar and liquids. From now on I would have to make a conscious effort to drink at least eight pints a day if I could, in order to lessen the possibilities of pulmonary oedema.

On the morning of 24 March, we were up early and making our way in the grey light up the moraine, threading our way through the seracs that rose threateningly on either side of us, crackling and groaning with the changes of temperature. Never, in all the times I have been to places like this, have I ever been able to accept cheerfully the loud cracking noises ice emits in the freezing cold when you first step close beside it. It is not unlike a pistol shot and is guaranteed to make the heart miss a beat. You feel sure that the ice beneath you is going to split open and swallow you into some black void, or that one of the giant ice towers will collapse on top of you. These moments, though, are soon forgotten when, after walking for an hour or two, the colours of the new day start to appear as warm light touches the higher mountainsides and gradually seeps downhill to engulf you. By the time the sun appeared on this particular morning, we had reached the boulder-stone, put on our crampons, and roped up. For the next two hours we steadily crunched our way up the glacier, following the line of flag poles left by the lead team the day before. The ice and snow was hard and crusty, allowing our spikes to bite in and give our boots perfect purchase on the ever-rising slopes.

As we got higher, so our pace slowed down and our breathing became more laboured. The mind tended to switch off, and life shrank to a mere counting of footsteps. To begin with, two or three hundred steps before stopping to catch our breath was OK, but as we moved up to around 20,000 feet, the number rapidly dwindled to fifty, and finally to only ten or fifteen. These are the times, when pushing up to new altitudes, feeling constantly nauseous and with a racking great headache, you begin to wonder why you do it. Surely this can't be fun?

Talking to myself in my mind, I declare, 'Stokes, you must be some sort of masochist. You have to be mad to want to do this.' Then I reason with myself, saying it won't feel like this in a day or two when I have got used to the new height. I know my own limitations and realise that I always feel lousy for twelve to twenty-four hours whenever I move up to a new level on the hill, and console myself that tomorrow I will begin to feel differently.

Stopping at yesterday's high point, just short of a crevasse, we were overhauled by Archie's team, who had started from camp a little later than us. They were going like trains and I could see that it was going to be a hard choice when it came to picking summit pairs. There was little to choose between any of them so far. They were all strong, fit – and young. At thirty-nine, Bronco and I were the 'old men' of the team and constantly ribbed about the fact. Our saving grace was that we invariably managed to be up and on the hill before the majority of them and breakfasted. This enabled us to retort, 'Don't matter how young you are, lad. You've got to get out of your sleeping bag to climb this *bukit*!' The banter was all good-humoured.

'We'll put one of our light ladder sections across this one,' said Bronco to Archie, indicating the crevasse in front of us.

'It don't need a ladder on that!' Dismissive, one of the young bucks was impatient to get on and made his way across a very unstable looking snow bridge. Luckily he was still roped up.

Whooompf!

'Hold it! Hold it! Agitation had replaced the bravado in his voice, as he now made a lunge for the opposite edge of the crevasse while the snow he had been standing on plummeted into the belly of the glacier. We laughed as he scrambled to safety and shouted to his Number Two to give him more slack on the rope.

'Think you might be right about bridging this one,' he conceded. Bronco and I swallowed the temptation to say, 'Told you so!' but stayed behind with our four porters while the others pushed on, and set about fixing the ladder-bridge over the crevasse. An hour and a half later we joined them below the North Face at 20,300 feet, our Advanced Base Camp.

We felt very insignificant there in the centre of a huge amphitheatre beneath the walls of Changtse, where it joined Everest and formed the North Col, and with wide eyes we followed the sweep of the Northeast Ridge to the point on the Second Step where Odell had last seen Mallory and Irvine heading for the summit all those years before. Towering thousands of feet above us, the Great Couloir disappeared into swirling spindrift as a small powder avalanche slid gently down its deep cleft and dropped harmlessly to the foot of the mountain, still some way above us. All eyes then returned to our face, and the chatting stopped as a lone *Lammergeier* soared its silent way past on wings of more than six feet across. It put everything into perspective, soon looking no more than a mere dot against the snow, and making us realise just how small we were in this vast and silent place.

My attention turned towards finding the best spot for our camp. Three other expeditions had used this site over the last two years: Americans had been here in 1982 when one of their women-climbers, Marty Hoey, had inexplicably unclipped herself from her harness high on the face and fallen to her death; and two Japanese teams came in 1981 and 1983. There was still a lot of rubbish and debris from one of the Japanese parties scattered about the place, so we found a spot some 100 yards further down the hill. Dumping our gear and erecting one tent, we set off back down, satisfied with the day's work. All we had to do now was stock up the camp and push on.

Three days later we had lifted up sufficient stores to allow five of us to occupy the camp and prepare to tackle the face. We were excited as we sorted loads of climbing equipment in readiness for an early start the next day. Merv and Graham were to form one climbing team; Andy and Tony another; and I was to fit in and assist where I was most needed. We were fully acclimatised to this new height now, and waking early next day, we set off towards the hill. There was a competitive feeling in the air as Graham, Merv, Andy and Tony raced for the bottom of the climb, each eager to rub noses with it first. Knowing that with only one kneecap, no toes and a few more years than they had, my chances of 'winning' any race were slim, I opted to sort out camp for an hour and follow up later with a load of rope. By the time I arrived at their high point, jumaring up the fixed ropes they had left in place, Tony had jumped across the *Bergschrund*, which was about ten foot wide, and was front-pointing on steep ice high above us. Seeing that they were all enjoying themselves and jostling for position out in front, I dumped my load and started back down again to bring up a ladder section to bridge the *'schrund*.

As I approached camp, I could see Archie's team and the porters making their way up towards it with more gear. I put on a brew for when they arrived and sat down on a ration box to survey the view. Down in the valley, the early morning mist and cloud was being lifted by the heat of the sun. It was 10.30 and the sunshine had only just reached the campsite as the pot of melted snow started to boil and the chill of the night was finally banished

221

from my bones. I loved moments like this when I was sitting on my own in silence with the sun warming by face. Life was so peaceful. By the time I had drunk my mug of hot tea, the others had started to arrive.

'How ya doin', mate?' I asked of John Bloom as he dumped his heavy load with a thud and plonked his sweating carcase upon it, taking the flask of hot drink I held out to him.

'It's a doddle,' he said with a twinkle in his eye, staring longingly up at the others, who were hammering in ice screws and fixing rope way above us. 'Be glad when we can get out in front, though.'

I could sympathise. From previous trips I knew what it felt like to have to lug up gear for weeks on end before finally getting your chance to do some of the leading.

'Never mind, John,' I consoled him. 'That's what expeditioning is all about. It won't be long now,' and borrowing an SAS Selection Course phrase, added, 'Stick it, mate, stick it!'

After they had all departed back down, I picked up the ladder and half-dragged, half-carried it up the slopes to fix it across the gap. Merv had mentioned that as the sun hit the snow higher up the hill, it had loosened some stones and they had been 'rained upon' for a little while, but that the majority of the debris had bounced off a bulge above them, out into the amphitheatre and out of harm's way. Later that night when everyone was back at the camp in our small bell-tent that acted as cookhouse, we decided that because of this 'rainstorm of stones' after the sun came up, we would be well advised to start climbing as early as possible in the mornings so that we would not be running the gauntlet for too long. Our routine was thus set, and over the next couple of days, early starts saw us pushing the high point up to 23,000 feet and searching for a platform on which to build the next camp.

Tired from the early start and long day, we descended to ABC once more, to find that some mail had been brought up and left in the cook tent. At long last, letters were filtering through the CMA mail system that I had almost given up on. There was a couple of letters from Lynn and a short note with rough drawings of 'Daddy climbing Mount Everest' from each of my boys. Finding a quiet spot, each of us crept off into a private world to read and re-read our mail. Lynn, in her usual amusing way, related how the boys were doing at school, what progress Sam was making with his karate, about Ben's new-found girlfriend. She said how much they all missed me, loved me, and wanted me to hurry up and climb the old mountain and come home safely. Her letters always cheered me up, but at the same time left me feeling lonely and far away. We had been gone for six weeks already and I was missing them all terribly. She was right, it was time we climbed this old mountain and started for home.

Lighting the Peak-one stoves and our large primus double-burner, I set about preparing the evening meal. I had decided that tonight I would make a speciality: kipper fillets as a starter, followed by mashed potato powder mixed with tuna fish and fried like potato cakes (this was my favourite), and to top it all off, we would heat up a tin of frozen fruit salad to have with a slice of Dundee cake. It took almost two hours to cook and eat this little lot, but afterwards it felt great as we drank our tea outside the tents, watching the shadows getting longer as the sun disappeared behind a ridge of mountains. I spoke to Bronco over the Radio on our nightly call and informed him of the day's progress, ribbing him about missing out on all the good food we were having in the peace and quiet of ABC. I told him to get the oxygen up here quick or we would be on the summit without it.

The rest of the evening was spent in relaxed conversation, watching the sky turn a peculiar mixture of yellow and mauve, with mares' tails blowing high. It was so peaceful as we made our way to our sleeping bags: no one could have had any inkling of what was to happen.

The Avalanche

DURING THE night the wind started to blow up, but sheltered as we were in our tents in the lea of the hill, we knew little about it as snuggled deep in our bags, we slept off the effects of our little yellow sleeping pills.

Pulling on my boots inside my tent at 6.15 the next morning, I heard Merv scream a warning, but it came too late. A chunk of ice whistled through the tent in front of my face and the whole world went crazy. The tent, with me inside it, was picked up and thrown down the mountainside by what I took at the time to be a big wind. I felt myself being lifted from the ground and rolled around inside the small blue capsule as it was flung down the hill, all my kit tossing and tangling around me as we went. I was screaming with panic, convinced I was going to die without seeing anyone ever again. My mind was racing: I had to do something.

Bouncing off the snow, I felt my shoulder jar as it hit something. I then noticed that a small hole had been made by the ice when it flew through the tent earlier. Pushing my hand into this hole, I ripped a large tear down the side of the bubble I was in, deflated it quickly and was half outside as tons of snow began piling in on top of me. I blacked out.

When I came to I was swimming for the surface through the suffocating snow. I fought my way clear, knelt up and opened my eyes. What I saw horrified and scared me. Snow and ice blocks were piled up everywhere, bodies lay crumpled and half-buried in the snow, and there were such strong winds blowing, it was almost impossible to scramble to my feet. A loud rumbling noise echoed in my ears and the high-pitched whine of wind as it tore savagely at my clothing. I stood up, but was immediately bowled over again.

'On no!' I thought. 'It's starting again!' Any minute now I

expected to be blown away once more, and cried out in anguish, 'God! No! No! Please don't make it now! Please, please don't make it now!'

I was shouting at the wind to stop, like a crazy man. I couldn't understand what was going on, what had happened. Later I learned that Merv, who had screamed the warning, had been standing outside his tent and had seen a 400-foot frontage of serac high on the mountain start to tumble towards us. The crash that followed after it had fallen free for a thousand feet shook the whole amphitheatre and triggered off avalanches of powdered snow from both Mount Everest and Changtse. The whole lot poured on to us, completely devastating our camp and sweeping it almost half a mile down the hill.

Still numb with fear and shock, I looked up the hill to where Merv was waving and yelled over the wind, 'I'm all right!' But he continued to wave, obviously trying to tell me something. I made out the words: 'Help me! Help me! Bring an axe!'

Dazed, I looked round at the tatters of my tent: no axe, no anything. It had all gone, all been buried. I turned to look down the slope and felt a hot iron in my head.

'Ohhh! My neck, my neck! It's broken!' It hurt so much, I couldn't move it, and I fell back to my knees clutching at my head, which seemed to be lying on my left shoulder. I had never felt such pain, but something in my mind insisted I get up and help Merv.

Staggering towards where he was bending over something, I felt the snow give way beneath me and fell into a shallow crevasse. Once more, panic rose almost uncontrollably. I hung on: a burst of adrenalin gave me the strength to drag myself out and over to Merv.

'An axe, an axe, we need an axe,' he was saying, but I had not understood why until I saw for myself that Tony had been killed and Andy's head was buried under an ice block. There were no tools anywhere with which to dig him free, and in desperation I pulled a plastic spoon from my pocket and scraped away at the snow covering the ice block that trapped Andy's head. He was conscious, but very dazed and did not really understand what was happening. We kept reassuring him as Merv and I scrabbled away at the solid ice until, with a crackling sound, the ice block moved and we had him free.

Learning from Merv that Graham, was alive, although badly

bruised and shocked, I wandered off to look for some oxygen and the remnants of a tent with which to protect Andy from the icy wind. Miraculously, the radio, my oxygen masking and one cylinder were located from the area where my tent had come to rest, and I quickly fitted the mask on to Andy's face and switched the control valve to maximum. There was instant reaction in Andy's eyes as the oxygen brought his body warmth.

'How's Tony?' His first words were for his friend and climbing partner. Choking back tears, I had to tell him that Tony was dead.

Merv appeared the least injured of us all. He pulled out a torn length of tent fabric from the rubble and wrapped it around Andy, doing his best to console him as he did so. I made my way over to Graham.

Just after seven o'clock I was able to make radio contact with Bronco at base camp. In what must have been an almost hysterical voice, I told him what had happened and begged him to get a rescue party up as soon as possible with tents and sleeping bags.

Archie and John, I learned, had left base camp already and so were on their way to us unaware of what had happened. They heard the roar of a large avalanche, but thought no more about it than to comment that it sounded like a big one. Two miles below our camp, they came upon the first signs that all was not well. A blue sleeping bag lay flapping in the wind on the glacier, not far from our boulderstone. The higher they got, the more debris they encountered. Bits of tents, hats, and, as Archie was to comment later, 'There were lumps of ice the size of Minis scattered everywhere; the camp had been pushed half a mile from where it previously stood.

Knowing by now that they had to expect tragedy, it must have been a harrowing experience for them to come up and find out what had happened: John later told me that they half-thought to find us all dead. Even so, we could read the extent of the damage by the expression in his face: Tony dead, Andy with broken ribs and shoulder, I with a damaged neck, Graham with frostbite on his fingers, Merv bruised, and all of us in a state of shock. Nothing had escaped the avalanche. Our kit lay scattered over a square mile. All we could do was gather up what clothing we could find to keep warm in, and get ourselves down to base camp as quickly as possible.

An hour and a half later, we spotted the others making their way slowly up the glacier towards us and, leaving Andy in the care of

Archie and John, the rest of us limped down to meet them. I tried to ignore the burning pain in my neck at each jarring step, and to put from my mind for a moment the horror of what had just happened. But of course, it would not go away. The whole thing had been so harsh, so brutal, and had happened so fast. So many things now needed to be done. Up till now I had been reacting instinctively, had kept going solely on the adrenalin. Now, away from any immediate danger, a wave of emotion swept over me and I felt absolutely drained. Dropping to the ground on the cold snow, I wept bitterly. Why, why, why had this happened? Just when all was going so well for us?

I pulled myself together as Bronco, Phil and the doctor reached me, and fighting tears, told Bronc that had happened. He looked almost as tired and drawn as we were. I had never seen him shocked like this before. The doctor examined my neck and informed me that it was broken. After placing on a surgical collar which took off some of the pressure and relieved the pain a little, Phil took my pack and escorted me down with Graham to the comfort and warmth of base camp. On the way we met the doctor and members of Pat Gunson's Cumbrian team, here to attempt the Mallory route, and they helped with the evacuation. It seemed that Pat was always on hand whenever I got myself into trouble on this mountain. It was he who had helped me from the bivi site on the other side in 1976 when we were descending from the top after our night out on Everest.

During the rest of that day, as we made our painful way down the hill to base camp, the team – helped by Gunson's Cumbrian lads – carried Andy on a makeshift stretcher down the moraine. He was constantly drifting in and out of consciousness. Once we were all safely esconced in camp, Ricky Villar, our doctor could better assess the damage. Not wanting to believe that I had got a broken neck, I kept insisting that it was 'only a crick, Rick', much to the amusement of the others.

It soon became apparent that Andy, Graham and I would have to be escorted off the mountain and transported to a hospital as soon as possible, so the wheels of organisation were thrown into motion. Bronco and Mel set about summoning up transport and arranging accommodation back in Lhasa via the CMA representative at the roadhead, our Mr Chen Ronchang.

The walk down the moraine to the roadhead where the vehicle was waiting for us, took a full day for the walking wounded, but two days for Andy, who had to be carried. The urgency and professional manner in which this evacuation was carried out, can only reflect credit on the team, who worked unstintingly in order to get Andy down without causing him unnecessary pain and suffering.

Three days after the accident, Andy was brought into the roadhead camp by the Rongbuk Monastery, where Mr Chen had prepared the vehicle and driver to take us on the Xegur. There was a clinic in Xegur, he told us, with medical facilities. Six of us were to travel out in the jeep next morning.

By now my neck had stiffened so that I could not move it at all (not that I wanted to, because of the pain), but even more worrying was the fact that my left arm and hand had become paralysed; I was worried I might lose the use of them. Graham's frostbite was already turning black and I tried to reassure him that he would not lose much, if any, of his fingers to amputations, a fact that later proved to be correct. The day before we left, Bronco led some of the team back up the mountain and buried Tony Swierzy on the Central Rongbuk Glacier, close to the place where he died. A small marker was left in place and later a memorial stone carved and built into a cairn near base camp with the inscription:

'IN MEMORY OF TONY SWIERZY,
FRIEND AND MOUNTAINEER,
DIED ON EVEREST 3.4.1984.'

Tony's death had saddened us all, and now we had to make sure that his close family received news of the tragedy in the right way, via our own people in Hereford and not through the national newspapers, as so often happens. We explained the problem to Mr Chen, who agreed not to disclose the information to the authorities until I had had a chance to break the news to the Regimental Headquarters in Hereford. They in turn would inform relatives of Tony's loss. But first, we had to get ourselves to the nearest telephone, which was a day's journey away in Xegur.

We collected up the mail from the rest of the team, who had all written to their families about the accident and assured them of their well-being, and bade them farewell. I felt for Bronco, my mate, who had been forced to abandon the climb due to the loss of six of us, and now had to remain to prepare for the withdrawal from the mountain whenever I could arrange for transport to come for them. Cramming ourselves into the tiny vehicle, we propped

Andy against the door at the back of the jeep, next to Graham and myself. With Ricky and Mr Chen fused on the front seat, the driver crunched into gear and set off in a cloud of dust.

The next ten hours were agony as we were buffeted left and right, crying out in pain, along the bumpy track that was to take us back to civilisation. Stopping to relieve ourselves on top of the Pang La pass. I looked back at the Everest massif, which now appeared calm, bathed in sunlight miles behind us. Through my mind, over and over again, I was saying, 'I'll be back, don't you worry. I'll be back!' It was a promise to a friend, rather than an adversary.

In Xegur over the telephone in a dusty, ill-lit room that smelled of dogs, I spoke first to the Guardroom Duty Sergeant at Hereford, outlining the situation and the actions that must be taken, and then to the Defence Attaché in Peking. Both agreed to help wherever they could and wished us a safe journey. Ricky then led me away to a room where I could wash off the dust and grime of the last few months, and tumble into bed. In no time at all, I fell into a deep sleep and dreamed of home.

Two more days of travelling by jeep brought us to Lhasa, a real bath, and a visit to the hospital where they had an ancient X-ray machine. This showed the extent of Andy's breakages and a hairline fracture in my neck – so it wasn't 'just a crick, Rick!'

Over the next two days our journey continued by aircraft to Chengdhu and on to the British Hospital in Hong Kong. I managed to speak to Lynn over the telephone and almost convince her that my injuries were not as bad as had been reported in the national newspapers. In a day or two's time, I told her, we would be flying home and she could judge for herself. I vowed to myself when the day came to try and appear better than I felt. For her sake.

The Northeast Ridge 1986

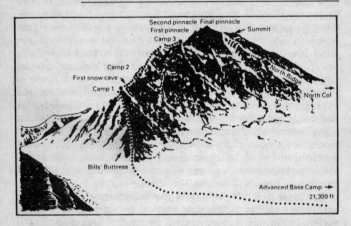

WHEN I got back to Hereford and reported to the Colonel, he expressed his deep sympathy over the loss of Tony Swierzy on the mountain, but was delighted that we were determined not to give up. We all wanted to return to the hill for another attempt and he would, he said, give us all the backing that would be required. But the first thing for me to do was to get over my neck injury.

It took a lot longer to mend than I anticipated, but was made bearable by all the tender loving care administered to me by Lynn. The normal rough-and-tumble games with my two boys had to be shelved for a while, though, as any movement of my head was agony. I felt for them both, realising that it is not much fun for a kid when Dad won't play the way he usually does. But six months later I was almost as good as ever and well on the road to organising the next climb.

I had already approached the Chinese authorities for a permit to return to the mountain when I was on the way home last time, and had been informed that a slot was available for the autumn of 1986 on the Northeast Ridge. It had been tentatively booked by an

American team who now found themselves unable to raise enough cash to go. If we could muster the necessary booking fee, the Chinese said, it was ours. Leaping at the chance, we staked our claim. The ridge, we knew, had only been attempted once before, by a team led by Chris Bonington, and that expedition had ended in tragedy with the deaths of two of Britain's best loved climbers, Peter Boardman and Joe Tasker. The pros and cons of the climb, however, did not matter to us at that time; we would look into those later. What was important was that the route was ours.

Backing was once again promised by George Williams, and he invited all prospective members of the team down to his house in Norfolk to get to know us. His main concern was not, as one might expect, for the failure of our earlier attempt and the fact that he had seen no return on his investment, but rather for the family of Tony Swierzy, and he had nothing but praise for all members' wives for the support they had given us. George was immediately accepted and respected by the lads as a true member of the team. His thoughts mirrored our own when he said aloud, 'We'll crack it next time, lads.' God willing, that is just what we would do.

By the time all our plans were finalised, Colonel Neville, as he was known, had unfortunately finished his time with the Regiment. There was a new hand steering the SAS ship, and I immediately sought an appointment with him to explain the Everest project more fully before flying off to Peking to sign the protocol and make last minute arrangements.

Over the telephone the new Commanding Officer told me that he would not have the time to see me before I went, but that I should fix up a meeting with him as soon as I returned from China. The Chinese Mountaineering Association saw no problem with the arrangements and gladly signed the protocol, wishing me a safe flight home and saying they looked forward to our return and success on Qomolungma – their name for Everest.

Excited that things were now so well under way, I bounded into the Headquarters building immediately upon my return to Hereford and fixed up to see the CO, as instructed. My enthusiasm was not returned by the staff in the HQ and I noticed tell-tale signs that things were not quite as they should be. Eyes were being averted and people seemed to avoid the issue when I asked, 'Is everything OK?'

I was soon to learn the reason for this edginess. When I was finally ushered into the main office, the CO informed me that he had changed his mind about this expedition continuing as an SAS-

231

only affair, and to that end, had given the whole thing away to a friend of his who was now running the Army Mountaineering Association. He would, he conceded, allow four members of the Regiment to go, but only if they were selected by a committee that the AMA would convene.

I was dumbfounded. I could not understand it; the previous Colonel had given it his blessing as a good venture for the SAS to undertake, and now here was this new broom telling me it was all a *fait accompli*. It had been given away, and that was that. No argument.

'Have you explained this turn of events to the team?' I enquired.

He had advised them of his decision while I was away, he told me curtly, and I suddenly realised why he had not wanted to see me before I went to sign the protocol. He knew that I would have refused to agree to the change of plan.

Later I learned that the climb had been given away at a cocktail party in London. I was livid, and told him I was not prepared to be treated in such a deceitful way. Learning that he had not informed the sponsor it was now to be an AMA project, I pointed out that since the money was not his to give away in the first place, the decent thing to have done would have been to have got the backer's permission first.

'Don't worry about him,' I was informed. 'I am a businessman, too. I will handle him.'

I had my reservations about that. George Williams had backed the SAS because he liked the type of people we were. He associated with us. I doubted that he would care for what was happening behind his back. Leaving the Colonel in no uncertainty that I thought he had mismanaged the whole situation, I announced I intended to explain to George myself that this nonsense was no responsibility of ours. With that, I stormed off to consult the rest of the team.

That night we all met in my home, where I learned that the reason they had been given during my absence for the climb being called off was that some of them were 'on operations' and would be unable to spare the necessary time for training. This they saw as an excuse, because only one of them would be on anything important during the time of the expedition. To a man, they felt let down and disgusted with the way things had turned out. Morale was at rock bottom.

My own feelings were the same, I told them, adding that I felt so strongly about the ethical aspect of the let-down – as regards both them and the sponsor – that I intended to resign if the decision were not reversed. Most of them said they would do the same; they felt that, for them, the magic had gone from belonging to the Regiment. I knew only too well that in the heat of the moment, decisions like this could be swiftly made, only to be regretted afterwards, so took time to point out that some of them only had a couple of years to serve before qualifying for a pension; they should think seriously before throwing that away. Three of them remained adamant, however, that they wanted no more to do with the new regime. They, too, would leave.

Armed with the facts, I returned to the office the next day to argue the case, but was told firmly that the subject was closed. There would be no more discussion.

Dejected and ashamed that someone in the Regiment I loved so much could act in this inflexible way and treat his soldiers, as I considered, so shabbily, I resigned, and went to visit George Williams.

My instinctive feelings about how he would react to the climb being given away behind his back proved right. We discussed the possibility of his transferring the backing to me personally, and of me putting together a different team to climb the mountain. George decided to fix a meeting with the CO himself, to make sure he knew both sides of the story, and I returned to Hereford. Some days later he rang to say that the climb and the permit from the Chinese had been transferred to me.

Sad at leaving the SAS, and not really knowing what the future would hold, I set about organising a new team around the few lads that had resigned with me. On reflection, I see it as having been rather a sordid affair, one that with a modicum of common sense and good manners, could have turned out quite differently. I am glad to say that I have since received a letter to say that management of the SAS had changed again and that everything is now 'back to normal' once more.

I was now faced with a bit of a problem. Here I was, an ex-SAS sergeant-major, complete with a pile of expedition kit, a protocol firmly in my pocket, but no team apart from the three who had made the stand with me. I could contact a few ex-members of the Regiment who were good climbers, but I knew that I was going to need help from someone who was familiar with the better civilian climbers. The obvious person was Paul Moores, whom I had met during climbing trips to Scotland. Paul was an accomplished climber, a mountain guide who worked in the Highlands, and I immediately went to visit him in his climbing shop in Glencoe to invite him to become the expedition's Deputy Leader. He readily agreed and we set about putting together the rest of the team.

Paul had climbed with many of the country's leading alpinists and produced a list of names, which included Joe Brown, Mo Anthoine, Paul Nunn, Bill Barker, Sam Roberts and Wal Thompson. One name led to another, and pretty soon Pete Long, Ali Kellas, Pat Green and Clive Rowlands had joined the ranks. Harry Taylor had reminded me of Paddy Freaney, who had left the SAS in the Seventies and was now running a climbing business in New Zealand. Soon a letter was winging its way to him with an invitation, which he accepted by return.

Philip Horniblow had been our doctor in 1976, when Bronc and I went to the top of Everest, and had performed his duties so well then that he was invited to take on the role of Expedition Doctor and Base Camp Manager. With him came John English as Climbing Doctor. With so many organising jobs to do in so little time, I enlisted the help of a friend from the SAS Territorial Army Regiment, Loel Guinness, to take over as Administration Officer. Trevor Pilling, a lad of about Harry Taylor's vintage and with a growing reputation as a climber, was asked along with the idea of bringing down the average age. We would need some young blood capable of keeping up with Harry, who was really strong. Trying to get the media involved, I approached Ronnie Faux of *The Times* and was told that the paper would allow him to participate in return for the story. So with the team more or less fixed, I set about travelling around the country to meet everyone and issue expedition tasks. We needed individuals to take overall responsibility for equipment, rations, fuel and stoves, oxygen, and packing. Everyone had a job of some description.

For me this was quite an exciting time as I was meeting for the first time climbers who I had only read about in books or heard other people talk about respectfully. In the back of my mind, I was anxious that whatever happened we should not take any prima donnas on the trip, since the secret of success on any large team is compatability. Everyone must be prepared to work for the common good. Too many times I had read about arguments and punch-ups among big national teams. Rather than have any nonsense, I was prepared to do without a climber, no matter how good he was. My fears were immediately dispelled when I met Mo and Joe in Llanberis. If anyone had a right to feel superior about his climbing prowess, it was Joe, but Britain's best known and liked climber turned out to be completely without affectation, modest and humorous. I got on with him and Mo from the start, and as it turned out, could not have wished for a better team all round. Soon I felt firm friends with them all.

While all this preparation work was going on, I travelled to London to explain the situation to David Stirling, telling him of my resignation from the military. He had his own reservations about the way things had worked out, and agreed to continue as one of the expedition's patrons alongside Lord Hunt, who led the first successful Everest expedition in 1953, the Hon. Angus Ogilvie and the Rt. Hon. the Earl Jellicoe. On David Stirling's advice, I contacted a film crew in London, Mind's Eye Productions, and started planning a film of the climb. Since our proposed route up the Northeast Ridge was the last major unclimbed line on the mountain, and obviously therefore an important part of history, it would be a shame not to capture it all on film. It did, however, mean that the budget would increase and that a further sponsor would need to be found. After much difficulty, this was achieved when we were contacted at the last minute by Seligman Harris, a firm of stockbrokers in the City, who felt this to be a worthwhile British venture. I was now morally contracted to both Seligman Harris and George Williams of Anglian Windows and would have to ensure that both parties received recognition for their support.

The next few weeks were spent racing around, tidying up last minute details. Things were coming together nicely, but first I had a run to do.

Some time before, I had been drinking in one of my locals in Hereford when an old friend remarked, 'Aren't you a bit over the hill for this climbing game, Brum?' Being a young forty-year-old, who always took care to keep himself in reasonable trim, I took umbrage at this and, as much to prove things to myself as to him, set about getting myself a place on the London Marathon. We would see who was over the hill or not!

My wife, Lynn, had run the marathon the year before and finished in under four hours. I was not sure that, without toes and one kneecap, I could do the same. The only thing I was sure of was that I would complete the course.

Lynn and I received our entries by the same post and set about training. Finally, the day came and we joined the thousands of other runners on Blackheath for the start of the race. We ran those London streets, cheered on by millions. I crossed the line at Westminster Bridge in 4 hours 38 minutes 17 seconds, a long way behind Lynn, but it did not matter. I had done it, that was the important thing. I was there at the end and had really enjoyed the atmosphere of the day. No one could now say that I was not up to it! I would confirm that on Everest – just as soon as my feet stopped throbbing and my body overcame this terrible ache.

The team was finally made up of eighteen climbers, one reporter and a three-man film crew. The idea behind taking such a large number of climbers was to be strong enough to do our own portering high on the hill; we preferred to spend our money on giving more Brits a chance to go to the mountain rather than on porters' fees. It was to be an all-British team, supported by British equipment. A Chinese contingent, comprising liaison officer, interpreter, and a driver would assist our passage as far as Base Camp, where to their number would be added seven yak herders and twenty-one yaks.

By the time we arrived, there had been two previous attempts on the ridge. The first had been in 1982 when Chris Bonington led a small team without oxygen. That was when Joe Tasker and Pete Boardman, the lead climbers, failed to return after attempting a traverse of the great rock pinnacles barring the ridge at 26,000 feet. Three years later another British team, this time led by Sandy Allan and Mal Duff, were forced to retire at the foot of these same pinnacles. This attempt, too, had been without the aid of oxygen. Looking at the geography of the ridge, I could see that more than a mile of it lay above 26,000 feet. To overcome this problem (which by now had become known as 'The Last Great Challenge of Everest'), we would need to work at very high altitude for extended periods and would be at high risk all that time. Ever one to learn from the experience of others, I took the decision that this expedition would use oxygen.

We met several times in Scotland to get to know one another better and try out our new gear, and to pack our six tons of food and equipment prior to its transportation to Peking, courtesy of British Airways. Some of us flew to Alaska for last-minute trials of film kit and acclimatisation. By this stage, I was formulating a plan in my mind of how to combine my love of of the outdoors with some form of business later on after the climb. Having been to

236

many places in my life, most of them somewhat off the beaten track, I had come up with the idea of escorting clients to the more remote areas of the world in company with tried and trusted friends, both climbers and ex-SAS soldiers. And to see whether 'Expedition Logistics' (as I proposed calling my new venture) was feasible, I invited my brother Graham to come to Alaska with us as a 'guinea pig'. I wanted to establish whether or not a reasonably fit person could in fact manage one of these trips and, more importantly, whether he would enjoy it.

Graham had never climbed before except to walk to the top of Snowdon one day in winter. As our training climb progressed, so his eyes widened further at the wonder of it all. With only ten of us, it was a nice relaxed, laid-back jaunt. Some of the team got to the top of Mount McKinley (20,320 ft) and Graham made it as far as 17,600 ft, which was a grand effort for his first time on a big hill. I was very proud of him. The trip was not without incident, though, as he first of all fell into a crevasse and later stole the show when, just below Windy Corner, his sledge toppled over for the umpteenth time into deep snow, and in his absolute frustration, he began shouting at the up-turned plastic carrier, angrily jabbing the snow off it with his ski pole. To the rest of us he looked like John Cleese in one of the *Fawlty Towers* sketches, frenziedly thrashing his mini-car for refusing to go, and we couldn't help roaring with laughter at his misfortune.

Alaska had been a great success: we had shaken down as a team, tested kit, and I had climbed McKinley again – it had also proved to me that my idea for future business was a viable idea. This was emphasised even more when a month later, back home, I visited my brother's house in Birmingham and found that almost every wall in the place had been turned into a photo gallery, recording his adventures in Alaska. There were blow-ups of him in an aircraft, on skis, high on the hill and by his tent – but nowhere could I see one of him beating his sledge!

August found us in Lhasa, having survived the rigours of the journey through Peking and Chengdu. Things had changed considerably since my last time in China: the regime had relaxed and individuals were now allowed to profit from small family concerns. This change was reflected, too, in the type of clothing people wore. Gone were the drab blue serge uniforms and Chairman Mao hats that everyone had then. Instead, the women were wearing dresses of red and green print, and the men, jeans and suits. Tourism was being catered for in a big way and many

237

multi-storeyed hotels had sprung up almost overnight. The only thing that had not changed was the food. I was glad to be back in Tibet, back to the friendly smiles of the Tibetans.

It is easy to see why the people of Lhasa appear so happy. Their home is a real Shangri-la, sitting as it does in such a beautiful mountain-locked valley. A life that moves only at walking pace is one of few pressures, except – that is – for the stress of having Chinese militia controlling the land. Despite the apparently blissful calm, one could see this was a melting pot. One day there would be big troubles here when the Tibetans finally tried to throw off the Chinese yoke. I did not want to be around when that happened – but for the moment, I could enjoy Tibet for itself.

By now I felt quite at home here; this was the fourth time I had visited Lhasa. I contented myself with ironing out last-minute details and transport arrangements with Mr Tang, the CMA official, leaving the rest of the team to explore the Forbidden City. Daily visits to the Potala Palace, the Jokang Temple and other places of local interest provided footage for our film. Most of the shooting here was being handled by Mo Anthoine, since our climbing cameraman Tony Riley was laid low with altitude sickness and the Mind's Eye trio were still some days behind us.

When people were not out sightseeing, we loaded up our vehicles for the three-day journey to the mountain. Being a different season from the last time I was here, we were able to buy fresh vegetables to take in with us. Someone came up with the bright idea of taking six laying hens in with us as well, so that we might enjoy fresh eggs at base camp before consigning the poor creatures to the cooking pot; but seeing them wilt away in their wicker basket on the back of one of the trucks, I pronounced a stay of execution. We gave them to some villagers along the roadside.

The overland trip was very much the same as it had been in 1984. The roads were still as dusty, the accommodation at Xigatse and Xegur just as spartan, and the sanitation only matured with age. It was enlightening for me as an ex-soldier on my first major civilian expedition to sit back in the mini-bus and listen to the comments of the rest of the team as we bumped and thumped our way along the Friendship Highway. Between them, our members had climbed all around the world: Kangchenjunga, Lhotse Shar, Mount Cook, Roraima, El Toro . . . The discussion ranged over climbs that people would most like to do, and who they would most like to climb with. It all helped give me an insight into the various personalities; I knew, if I was to make the correct decision later on about who should go to the summit, and with whom, I was going to need to know this team inside out. But I did not foresee any real problem over this, since all the people here had been picked because they were potentially capable of getting to the top. I knew also that it tends to be a self-selecting process. Whoever is going strongest at 25,000 feet would be the obvious choice. I wondered how I would fare: how would I go at 25,000 feet? Could I get to the top again and become the first Brit to do the *bukit* twice? We would just have to wait and see.

Humour was the overriding factor in all the conversations I eavesdropped on. Paddy, Mo and Joe kept up a hilarious stream of deadpan banter, and Bill had taken to ribbing Harry about his SAS background, dubbing him 'Dirty Harry'. Harry bore it stoically and, true to form, said nothing unclean. It appeared there were culinary delights in store as Pat Green outlined some of his menus: I had never experienced home-baked bread and pastries at 21,000 feet and certainly not on top of honey-roasted ham. I could hardly wait. It made me hungry just thinking about it, and I tucked into the box of 'travelling food' that Pat had so thoughtfully prepared. The obligatory Chinese fare, for which we had paid dearly, lay conspicuously untouched in a large plastic bag at our feet.

Our second night was spent in the same bug-infested beds in Xigur in which I had itched my way through the night two years earlier when returning from the mountain with my neck in a collar. My mind flashed back to that horrendous journey, and I prayed that the same thing would not happen this time. I thought too of Andy Baxter, who had since died of a brain tumour, and inevitably of Tony who was killed in the avalanche on the North Face. In my pack was a brass memorial plaque that I would erect to his memory at some suitable place on the hill.

In the darkness of an early Tibetan morning, we prepared to board lorries for the last leg of the trip to base camp. I had organised things with the CMA so that I could get as many climbers into the cabs of the vehicles as possible, out of the cold winds encountered when travelling in the back of these cumbersome giants.

The sunshine of the new day found us parked on top of the Pang La, gazing at Everest in the distance. I was surprised at the amount of snow that still lay on the mountain. The view was perfect in the clear blue of a cloudless sky. Cameras clicked and the whir of the film-camera captured the moment forever. Like bison smelling water, the team started to kick up the dust around their feet, eager to get to grips with the Ridge.

By the time we arrived at base camp, there were already a couple of teams on the mountain. Chilean climbers were attempting the North Col Route and a joint Franco–Swiss party was on the North Face. There was also a lone Englishman – Roger Marshall – hoping to make a solo ascent. It did not take long before we had our camp sorted out alongside theirs: tents up, cookhouse erected and a meal of hot soup and corned beef hash, served up by our singing chef.

Looking up at the mountain later that day, I could not help noticing how similar the outline of Everest was to the shape of the old pit mound in Hamstead, where I grew up. Just grander, that was all. It wasn't something that had struck me last time I was here, but now, seeing it from a slightly different angle, I could see the resemblance. Our base this year was further up the valley, at the foot of the moraine, well out of the way of the Rongbuk Monastery and the begging monks. This time we would keep ourselves away from the 'madding crowd'.

The next week was spent acclimatising, sorting out our gear and preparing yak loads to go up the hill to ABC. We were visited by the Franco–Swiss team and I was pleasantly surprised to find that one of their climbers was Jean-Pierre Troillet, whom I had met on McKinley several years before. Over a brew of tea, we discussed the North Face and I wished him luck, remembering once more the avalanche and Tony's death. I resolved to find a nice quiet spot the next day, at which to erect the memorial plaque. Harry was the only other person on this trip who had been with me in 1984; together we walked up the moraine track to a place where the North Face can best be seen. There, in a moment of quiet dignity, we fixed the brass plate to a large granite rock where it would be visible to climbers as they made their way towards the great peak.

Eager to move higher, some of the team had already started to follow the old yak track up the moraine in the direction of ABC, but because it was still some twelve miles away at the top of the East Rongbuk Glacier, it became increasingly obvious that we would need an interim camp at 19,000 feet. This was established and a couple of tents set up at the foot of Kellas' Rock Peak, a mountain named after Dr Kellas, who had died on the walk-in to Everest during the first reconnaissance expedition of 1921. He was a relative of our own Ali Kellas, for whom this must must have been an emotional moment, coming to the spot so many years later.

As the interim camp was being established, so our twenty-one yaks with their seven yak-herders arrived at base camp. Characteristic whistles and shouts, echoed off the valley walls to herald their arrival. As this hardy bunch of Tibetans set up a tarpaulin tent, bedouin-style, Pat arranged a meal for them and a kettle of sweet tea, while Paul and I, with the help of an interpreter, welcomed them and began discussing our requirements. We were in luck, this crew were great. It was the first time they had ever been to Qomolungma, and they proved extremely helpful and honest. Not one scrap of equipment was lost throughout the trip. Their leader was a man called Jobbie, who became everyone's friend over the next weeks.

As our yak-men ferried the kit up the moraine to the interim camp, so Mo, Joe, Paddy and Bill started to push on up to ABC. The route was not too difficult to find as the Chilean team, who were ahead of us, had left the odd marker flag along the way. The scenery was constantly changing as the track wove in and out of huge ice towers and ended up passing through a narrow gap with the glacier to the left and overhanging ice towers on the right. This corridor soon earned the nickname 'the Tubes'.

Now above 20,000 feet, progress had slowed to the familiar plod of altitude. Once we were acclimatised properly, we would fly up and down this section – no problem – but meanwhile, it was heavy going. Approaching the site of ABC, our advance party were greeted by the leader of the Chilean expedition, Rodrigo Jordan. It was not a happy moment, for one of their young climbers had just stepped through a cornice climbing up to the North Col, and fallen to this death. Putting on a brave face, his friends had buried him on the mountain and now prepared to abandon their climb. This had been the first Chilean team allowed to visit a major peak outside South America and they were worried that, because of the accident, their government might refuse other groups permission to climb abroad.

Joe and the others assisted the Chilean evacuation from the mountain as best they could, and then set about establishing our own ABC at the foot of Changste, at 21,500 feet. This was the same site used by the two previous Northeast Ridge expeditions as well as by parties going up the North Col, and it was in an appalling mess. Our team spent two days on 'conservation duties.'

The rest of us meanwhile were stockpiling equipment at interim camp and organising yak loads on from there. We found enough free time to climb some of the surrounding peaks, giving us a better look at the Ridge. From the glacier, it rises sharply from the Raphui La in a series of steps of varying heights and difficulty until the way is barred by the line of pinnacles at 26,000 feet. Above that the ridge continues ascending steadily towards the First and Second Steps (where Mallory and Irvine were last seen on their famous attempt from the North Col in 1924), and from there on finally to the summit pyramid. It was easy to see why this route had not yet been climbed. Through our binoculars and mirror-lens cameras, we obtained a close view of the savage pinnacles on which Boardman and Tasker were last seen. The wind was cutting through the gaps in the rock and hurling plumes of spindrift high into the air.

I could imagine what conditions would be like up there without oxygen. I was glad now that I had decided we should use it. Even Reinhold Messner, who had twice been to the top without oxygen, thought better of trying this route. (He was, even now as I contemplated the ridge, just on the other side, attempting Makalu.) It was easy to imagine what the early British pioneers must have felt like as they stood here in their Harris tweed jackets and putties, sustained by Fortnum and Mason hampers. They must have looked hard and long at this classic line and dismissed it as impossible, but at the same time secretly thought, 'What a challenge – oh, what a challenge!' And it certainly was, this 'Last Great Challenge of Everest'. Now here we were, determined to take it up.

Standing here again, amid all this grandeur, made me feel humble. Mountains are great levellers: they certainly bring you to an awareness of your own fragility. Sometimes in life you can become swollen-headed over achievements you have made – maybe you run a big business, maybe you have written a book, maybe you have climbed Mount Everest – whatever you have done, here amongst these hills, it makes no difference. You are as everyone else. It doesn't pay to give yourself airs.

Up at ABC Joe's advance party was making good progress and was well ahead of schedule even though there had been a logistical mix-up at the beginning. The first yak loads up to ABC had failed to include all their necessary personal gear. Mo and Jo were left without altitude boots and crampons, although they did have an umbrella apiece; and stores, too, were uneven. For some inexplicable reason, almost two hundred packets of pear drops had gone up, but very little in the way of real food and no teabags! The only cutlery between the four of them up there was a single spoon that Joe had found in the lid of his rucksack and with which they ate all their meals turn and turn about. A few more spoons came up some days later, but then there was another long delay before they got knives and forks as well! There is no water at ABC, of course; everything we needed up there had to be melted from snow or ice.

By the time I had moved up to ABC, we had ferried up enough gear to feed an army. The lead team had forced a route across the glacier and were fixing rope up the right-hand edge of a rock buttress, some 1,525 feet high. This new route, which was quite steep but on good snow, avoided the long traverse over suspect avalanche-prone ground up to the Raphui La, which was the route taken by the two previous expeditions. By going this way, we could cut out two sides of a large triangle and save ourselves many hours of load-carrying. Out of respect for Bill Barker, the man who did the majority of the lead climbing on it, we called this new line 'Bill's Buttress', a name I hope will stick. But even though we had drastically shortened the distance we needed to go across the glacier, it was still a gruelling plod. During the day the sun burned down so fiercely that, as Joe said, it seemed to drill holes in your back; it also softened the snow so that you were continually sinking in up to your knees. We had thought at first that this must be one of the easiest glaciers to cross, being relatively even and flat and with no obvious crevasses, but bent under our heavy loads, it seemed endless. It also had the curious quality of appearing to be uphill in whichever direction you were going. 'None of us would do this for money,' commented Joe. 'You couldn't pay us enough for such punishing work.'

Joining the lead, Harry Taylor, myself, Pete Long and Trevor Pilling ferried up hardware to a point where Joe Brown was pushing out a length of rope up and around two big boulders that jutted out of the nose of the buttress like two large teeth. As he was descending the ropes, having placed a piton in the top of the boulders, I remarked to Joe that we should call these the 'Tombstones'.

'Why's that?' he enquired, and I told him how they reminded me of giant teeth. For a moment, he had thought I was referring to the famous old photograph, in which he looks so grotesque that he has been described as having 'arms like a gorilla, fingers like bananas and teeth like tombstones!'

'Not only that,' I teased him, 'the way you were sprawled across them out of breath at the end, I thought they were going to be the death of you!'

'Go on, get up there!' he retorted, pointing with his chin towards the top of the rope, and continued his descent muttering something like 'Cheeky monkey!' Actually, Joe looks nothing like that description at all – he's uglier!

After seven days of forcing the route, Harry and Trevor finally reached the point of 23,200 ft where the buttress joins the Northeast Ridge proper, and dug a small platform for a tent. We had reached our Camp I despite bad weather and several snow storms. Joe, Paddy, Mo and Bill trekked off down the hill to base camp for a well-earned rest.

Paul Moores, Sam Roberts, Will Thompson and John English had by now moved up to ABC and were soon ferrying loads up to camp I. Before long a snow hole had been dug close to the tiny tent and the camp occupied. From here, high on the ridge, we gained an incedible panoramic view eastwards down the Karma Valley towards Makalu, which stood proud and squat in the foreground. Kangchenjunga, the peak that Joe Brown had first climbed in the fifties, sat alone in the far distance. A glance to the right rewarded us with another spectacular view up the Northeast Ridge as it ran away in a heavily-corniced and delicate flying-buttress towards the great white plume which marked the summit of our mountain. Looking back down the way we had come always made me hold my breath when I stared over the North Col and Changtse and followed the course of the glacier down the valley towards base camp. The setting was perfect for our cameraman, the air so thin it gave everything a clear, sharp look; it was like a wonderland set. All he had to do was run the camera and point it, no matter what he filmed it would all provide excellent footage for our film.

With the winds blowing constantly at this altitude, the snow cave soon became the favourite living place, sheltered as it was from the battering, noise and snow flurries. Once inside, it became noticeably warmer too, with the Bluet stove merrily brewing up tea and melting snow to make water. Taking the snow from the inside of this 'igloo', meant that our domain daily grew in size.

Moving out of the camp and fixing the route along the heavily-laden ridge proved more of a job than we had anticipated. Several feet of fresh snow had left the route in a very unstable condition. We were glad of the protection of our fixed ropes on more than one occasion as sections of snow collapsed underfoot and cascaded down the steep slope towards ABC two thousand feet below. Being on a ridge, however, meant that we were free of any avalanche danger from above, but with the crusting up of the snow, progress was slow and laborious. We would constantly fall through the soft crust up to our knees. What had taken the two previous expeditions a few hours to traverse, was now taking us half a day. High winds and near white-out conditions twice forced us to beat a hasty retreat to base camp before a snow-hole was finally dug to give us Camp II, just below the First Buttress at 24,000 feet. The winds were so strong now that at times we were forced to crawl on all fours back to the safety of Camp I, and eventually to pull off the ridge altogether and descend the fixed ropes of Bill's Buttress to the glacier below. When there was no let-up in the weather, we decided to keep on going down. It was a good job we were still slightly ahead of our expected schedule.

By the time we reached base camp again there were two more expeditions in the vicinity. Both were American, one attempting to hang-glide off the West Ridge, and the other – led by Andy Harvard and Tom Holzel – to follow the North Col route in the footsteps of Mallory and Irvine. This party included a number of women climbers, each hoping to become the first American woman to reach the top, and two Brits, Audrey Salkeld, a writer I had read about in *Mountain* magazine and who was the expedition's 'historian', and Alistair Macdonald of the BBC. Base camp was a hive of activity with all this to-ing and fro-ing and visits from other teams, most of them to see our doctor, Philip Horniblow, or to sample the delights of Pat Green's soup kitchen. His powers with pot and pan had become legendary, and every trekker and hippy for miles around was soon heading in our direction for free handouts. Not being very sociable, nor free with our sponsors' cash, I soon acquired the reputation of a meanie as I chased them off. One trekker actually argued with me that I had no right to stop him wandering around our camp and inspecting the inside of my tent so that he could see how we lived. He left abruptly soon after that.

It was now that I learned that Jean-Pierre had managed to climb the mountain by the Hornbein Couloir with his friend Erhard Loretan during a lull in the bad weather. They had made an exceptionally fast unroped ascent, climbing mostly at night, and had beat it down to the bottom again in about three and a half hours – on the seats of their pants! I was glad for him, congratulating him on the achievement, and was able to reassure him that the minor frostbite he had sustained on his toes would only result in the loss of his toenails for a while.

As soon as the weather abated, we set off back up the hill, wading through the freshly-fallen snow. Digging out the tents at ABC did not take long, and soon we had pulled out the buried ropes on Bill's Buttress and along the Ridge between Camps I and II, and were busy stocking up the top camp in order to push on further. Camp 2 was always a windy and insecure spot. We had a tent up there as well as the snow-hole which was in a yawning crevasse dramatically overlooking the East Face. Joe found he couldn't sleep a wink there: if he was in the snow-cave, he thought it was going to fall down the face in the night, and if he was in the tent, he was frightened it would blow away. The next week saw fixed ropes on the First and Second Buttress and Pete Long and myself got almost as far as the connecting ridge leading to the Pinnacles before being forced down to ABC once more by high jetstream winds that whipped up the spindrift and threw it into our faces with ferocious force. We were all now getting extremely tired. By this time, it was already mid-October and we had been on the hill for two and a half months. Our initial advantage had long since been conceded and with our high point still only 26,200 feet, we were fast running out of time. We would only be able to make one more stab at it.

At about this time we had a fortunate windfall, or to be more precise a fortunate yakfall. To be even more precise, it was fortunate for us, but not the yak. One of the American team's animals fell into a crevasse, broke its neck and died instantly. We joined forces to mount a recovery operation and afterwards Pat and Harry butchered and divided it. Half a yak goes a long way in steak sandwiches and yakburgers.

After the storm we put all our efforts into one last push as Paul led a team back up to Camp II with Mo, Pete and Joe to back-up Harry and Trevor, who were going the strongest by now and would make the actual push. Hoping that conditions would improve, and that the longed-for 'window' of good weather would finally materialise, they pushed on up the ridge, carrying fifty-pound loads and using oxygen, to set up Camp III at a high point of 26,200 ft, close to the first steep slope of the Pinnacles. A bold bid the next day (16 October) by Harry Taylor and Trevor Pilling to cross the ice-glazed Pinnacles, the difficult crux of the Northeast

Ridge, was thwarted as violent winds hammered the Ridge, growing to almost hurricane strength and creating a chill factor of minus seventy degrees. Progress across the Pinnacles was impossible, even though Trevor estimated that technically the climb was feasible. Exhausted and disappointed, they turned back and struggled to safety, at times forced down on all fours by the wind.

I made the final decision to abandon the climb after a Sherpa working with Andy Harvard's American expedition was killed by an avalanche when descending from the North Col.

What a climb it had been! We had been hit by no less than four fierce storms which deposited eight feet of fresh snow; avalanches of hundreds of tons of snow had thundered around ABC, threatening to wipe it out, and horrendous winds of 130 miles an hour and more had screamed over the mountain. Despite this, morale and team spirit had remained astonishingly high and we were all still friends at the finish. There are images that will remain forever: Mo and Jo crossing the glacier with their umbrellas against the sun; Philip Horniblow, dressed as always in the green turban of his desert days, dispensing an endless stream of pills and paternal advice from his gentlemanly tent; and John English, our other doctor, who always greeted 'patients' with a brusque, 'What's wrong with you?' A dermatologist in 'real life', he could never work up much enthusiasm for ailments not connected with the skin – however, he was able to make his medical mark by discovering a species of high altitude wart that had not been described before; Ali Kellas a bit 'stir-crazy' after three long days alone at Interim Camp, so pleased to see people that he couldn't stop talking and rattled on at about two hundred words a minute; Pat Green butchering the dead yak with a bread knife and an ice saw; the 'low altitude headaches' we all suffered after cracking the *Glenmorangie* while resting and recuperating at base. We had not climbed our Northeast Ridge, but I still considered the expedition to have been a success. We had given it a fair and honest go, and were all still alive and smiling. Each of us had learned a little more about himself and enjoyed Nature in its rawest state.

For all the hard work and sheer guts shown by everyone involved with this climb, sponsors, climbers, cameramen, patrons, wives and children, I want to put on record my gratitude, and thanks for being part of our Team. Rest assured Everest and the Northeast ridge will not go away. And neither shall I.

Epilogue

In the summer of 1988 I returned to the Northeast Ridge with many of the old hands from the previous trip. The 'slot' I had been given was for the monsoon period, which is not normally considered the best time to be climbing in the Himalaya.

This time I had decided to bring in a strong team of climbing sherpas to help establish the chain of camps along the ridge. I also hired two sherpa cooks. The addition of ten Nepalese brought our party to nineteen. Paul Moores was again my deputy and Mo, Joe, Harry, Bill, Sam, Ali, Pete, Loel and our two doctors, Philip and John, would all be there. Paddy Freaney from New Zealand was coming again, too, bringing with him Russell Brice, who, Paddy assured me, would be 'worth his weight in sweat'. I invited my brother Graham to be Base Camp Manager and he leapt at the chance.

It was also my intention to take along six youngsters from the National Association of Youth Clubs as far as Base Camp, but when I had costed everything out, I was horrified to see a total of £178,000 staring up at me from the page. The bulk of this was money due to the CMA (Chinese Mountaineering Association) for our Chinese and Tibetan arrangements. I began crossing off those items for which I believed I might pick up sponsorship: flights, clothing, food, oxygen. By the end of the day things looked brighter and I considered £100,000 should do it, but it meant I would not be able to take the youngsters after all.

The long-suffering George Williams again chipped in with £25,000 from Anglian Windows; and Trevor Williams, one of our new climbers who worked for Tetra Pak in Wrexham, managed to persuade his employers to donate another substantial sum. Things were coming along, but fund-raising is always a slow business. We managed to secure a television contract with HTV, but even so, by the time it came to leave, Lynn knew I was cutting it finer than I had ever done before.

Mo had already gone on ahead to Kathmandu. I wanted him to take over some rations and oxygen equipment from a returning Army expedition. They had a prefabricated hut, too, which sounded as if it would be great for Base Camp. Together with a sherpa, Mo would take the first truckload to Everest and begin setting up. We followed him to Nepal about a week later, only to be told that the road to China was closed and would not reopen for another fifteen days at least. We went backwards and forwards between embassies and police posts, protesting and pleading by turn; we even turned up at the border, but were sent away. I failed to see how we could ever reach our hill in time to climb it. A telex from the CMA in Lhasa advised us to fly team and equipment to Lhasa and travel overland from there. This would cost an extra £8,000, which we did not have. I was desperate and called Loel Guinness to relay the bad news (Loel had remained in the UK to raise last-minute cash). He did not wait to hear my woes, but jubilantly informed me that newspaper rights to the expedition had just been sold. This put a different complexion on things! We could go to Lhasa after all.

When we finally pulled into base camp, there was Mo smiling a welcome as he stood proprietorially outside his prefabricated shelter. He had almost

248

given us up. 'The bad news,' he informed us, once we had unloaded, 'is that the oxygen masking we collected from the Army expedition is nothing but rubbish.'

I had only agreed to sell our 1986 equipment to the team attempting the West Ridge on the understanding we could buy it back afterwards. It appeared that all we had inherited from them were a few bastardised bits and pieces they had cobbled up themselves. Our good stuff must have gone home with them. I was flabbergasted. In my book, this was nothing short of sabotage and placed our whole enterprise in jeopardy. I took myself to bed early to ponder what to do about it, slept fitfully, and woke next morning with a headache from the altitude.

Over the next few days our communications expert, Glynn Davis, set up the satellite radio system that enabled me to speak to Loel back home. I urged him to get working on the oxygen problem. Again, he had good news for me: a prominent figure, who wished to remain anonymous, hearing of our difficulties, had made the expedition a donation of £10,000. He would probably never know how he had just saved me from personal ruin.

By 29 June, ABC was established and our lead climbers were starting up Bill's Buttress. The snow was good and their progress steady. I could not wait to be up there with them. All the organising had kept me down at Base and I made the sudden decision to put in one more call to our expedition sponsors then head off up the hill.

Walking slowly up the moraine in the crisp morning air, I was at last able to relax and feel at home with the mountain. Since the last time we were here, the Northeast Ridge had been attempted by Doug Scott's lightweight expedition of autumn 1987. It had experienced the same appalling conditions as we had in 1986 and, like us, failed to cross the Pinnacles. One of his cook sherpas was killed in an avalanche walking up to Advance Base and looking around, I wondered where this had been. Everything appeared the same until I crossed the meltwaters of the river that runs from the East Rongbuk Glacier. Suddenly, I found myself in the middle of a huge area of crushed rubble and powdered rock that obviously marked the spot of a substantial avalanche. Looking up, I could see where two or three large towers had broken off and cascaded down to pepper the ground on which I stood. This, I thought, must have been the place.

It still felt threatening and I moved quickly away. It had caused me to remember that several climbers who were here with us in 1986 had since been lost in the mountains. Trevor Pilling, who had climbed so well with Harry Taylor towards the end of the expedition, failed to return from a climb of Pumori with his girlfriend; Roger Marshall was killed making another solo attempt on Everest in 1987; and two climbers from the American teams – Dave Cheesmond and Cathy Freer – disappeared on the formidable Hummingbird Ridge of Mount Logan in the Canadian Yukon. These were stark reminders that mountains can never be taken for granted.

Once up at ABC, I began throwing boxes around, as I do, and the next thing I knew I was on my back, suffering from cerebral oedema. My head felt three sizes too large, my eyes were puffy and ultra-sensitive to light. The throbbing inside my brain, like Zulu war drums, was made worse by constant vomiting.

The only cure for this type of altitude sickness is to get downhill fast, so for me it was, Base Camp here I come! Descending next morning the pain receded with each foot of height I lost. I felt sure if I stayed at Base for a few days things would be OK. After a week I felt well enough to go back up the mountain. At first light, I was up and away, trudging at my own pace with Irish folk music blasting on my Sony Walkman, and the sun warm on my back. Life seemed worth living once more.

My joy was short-lived. As I reached interim, where my brother Graham was holding the fort, I felt a slight, tingling sensation down my left arm and hand, the side of my face went numb and my vision blurred-another attack of the cerebral oedema. My words were coming out all jumbled because of pins and needles in my tongue, and my head had started to throb incessantly. Soon I began vomiting again and the world was swaying wildly. Everest toppled over before my eyes and as I put out a hand to save myself, I seemed to fall into a huge crevasse. Avalanches were crashing inside my head as I slipped into total blackness.

'Come on, kid, I've got a brew for you.' I opened my eyes and saw the blurred outline of my brother kneeling at my side. 'You all right?' There was an edge of anxiety in his voice, as he urged, 'I think you ought to go down.'

Even in my befuddled state, I knew he was right. Something had gone wrong in my head, which if I stayed up here, could very well kill me. With Graham to escort me, I staggered back into Base just as it grew dark.

Next morning, though a little better, I still had no feeling in my arm or hand. I felt as though I had been beaten all over, but weak as I was, I refused to be sent back to Kathmandu. Too much was happening on my mountain. Over the following days Harry and Russell pushed the route up to the bottom of the Pinnacles at 26,000 ft. From here, we were on new ground, and if all went well, could hope to see someone on the summit within a week. Excitement mounted and our satellite was kept busy sending updated reports back home.

Natural impatience is hard for me to curb, and one day without thinking I set about helping to load a yak. Stupidly, I lifted a sack of oxygen cylinders and brought on another haemorrhage in my brain. This time there was no arguing with my body. One side of my face and my left arm became paralysed, the numbness was back in my tongue, and pressure was building in my head. Despite being on oxygen, my body seemed to be deflating. This was my third attack and I knew that I was dying. I was immediately evacuated in the expedition jeep, and in Kathmandu I was given massive doses of steroids to reduce the pressure in my brain. By the time I reached England, my condition had stabilised. A brain scan showed an enlarged blood vessel which should cause no long-term harm, but I would need a long recuperation before returning to the high mountains.

I was devastated. All my hopes of being the first Briton to climb Everest twice had been dashed. My expedition was in Tibet and here was I, taking things easy at home. Life seemed very unfair. Now I knew what it must be like for Lynn and the other wives.

And how did the team fare on the mountain? Well, when you have a team of that calibre, it can only do one thing. It succeeded in climbing through the Pinnacles and cracking, finally, the Last Great Challenge of Mount Everest's Northeast Ridge. But that's another story.